1 -3, 213-216, 243-248

The World's Great Wisdom

TM mantra for 18-20 years

Acm

20-22 years

Aenga

Ā-nga

SUNY series in Integral Theory

Sean Esbjörn-Hargens, editor

The World's Great Wisdom

Timeless Teachings from Religions and Philosophies

Edited by

Roger Walsh

Published by State University of New York Press, Albany

For information, contact State University of New York Press, Albany, NY
www.sunypress.edu

Production by Eileen Nizer
Marketing by Michael Campochiaro

Library of Congress Cataloging-in-Publication Data

The world's great wisdom: timeless teachings from religions and philosophies /
   edited by Roger Walsh.
      pages cm. — (SUNY series in integral theory)
   Summary: "Surveying spiritual and philosophical traditions, revives the search for
wisdom for modern times"—Provided by publisher.
   ISBN 978-1-4384-4957-9 (hardcover : alk. paper)
   ISBN 978-1-4384-4958-6 (pbk. : alk. paper)
   1. Wisdom.   2. Religions.   3. Philosophy.   4. Conduct of life.
I. Walsh, Roger N., editor of compilation.

BJ1595.W84 2014
200—dc23   2013006242

10 9 8 7 6 5 4 3 2 1

This book is dedicated to
Angeles Arrien and Tracy Gary
two wise women who have helped, healed, and benefited so many

Contents

1

Introduction

ROGER WALSH

> Happy are those who find wisdom . . .
> She is more precious than jewels,
> And nothing you desire can compare with her. . . .
> Get wisdom, get insight: do not forget.

—Book of Proverbs: The Bible

What is wisdom and how can it be cultivated? These are two of the most important questions of human existence, yet they are tragically neglected in our contemporary culture. We are inundated with information and drowning in data, yet largely bereft of wisdom. As T. S. Eliot (1936) put it:

> Where is the wisdom we have lost in knowledge?
> Where is the knowledge we have lost in information?

This is a dangerous imbalance, and the fate of our species and our planet may well depend on giving wisdom a more central place in both our personal and public lives.

How did wisdom fade from our awareness? After all, for centuries it was revered as one of the greatest of all human virtues. Thousands of years ago, sages such as the Stoic philosopher Epictetus urged, "Content yourself with being a lover of wisdom, a seeker of truth" (Epictetus, 1995, p. 31), while Jewish proverbs exclaimed, "Wisdom is the principal thing; therefore get wisdom" (Proverbs 4:7).

1

Yet in recent centuries, wisdom slipped from Western awareness. Dazzled by the flood of scientific discoveries and technological breakthroughs, people dreamed that science would answer all questions and technology solve all problems. Science became scientism, technology the new savior, and knowledge—not wisdom—the key to living well.

Science and technology certainly delivered miracles. Yet in unwise hands, they also delivered unpredictable and unprecedented disasters, as the awesome power of modern technology dramatically multiplied the impact of human actions. As a result, populations exploded, pollution spread, resources were depleted, wars became genocidal, and the very health of the planet deteriorated.

Like the sorcerer's apprentice, humankind now possesses enormous knowledge, awesome power, and little wisdom. And that is a potentially lethal combination. As Robert Sternberg, former president of the American Psychological Association, lamented, "If there is anything the world needs, it is wisdom. Without it, I exaggerate not at all in saying that very soon, there may be no world" (Sternberg, 2007).

Fortunately, recent years have seen the beginnings of a major reevaluation. Science is no longer worshiped as simply a savior, technophilia and technophobia jostle ambivalently, and wisdom is coming out of the closet. In society at large, there is talk of, for example, elder wisdom, native wisdom, and wisdom cultures.

Scientists have recently joined the quest. Though they long regarded it as too abstruse for investigation, research on wisdom is beginning. But though there is growing interest, the research is as yet preliminary and the information obtained is, by traditional standards, far from profound. The great questions of life and death that sages ponder are as yet unasked in modern laboratories. Of course, this is not surprising for a new research field. Moreover, science must measure and count. Yet what really matters can't always be measured, and what really counts can't always be counted.

If our contemporary culture has only a superficial understanding of wisdom, then the obvious question becomes, "Where can we go for the deepest understanding of wisdom and of how to develop it?" The answer is clear: to the world's great religions and their accompanying philosophies and psychologies. For here, often hidden behind conventional beliefs and rituals, are preserved records of the insights of sages, the depths of existential exploration, and the heights of human understanding.

Of course, the world's religions contain a curious mix of high and low, transcendence and nonsense, sagacity and stupidity. Yet the quest for wisdom has long been one of their central goals. For example, Jews and Christians claim that wisdom "is more precious than jewels" (Proverbs 3:15), while the Koran declares, "[T]those to whom wisdom is given; they truly have received abundant good" (Koran II: 269). In Hinduism the cultivation of wisdom constitutes a major spiritual path or yoga, while in Buddhism wisdom is regarded as the preeminent spiritual capacity.

But what we need above all else are methods to nurture wisdom. Fortunately, the contemplative core of the great religions contains these methods. Each tradition preserves methods for actually cultivating wisdom through systematic practices such as contemplation, meditation, yoga, and reflection on the great mysteries of life and death. These practices constitute a veritable "art of wisdom" or "science of wisdom." At their best, therefore, the great religions contain both timeless treasuries of humankind's accumulated wisdom and effective methods for fostering it.

How can this treasury be brought to the contemporary world? One strategic method is to gather distillations of wisdom from each of the great religions and their accompanying philosophies and psychologies. In short, to create a book that offers summaries of each tradition's sapiential principles and practices. These are the goals of *The World's Great Wisdom*.

To achieve these goals, I sought outstanding scholar-practitioners from each of the great religions, as well as from Western philosophy, to contribute chapters. These contributors are all both noted scholars with expert intellectual knowledge of their tradition as well as practitioners who use their tradition's reflective and contemplative techniques themselves. They therefore have both intellectual and experiential expertise in their traditions. This direct experience and prolonged practice is essential, because if there is one thing on which the world's wisdom traditions agree, it is that to fully comprehend deep wisdom requires careful preparation and practice.

Having found these contributors, I asked them to address several topics from the perspective of their traditions, and especially the major questions:

- What is wisdom?

- How is it cultivated?

- What are its implications for individuals, society, and the world?

The book's final section compares these chapters and examines wisdom from an integral perspective. This comparison allows us to identify unique features and common themes among traditions, and to extract general principles and practices.

Wisdom is both vast and profound, potentially encompassing all of life, and consequently we need a large framework from which to examine it. Integral theory offers a remarkably encompassing conceptual framework, and so the final chapters introduce integral theory and use it to enrich the comparative analyses.

The World's Great Wisdom, therefore, offers a distillation and examination of the world's priceless heritage of humanity's deepest insights into the great questions and issues of life. It constitutes a unique resource that, for the first time in history, brings together one of our most priceless treasures: humankind's understandings of wisdom and the ways to nurture it.

References

The Bible. King James Version.

The Bible. New Revised Standard Version.

Eliot, T. S. (1936). *Collected poems 1919–1935.* London: Faber & Faber.

Epictetus. (1995). *The art of living* (S. Lebell, Trans.). San Francisco: Harper San Francisco.

The Koran.

Sternberg, R. (2007). *Wisdom, intelligence, and creativity synthesized.* New York: Cambridge University Press.

2

Judaism and Its Wisdom Literature

Rabbi Rami Shapiro

Jewish wisdom, *chochmah* in Hebrew, isn't as much a body of knowledge to be mastered, as it is a lifelong project to be undertaken. The aim of this project is spelled out in the opening verses of *Sefer Mishlei,* the Book of Proverbs:

> These are the proverbs and parables of Solomon,
> son of David, King of Israel, offered as
> a guide to insight, understanding, and spiritual discipline
> to help you become generous, honest, and balanced.
> (Proverbs 1:1–3; author's translation)

Wisdom and the pursuit of wisdom are valuable to all people, from the simple and the young to the seeker and the sage. Much of what is contained in Jewish wisdom literature is clearly aimed at the former, offering practical insights into the workings of the world that will benefit them as they mature and take their place as productive citizens of their communities. This is not the wisdom with which we will be concerned. Our goal is to reveal the core teaching of *chochmah* and a method for actualizing it in one's daily life.

Chochmah, despite all attempts to tame her, is seditious. This is why the wise speak in parable and puzzle; to speak clearly is to place themselves at risk. For what they teach is not simply an alternative worldview, but a series of observations that eat at the foundations of the official worldview until that worldview collapses under its own weight, and with it the power of those who preach it.

Following the schema of Lawrence Kohlberg, director of Harvard's Center for Moral Education, there are three categories of worldview: Preconventional, Conventional, and Postconventional, each with its own sense of wisdom and morality. The Preconventional worldview is rooted in the notion that those with superior power determine what is true, wise, and good. You know an action is good because compliance is rewarded, and resistance is punished. Wisdom is the system that identifies what is good and what is not based on reward and punishment, and truth is simply that set of ideas insisted upon by those with the power to enforce them.

One of the clearest expressions of Preconventionalism in the Hebrew Bible is the rebellion of Korah and the Elders of Israel against Moses found in the Book of Numbers (1–40). Relying on the notion, revealed by God, that all Israelites are holy and equal in the sight of God, Korah and 250 of the leaders of Israel demand that Moses replace his autocratic rule with a more democratic style of leadership (Numbers 16:3). The rebellion spreads to the entire people, and they gather behind Korah to confront Moses at the Tent of Meeting. Moses address the people this way:

> "This is how you shall know that the LORD has sent me to do all these works; it has not been of my own accord . . . if the LORD creates something new, and the ground opens its mouth and swallows them up, with all that belongs to them, and they go down alive into Sheol, then you shall know that these men have despised the LORD." As soon as he finished speaking all these words, the ground under them was split apart. The earth opened its mouth and swallowed them up, along with their households—everyone who belonged to Korah and all their goods. (Numbers 16:28–33, NRSV)

A more sophisticated expression of Preconventional thinking, one that arises on the heels of the "might makes right" model mentioned above, is transactional: I do to you what you do to me. The classic example of this in the Hebrew Bible can be found in Leviticus:

> Anyone who maims another shall suffer the same injury in return: fracture for fracture, eye for eye, tooth for tooth; the injury inflicted is the injury to be suffered. One who kills an animal shall make restitution for it; but one who kills a human being shall be put to death. You shall have one law for the alien and for the citizen: for I am the LORD your God. (Leviticus 24:19–22, NRSV)

In Preconventional worldviews right and wrong are determined by power and personal satisfaction. In Conventional worldviews a more sophisticated level of thinking is required that subsumes individual happiness to group cohesion. The community rather than the powerful individual determines what is good and true and wise. Adherence to the community's rules and laws, rather than the often arbitrary whim of the powerful, now constitutes morality.

This is the worldview to which most people ascribe, and upon which much of Judaism in its contemporary form rests. The central teaching of the Conventional worldview is that wisdom and morality lie with group conformity. The official worldview of Judaism, then and now, clearly falls within Kohlberg's category of Conventional. It is articulated in the Book of Deuteronomy and read twice daily in the liturgy:

> If you will only heed his every commandment that I am commanding you today—loving the LORD your God, and serving him with all your heart and with all your soul—then he will give the rain for your land in its season, the early rain and the later rain, and you will gather in your grain, your wine, and your oil; and he will give grass in your fields for your livestock, and you will eat your fill. (Deuteronomy 11:13–15, NRSV)

Simply put, the official worldview of Judaism is this: do good, get good; where "doing good" is defined as keeping the *mitzvot* (divine commandments), and "getting good" is defined as material success. The problem with this theology is that it doesn't hold up under the contingencies of everyday life. It doesn't take much investigation to see that good people often suffer while wicked people often prosper. Nor does it take a detailed examination of Jewish history to see that even the most observant Jews fall victim to God's blazing wrath. Unless we assume that God's angry fire, manifest in our time as the flames of the Nazi crematoria, took the lives of nonobservant Jews only, it is terrifyingly obvious that the "do good, get good" theology is farcical. But you don't have to be a Holocaust historian to question this theology, as the ancient wisdom sages, especially the author of the Book of Job, make clear.

The worldview of the wisdom sages falls into Kohlberg's category of Postcoventional. The Postcoventional thinker seeks to identify universal moral principles, and to use these to guide her actions. The Hebrew Wisdom sages did not find wisdom in the covenant with God, the sacrificial service of priests, or even the revelations of prophets. They were independent observers of life, and their teachings reflected what they saw to be true rather than what the official arbiters of truth insisted is true. As we shall see, life is more than a matter of trusting in God, adhering to the commandments, or even doing good and receiving good. Life was, and is, a wild chaotic struggle for survival that can be neither tamed nor avoided, only well traveled.

The Wisdom Library

The Wisdom literature consists of the Hebrew books Proverbs, Job, and Ecclesiastes, and the Greek books Wisdom of Solomon and Ben Sirach. I shall present each book of wisdom in turn, highlighting its primary message, and pointing each toward a shared insight that will occupy us in the final section of this essay.

Proverbs

Even a quick glance at the thirty-one chapters of *Sefer Mishlei,* the Book of Proverbs, makes it clear that this is an anthology of sayings. While traditionally ascribed to King Solomon it is impossible to take this claim seriously as the entire collection spans some eight hundred years.

Despite the plurality of voices contained in these collections, one can detect a common thread captured in the phrase *yirat HaShem,* commonly, albeit misleadingly, rendered into English as "fear of the Lord." For example: "*Yirat HaShem* is the beginning of knowledge, wisdom, and character that the foolish scorn" (1:7); "*Yirat HaShem* is hatred of evil" (8:13); and "*Yirat HaShem* is the beginning of wisdom, and the knowledge of the Holy One is insight" (9:10).

Translating *yirat HaShem* as "fear of the Lord," while quite common, is more than a little problematic. First, *yirat* can mean both "fear" and "awe," and either would be a legitimate translation of the Hebrew. Choosing "fear" over "awe" gives the phrase *yirat HaShem* an emotional quality of alarm that "awe" clearly lacks, and which the authors of these sayings may not have intended.

Second, translating *HaShem* as "Lord" assigns gender to God and places "him" at the head of a hierarchical system reflective of the patriarchal hierarchy operative in ancient times. Such a rendering, however, is completely independent of the actual Hebrew of the text.

The actual Hebrew, rendered here as *HaShem,* literally "the Name," is the four letter ineffable name of God: *Yod-Heh-Vav-Heh.* Because of the prohibition against pronouncing the name of God, sometime in the third century BCE the euphemism *Adonai,* "Lord," became the accepted stand-in for the unpronounceable four letter Name of God. So, *yirat HaShem* is not "fear of the Lord," but "fear of *Yod-Heh-Vav-Heh.*"

Yod-Heh-Vav-Heh is the singular, future imperfect form of the Hebrew verb "to be," reflecting the self-revelation of God to Moses at the Burning Bush, *ehyeh asher ehyeh*, "I will be what I will be" (Exodus 3:14). Hebrew lacks a present tense for the verb "to be," and thus the more common translation of Exodus as "I am that I am," locks the biblical notion of God into a static mode that the Hebrew does not allow. The Hebrew God is not a noun but a verb; not a being or even the Supreme Being, but be–ing itself.

This grammatical insight is the basis for the panentheism of much of Jewish mystical teaching. The sixteenth–century kabbalist, Rabbi Moshe Cordovero, for example, defines God this way: [God] is found in all things and all things are found in God, and there is nothing devoid of divinity, heaven forfend. Everything is in God, and God is in everything and beyond everything, and there is nothing beside God (Cordovero, 1881).

Similarly Rabbi Schneur Zalman of Liadi (1745–1812), the founder of Chabad Hasidism taught, "Everything is God, blessed be He, who makes everything be, and in truth the world of seemingly separate entities is entirely annulled" (Zalman, 1979).

If we were to conjure a modern euphemism for *Yod-Heh-Vav-Heh* and *ehyeh asher ehyeh* we might be better served with "that which is happening," or "Be–ing" where be–ing implies the ongoing creative process of life, death, and new life rather than a static source outside the process.

> The absolute reality of God, while extending beyond the conceptual borders of "existence," also fills the entire expanse of existence as we know it. There is no space possible for any other existences or realities we may identify—the objects in our physical universe, the metaphysical truths we contemplate our very selves . . . do not exist in their own reality; they exist only as an extension of divine energy. . . . (Cooper, 2005).

With this understanding of *Yod-Heh-Vav-Heh* we might more accurately read our proverb to say, "Awe of reality (*yirat HaShem*) is the beginning of knowledge, wisdom, and character disdained by fools." Standing in awe of reality is quite different than standing in fear of the Lord.

The question now becomes, what is the correlation between *Yod-Heh-Vav-Heh* and Chochmah, Wisdom? Let me suggest that Chochmah is the personification of *HaShem*. While God is clearly anthropomorphized in Torah, the first five books of the Bible, there is no corresponding understanding of God in the Book of Proverbs. God as *Yod-Heh-Vav-Heh* is the abstract reality of which we are comprised and in which we function. *Yod-Heh-Vav-Heh* is far closer to St. Paul's notion of God as that "in whom we live and move and have our being" (Acts 17:28, NRSV), than to the all too human God of Torah. Yet it is difficult for people to relate to such an abstraction. We need a sense of divinity with whom we can interact. Jesus, God's son, plays that role in the Christian Gospels; Chochmah, God's daughter plays it in Proverbs:

> I fill the hearts of those who love me,
> they will never lack for insight.
> I am the deep grain of creation, the subtle current of life.
> God fashioned me before all things;
> I am the blueprint of creation.
> I was there from the beginning, from before there was a beginning.
> I am independent of time and space, earth and sky . . .
> My nature is joy, and I gave God constant delight.
> Now that the world is inhabited, I rejoice in it.
> I will be your true delight if you will heed my teachings.
> (Proverbs 8:21–31; author's translation)

The choice of personifying wisdom as a woman may reflect the cultural influence of the Egyptian Goddess *Ma'at* who, like Chochmah, represents order, balance, and justice.

In the twenty-fifth-century BCE text, *The Proverbs of Ptah-hotep* (Jacq, 1999) we learn that Ma'at, justice, is the foundation of creation (1.6, 5), and she alone endures (1.6, 7). Aligning oneself with Ma'at assures long life for both oneself and one's children (1.18, 1). We can see parallels with Chochmah: She too was the foundation of creation (Proverbs 8:23); walking Chochmah's path is the key to a righteous and long life (Proverbs 2:20:22). In the Egyptian hymn to Amon-Re, the Egyptian Creator and Sustainer of life, Ma'at is revealed as Truth who comes forth from Amon-Re and burns up the wicked. Proverbs 2:20–22 tells that Chochmah comes from God and cuts off and uproots the wicked.

Chochmah was not simply the first of God's creations; she is the means of creation itself, the "master builder" (Proverbs 8:30, the Hebrew can be read as "child" or "craftsman"). To know wisdom is to become wise. To become wise is to find happiness and peace: "Her ways are ways of pleasantness, and all her paths are peace. She is a Tree of Life to those who lay hold of her; those who hold her close are happy" (Proverbs 3:17–18).

This last claim is testable. You don't believe in Wisdom, you engage with her. If your engagement with Wisdom leads to pleasantness and peace, then you have proof that her teachings are true.

As I understand the matter, the key to the awakening that is Wisdom is having a clear perception of reality. Wisdom not only leads you to this clarity; she is this clarity. Imagine you wake up in the middle of the night to find a snake coiled at the end of your bed. You freeze in fear, and spend the rest of the night awake, afraid, and frozen in place. As dawn bathes your bedroom in soft light you suddenly realize that the "snake" is simply the belt you forgot to put away as you undressed the night before. The fear ends as quickly as it arose. Nothing has changed but the quality of your perception.

Changing the quality of perception is the key to Job's awakening in the Book of Job. While it is true that what Job sees is beyond the descriptive capacity of language, that he saw it is central to his spiritual realization.

Job

The Book of Job, dating in its current form to the fourth century BCE, consists of two distinct elements: the narrative that opens and closes the book, and the epic poem that is its primary focus. The narrative is the older of the two. In it Satan, God's prosecuting attorney, reports to God on the doings of humanity. Asked about Job, God's favorite, Satan suggests that the pious Job would curse God to His Face if God were not so gracious to him. To test Satan's hypothesis, God empowers Satan to do whatever he will with Job's businesses and family, but must leave the man himself untouched (Job 1:12). Satan destroys Job's businesses, kills his flocks and herds, sends marauding bands to attack and destroy his caravans, and kills his children via a tornado that flattens the home in which they were eating. Job is devastated, but does not curse God, saying instead, "Naked I came from my mother's womb, and naked shall I return there; HaShem gave, and HaShem has taken away; blessed be the name HaShem" (Job 1:21).

Reporting Job's continued loyalty to God at their next meeting, Satan suggests that Job has held his tongue because Job himself was not physically harmed. God tests Satan's claim by placing Job's health, but not his life, in Satan's hands. Job is suddenly covered with boils from the soles of his feet to the crown of his head. Job's wife finds her husband scratching his sores with the sharp ends of broken pottery. The horror of his plight stuns her, and she says, "You still keep your integrity? Curse God and die!" (Job 2:9).

Job refuses to do so, however, saying, "Should we accept only good from God and not evil?" (Job 2:10). For his loyalty, God rewards Job with renewed health, financial success, and a new brood of healthy and righteous children. While the overt message here is that loyalty to God results in material reward, the theological insight that God is the source of all things good as well as evil is the more important teaching. Job is confirming the teaching found in Isaiah 45:7 where God says, "I form light and create darkness; I make peace and create evil; I am HaShem, Maker of all things." Isaiah and Job offer us a theology that sees God as beyond good and evil even as God is the source of good and evil.

The message of the narrative section of Job maintains the "do good, get good" theology even as it hints of something more. The bulk of the book, the poetic heart of Job, explores that something more.

The poetic section of Job is a series of conversations primarily between Job and four friends who come to "comfort" him. Their comfort, however, is simply an attempt to get Job to admit that he is concealing some evil, and it is this evil that is the cause of his plight. God only punishes the wicked, they argue; Job is clearly being punished; so Job's supposed righteousness is a mask, and he must be wicked. If Job would confess his wickedness, God would surely forgive him, and his torment would cease. Job clings to his innocence, however, and demands that God show himself and explain what is happening.

Despite the phrase "the patience of Job," Job himself is anything but patient, "As for me, I will not hold back my tongue; I will give voice to my torment; I will protest the bitterness of my life" (Job 7:11).

The climax of the Book of Job is the appearance of God. It is crucial to the message of the story that God appears to Job from out of a whirlwind (Job 38:1). Job is looking to make sense of things, and God further blinds and disorients him. Imagine Job engulfed in the skin-tearing sands of this whirlwind and hearing the voice of God demanding that Job answer God's questions.

The poet has reversed the setting. It was Job who was questioning God all this time, and receiving no answers. But now that God arrives it is not to answer Job's questions but to pose his own. God's questions are, on the surface, irrelevant to Job's situation. God doesn't address Job's concerns at all, but peppers him with questions about the enormity of the universe, "Where were you when I set the foundation of the earth? Speak if you know!" (Job 38:4–7). Job wants justice; God offers only awe.

But as we read in the Book of Proverbs, the beginning of wisdom is awe. God is going to bring Job to wisdom, and to do so God has to strip Job of his anthropocentric view of reality. God cannot be reduced to human ideas of right and wrong, just and unjust. Creation does not run in harmony with human notions of law and order. Creation is irreducibly wild—*tohu v'vohu* as Genesis 1:1 tells us, chaotic and unformed. There is no conquering the chaos of life. There is no avoiding the terror of merely being alive. There is only learning how to make meaning in the madness.

Job's clinging to his integrity (Job 2:9), and his understanding that both the good and the horrible come from God (Job 2:10), prepare him for the climactic encounter with God in the whirlwind. Job is not willing to surrender to injustice, but neither is he willing to plead guilty to crimes he didn't commit in order to bolster the conventional worldview of his friends who insist that if you do good you will get good, and if you do evil you will be punished.

The author of Job is telling us that there is no *quid pro quo* in the universe. God is not human. Nature is not human. For all humanity's ideas to the contrary, humans are a tiny part of a vast and cosmic frenzy. Whatever justice and order there may be in the universe it is beyond the limited anthropomorphic fantasies of the conventional worldview.

Yet do not imagine the Book of Job to be promoting a kind of nihilism. As I read the Book of Job, especially when read alongside the rest of the Hebrew Wisdom Books, I don't see these books propounding a pointless universe and a meaningless life, but rather a vast and wild universe that transcends human categories of justice. It isn't that life has no meaning, but that only when you see life for what it is are you able to make meaning in the midst of it. Yet seeing the truth can be frightening, and our initial response, like that of Job, may be to hide from it.

Having gotten what he wished for, an audience with God, Job now wants it all to cease. He cannot answer any of God's questions, and wishes only that God stop asking them. Job says, "Enough! I see I am puny and worthless. How can I possibly respond to you? I slap my hand across my mouth to silence my speech. I spoke once, but no more; twice but not again" (Job 40: 4–5).

You might expect God to leave Job alone at this point, but the opposite is true. God redoubles his efforts and begins the questioning all over again. But why? What has Job left to learn from the wildness of God and his creation? The key is in Job's proclamation of humanity's worthlessness. This is not awe, but fear. God wants Job to move through the fear toward awe. And he does. After a second round of terrifying questions Job says, "I had heard of you by the hearing of the ear, but now my eye sees you; therefore I despise myself, and repent in dust and ashes" (Job 42:5–6, NRSV).

We have to go carefully into these, the final words of Job, if we are to discover the wisdom they contain. Job "heard of God," that is, he had ideas about God. He knew the standard theologies of his friends, and tried unsuccessfully to reconcile them with his own experience. Stripped of what he had heard, he is now fully engaged with God, seeing God with his eyes. But what could Job see? God was speaking from a whirlwind. Job was blinded by the burning sands tearing through his already ravaged flesh. Job isn't talking about physical sight. God didn't show him anything, but only asked questions. Job is speaking of an inner seeing, and what he saw was that he, and all creation, was nothing but dust and ash.

Now there are two possible realizations that this seeing can call forth. Either Job passes through fear into awe, the beginning of wisdom, or he passes into self-hatred. Most English translations, such as the New Revised Standard Version quoted above, lead us to believe he falls into the latter, but they are wrong.

The Hebrew verb *'em'as* does not mean "to despise," but "to reject," and what Job is rejecting is not himself, but the ideas about God he had heard with his ears. Job now knows that God cannot be reduced to theology. The second verb, *nichamti,* means "to comfort or console" rather than "repent." Somehow, being stripped of theological notions is comforting to Job, why? Because it reveals that he is dust and ash, *'afar va-'efer.* The NRSV makes it appear that Job is repenting of his arrogance in the surrounding dust and ash; Job is groveling in the dirt. But the phrase *'afar va-'efer* appears earlier in Job (30:19) as a reference to Job's body, not the place in which he sits. What Job realizes is that he and the universe are both dust and ash, and that dust and ash are the very stuff of awe and wonder. Job is led by God to the transcendent realization that God and creation are greater than humanity but nonetheless include humanity. Job is part of the wildness of the divine manifestation; and so are we.

A parallel teaching may be found in the Heart Sutra, a central text of the *Prajnaparamita* (Perfection of Wisdom) literature of Buddhism. Composed in China sometime in the first century CE, the Heart Sutra speaks to the core philosophical principle of emptiness (*sunya*). The most famous line of this sutra is, "Form is emptiness. Emptiness is form." The seeming paradox of the teaching fades when you realize that emptiness is not a state but an action. Like *Yod-Heh-Vav-Heh,* emptiness is best understood as a verb rather than a noun. Rather than the standard "form is emptiness, emptiness is form," a more philosophically accurate rendering of the text would be "form is emptying; emptying is forming."

Nothing in the world of Wisdom, Jewish or Buddhist, is fixed; everything is in flux. Problems arise only when we seek to make permanent that which is intrinsically impermanent. The suffering of Job and the self-righteousness of his friends arose because both clung to an abstract and fixed notion of justice laid waste by the wildness of God manifest as creation. Job's insight that the rising and fading of things both comes from God (Job 1:21), and that one cannot take precedence over the other, is what allows him to move deeper into truth until he realizes that all reality is a whirlwind of rising and fading, coming and going, birthing and dying. Job's ultimate realization that he is nothing other than this cosmic dance brings him a sense of peace by shifting his identity from the microcosmic dimension of humanity to the macrocosmic dimension of God. While it is, admittedly, a stretch, I can imagine Job spontaneously shouting a Hebrew equivalent to the central mantra of the Heart Sutra: *gate, gate, paragate, parasamgate, Bodhi swaha!* "Gone, gone, gone beyond all notions and categories, gone beyond even the idea of beyond—Enlightenment! Hail!" (author's rendering).

Going beyond, realizing that form is emptying, doesn't yet tell us how to live with the forming. While the Book of Job does a fine job decimating the conventional worldview of Job's friends, and pointing us to the possibility of enlightenment and a true understanding of "dust and ash," it does not offer a way to live in the midst of the chaos it reveals. For this we turn to the Book of Ecclesiastes.

Ecclesiastes

The author of Ecclesiastes claims to be King Solomon, but the language of the text—specifically the use of Aramaic and Persian words, and Hebrew grammatical forms unknown in Solomon's time—makes this impossible. While scholars disagree as to the exact date, it is safe to say the book was written sometime around 250 BCE.

Koheleth, the Hebrew name of the book, and *Ecclesiastes,* its Greek counterpart, are titles rather than proper nouns. Both terms mean "Assembler" or "Compiler," suggesting that the author wove together wisdom from multiple sources. Whoever the author was his book takes the teaching of wisdom to another level.

Nowhere does Koheleth use the Israelite name of God, *Yod-Heh-Vav-Heh,* preferring instead the term *HaElohim,* literally "The God." This is both striking and provocative: striking in that a Jewish text does not refer to the Jewish god, and provocative in that the formulation *HaElohim* rather than the more common *Elohim* found throughout the Bible implies a more abstract and impersonal understanding of God.

Elohim is the creator God of Genesis: "In the beginning *Elohim* created the heavens and the earth" (Genesis 1:1). Elohim belongs to no tribe or nation, and is associated with no religion or cult. It is Elohim in whose image women and men are created (Genesis 1:26). It is Elohim who blesses the new creation and proclaims it "very good" (Genesis 1:31). And it is Elohim who creates the Sabbath by resting on the seventh day, but does not impose it upon the Hebrew people as their personal Sabbath. Elohim is a global deity, not a tribal one. Over time, Elohim, the God worshipped by the northern tribes and *HaShem* (*Yod-Heh-Vav-Heh*), the name of God preferred by the southern tribes are linked, appearing in much of the Bible as *HaShem Elohim*, or as most English Bibles translate it, Lord God.

Koheleth, however, opts for neither *Elohim* nor *HaShem,* choosing instead the rare form *HaElohim.* Koheleth is not abandoning *HaShem,* but is pointing to something more impersonal. Take note of Deuteronomy 4:35 where we read, "You have been shown [all this] in order to know that *HaShem* is *HaElohim*! There is nothing else (*ayn od*)." *HaShem,* the ineffable and unconditionable one who chose the Jews as the vehicle for carrying the divine wisdom into the world, is none other than *HaElohim,* the global, trans-tribal Reality that cannot be bound by word or tribe. And this divine reality is all there is (*ayn od*): all life is an expression of the singular reality of God.

Koheleth is pointing beyond the gods of any nation to speak of the singular reality that embraces all creation. It is the nature of this reality that concerns Koheleth most. He calls it *hevel havalim* (Ecclesiastes 1:2). While most English Bibles render this phrase as "vanity of vanities" or "futility upon futility," Koheleth's Hebrew is far subtler. *Hevel* means "breath" or "vapor" and suggests neither vanity nor futility, but impermanence: life is as fleeting as breath, as temporary as dew.

Hevel occurs some seventy times in the Hebrew Bible to indicate the brevity of human life. Job says, "my life is a breath," and "my days are a breath" (Job 7:7, 16, NRSV); the Psalmist tells that human beings "are like a breath; their days are like a passing shadow" (Psalm 144:4, NRSV); "Men are mere breath; mortals, illusion; placed on a scale all together, they weigh even less than a breath" (Psalm 62:10, JPS). As Gerhard von Rad puts it, "[Koheleth] lumps all of life's experiences together and then labels the sum nothingness (hevel)" (von Rad, 2006).

HaElohim and the universe *HaElohim* creates is one of continual emptying. This is why HaShem is *HaElohim.*

As we have seen, HaShem (*Yod-Heh-Vav-Heh*) is defined in Torah as *ehyeh asher ehyeh,* "I will be whatever I will be" (Exodus 3:14), that is to say, HaShem cannot be restricted to this or that label or concept or form. Koheleth is saying this and more: not only is HaShem in perpetual flux, so is life itself. By using the term *HaElohim,* Koheleth is asking us to recall the reality that spoke to Job from the whirlwind, that reality that cannot be managed or made part of a religious system. Indeed, Koheleth never asks us to pray, to observe *mitzvot* (divine commandments), to attend the festivals or make sacrifice in the Temple.

So what can we do? First here is what we can't do: we can't win. If you expect life to conform to the "do good, get good" ideology, you will be disappointed. Koheleth makes it clear that everyone suffers, everyone grows old, and everyone dies. The rich can lose all they have in a bad investment, or accumulated wealth will fall to children who will spend wildly and foolishly. There is no escaping the absurdity of life. So don't try. Don't expect things to work out the way you wish. Don't expect the courts to be just (3:16), the government to be caring (5:7), or nature to cooperate with your hopes and dreams (3:19–20). Wishing things to be other then they are leads to *re'ut ruach* or *ra'yon ruach*. These idioms, often translated as "chasing after wind," actually mean "disturbing the breath." When you work against *hevel*, the impermanent nature of reality, you end up vexing your own breath; gasping for air as you engage in an endless and futile grasping for permanence in an impermanent world. Working against the way of things is *ahmahl*, needless effort or toil, and there is no benefit to it at all (4:6). It is the opposite of following the path of Chochmah.

Where the Book of Proverbs tells us there is wisdom to be found in the midst of life's turmoil, and where the Book of Job tells us that we will find comfort and contentment in our own impermanence (dust and ash), Koheleth tells us how to achieve *simcha*, joy (5:19). When we stop fighting reality by insisting it conform to some generally agreed upon notions of right and wrong, we can then learn instead to navigate it, we find joy. And how do we manage this? By accepting the reality of impermanence, by ceasing to grasp and gasp, and by doing the four things that Koheleth says will bring us joy: eating and drinking moderately (3:13), engaging in meaningful work (3:13), and bonding with two or three good friends (4:9–12).

Is that it? Can that be all there is to living? Does all of Koheleth's rhetoric lead simply to the mundane? In a sense, yes, but there is nothing mundane about this; it is in fact marvelous. When you realize you are part of the cosmic that embraces and transcends the microcosmic everything you do is imbued with meaning. Hence, the Zen saying: "How wonderful! How marvelous! I chop wood! I carry water!"

This is what the Sufis call the Supreme Identity. You have realized your fundamental identity with the Condition of all conditions and the Nature of all natures and the Being of all beings. Since spirit is the suchness or condition of all things, it is perfectly compatible with all things. It is even nothing special. It is chop wood, carry water. For this reason, individuals who reach this state are often depicted as very ordinary people, nothing special about them. This is the path of sages, of the wise men and women who are so wise you can't even spot it. (Wilber, 2001)

Job taught us that life is impermanent and chaotic: it and we are but dust and ash. He found comfort in this realization because it freed him from having to conform his life and his worldview to the conventional worldview of his community: do good, get good. But Job does not tell us how to live with the wisdom he attained. What do we do, now that we know we are but dust and ash? We eat, we drink, we work, and we befriend. In a sense, Job tells us what life is, Koheleth tells us how best to live it. Nothing special.

Ben Sirach

Sometime around 175 BCE, Ben Sira, a Jewish sage living in Alexandria, Egypt, wrote a book of instruction for his students. Ben Sira's grandson translated the original Hebrew text into Greek, thus expanding its audience. While held in high regard by Jews of his time and for generations thereafter, *Sefer Ben Sira* (the Book of Ben Sira) was never considered canonical by the Jews. The Greek translation of his grandson Jesus, however, did become part of the Septuagint, the Greek translation of the Hebrew scriptures, and entered into the Catholic and Orthodox Christian canons as part of the Apocrypha under the Greek name *Sirach* or the Latin *Ecclesiasticus*.

The Book of Ben Sira is a collection of ethical teachings along the model of the Book of Proverbs. While useful as a guide to life and ideas extant in Ben Sira's time, the most important aspect of the book for our purposes is its attempt to "Judaize" wisdom. Where Proverbs, Job, and Koheleth offer a universalist notion of wisdom unchained to Jewish life, the Book of Sira seeks to link *chochmah* with Torah. Speaking of herself in a manner similar to Proverbs, Chochmah says,

> I came forth from the mount of the Most High, and covered the earth like a mist. I dwelt in the highest heavens, and my throne was in a pillar of cloud. Alone I compassed the vault of heaven and traversed the depths of the abyss. . . . Among all these I sought a resting place; in whose territory should I abide? (Sirach 24:3–7, NRSV)

The notion that wisdom needs to abide in a territory and hence to be associated with a people is new. Not surprisingly, given that Sira is a Jewish sage, it is among the Jews that wisdom dwells:

> Then the Creator of all things gave me a command, and my
> Creator chose the place for my tent. He said, "Make your dwell-
> ing in Jacob, and in Israel receive your inheritance." Before the
> ages, in the beginning, he created me, and for all the ages I shall
> not cease to be. In the holy tent I ministered before him, and
> so I was established in Zion. Thus in the beloved city he gave
> me a resting place, and in Jerusalem was my domain. I took root
> in an honored people, in the portion of the Lord, his heritage.
> (Sirach 24:8–12, NRSV)

If any doubt should linger regarding the identity of Wisdom with
Judaism, Sira puts it to rest saying, "All this is the book of the covenant of
the Most High God, the law that Moses commanded us as an inheritance
for the congregations of Jacob" (Sirach 24:23).

As we shall see shortly, linking wisdom with Torah will prove central
to the cultivation of wisdom's central revelation: the nonduality of reality
in, with, and as *HaElohim*.

Wisdom of Solomon

Written by an unnamed Alexandrian Jewish sage perhaps a century after the
Book of Sira, the Wisdom of Solomon carries on Sira's attempt to uphold
the viability of Torah by linking Torah with wisdom, but does so without
reducing wisdom's universality. Written during a period when Greek philosophies competed with Judaism for the loyalties of many Jews, especially
those living outside the Promised Land, the Wisdom of Solomon defends
Judaism by essentially equating God with Wisdom:

> For it is he [God] who gave me unerring knowledge of what
> exists, to know the structure of the world and the activity of
> the elements; the beginning and end and middle of times, the
> alternations of the solstices and the changes of the seasons, the
> cycles of the year and the constellations of the stars, the natures
> of animals and the tempers of wild animals, the powers of spirits
> and the thoughts of human beings, the varieties of plants and the
> virtues of roots; I learned both what is secret and what is mani-
> fest, for wisdom, the fashioner of all things, taught me. (Wisdom
> 7:17–22, NRSV)

The Wisdom of Solomon defines wisdom as one might define God:

intelligent, holy, unique, manifold, subtle, mobile, clear, unpolluted, distinct, invulnerable, loving the good, keen, irresistible, beneficent, humane, steadfast, sure, free from anxiety, all-powerful, overseeing all, and penetrating through all spirits that are intelligent, pure, and altogether subtle . . . for God loves nothing so much as the person who lives with wisdom. (Wisdom 7:22–28, NRSV)

The Nature of Wisdom

Having briefly outlined the texts comprising Jewish Wisdom literature, we now turn to the Lady herself. Just who is Chochmah and what does she teach?

Chochmah is both the way and the way-pointer:

I fill the hearts of those who love me,
they will never lack for insight.
I am the deep grain of creation, the subtle current of life.
God fashioned me before all things;
I am the blueprint of creation.
I was there from the beginning, from before there was a beginning.
I am independent of time and space, earth and sky . . .
My nature is joy, and I gave God constant delight.
Now that the world is inhabited, I rejoice in it.
I will be your true delight if you will heed my teachings.
(Proverbs 8:21–31; author's translation)

Chochmah exists before time and with it. She is the archetype of creation and the way creation functions. To know Her is to know

the structure of the world and the activity of the elements; the beginning and end and middle of times, the alternations of the solstices and the changes of the seasons, the cycles of the year and the constellations of the stars. . . . I learned both what is secret and what is manifest, for wisdom, the fashioner of all things, taught me. (Wisdom of Solomon 7:17–22, NRSV)

Chochmah is the "breath of God," a "spotless mirror" reflecting divine creativity. "Although she is but one, she can do all things, and while remaining in herself, she renews all things; in every generation she passes into holy souls and makes them friends of God, and prophets; for God loves nothing so much as the person who lives with wisdom" (Wisdom of Solomon 7:27–28, NRSV).

Our question now becomes, how do we live with wisdom? We opened our discussion of the Hebrew Wisdom tradition with the claim that it was a postconventional worldview depending on neither personal gratification nor compliance with communal norms, but on universal principles available to all: Chochmah translated into a way of living.

Like the grain in wood, Chochmah "pervades and penetrates" all things (Wisdom of Solomon 7:24, NRSV). Just as the experienced woodworker learns to cut with the grain, so the wise learn to work with Chochmah. You do not pray to her or choose her, you simply see her and work in harmony with Her. Wisdom operates for you whether or not you appreciate her. What distinguishes the wise from the foolish is their ability to distinguish between a belt and a snake.

How do you become wise? "The beginning of Wisdom is this: Get Wisdom!" (Proverbs 4:7). While this teaching may seem solipsistic, it actually reveals an important aspect of Chochmah: the way to Wisdom is Wisdom herself. The way of Wisdom is study, observation, and clear perception. What you study, observe, and perceive is Wisdom as well, for she is both the Way to and the Way of. Wisdom "knows and understands all things," (Wisdom of Solomon 9:10, NRSV) because she is the creative energy through which God fashions all things. To know her is to know the Way of all things. But you cannot study Chochmah in the abstract, for there is no abstract with her. You study Chochmah by studying life and the myriad living beings that comprise life.

Chochmah is not a reluctant guide or a hidden guru. She is not hard to find, nor does she require any austere test to prove you are worthy of her. Rather she "stands on the hilltops, on the sidewalks, at the crossroads, at the gateways" (Proverbs 8:1–11; author's translation) and calls to you to follow her. Wisdom's only desire is to teach you to become wise. Her only frustration is your refusal to listen to her.

The Bible is not reticent to sing Chochmah's praises. She is "intelligent, holy, unique, manifold, subtle, active, incisive, pure, lucid, invulnerable, gracious, keen, irresistible, loyal, trustworthy, all-powerful, all-pervading, and all-penetrating" (Wisdom of Solomon 7:22–23, NRSV). Clearly, Chochmah rivals God in many ways, but this is not surprising, for she is the Way God is manifest in the world. To know her is to know God as well.

> Search for Her and seek Her out, and She will reveal Herself to you. When you lay hold of Her do not let Her go. Take your rest with Her at last, and She will become ecstasy for you. (Wisdom of Jesus ben Sirach, 6:27–28, NRSV)

If Wisdom is both the teacher and the taught, then following her is becoming intimate with her. The Hebrew verb "to know" means both intellectual knowing and sexual intimacy. To know Wisdom is to be her lover, and by loving her you become God's beloved as well for "the Lord loves those who love Her" (Wisdom of Jesus ben Sirach 4:14, NRSV).

How are you to love Chochmah? By knowing her. You know her by knowing how she manifests in the world as the world. You know her, the Way of Life, when you know the ways of the living.

Practicing the Way of Wisdom

With the rise of rabbinic Judaism as the de facto Jewish standard bearer following the destruction of the Temple and its priestly class by Rome in 70 CE, the wisdom tradition became part of rabbinic teaching, and Chochmah was equated with Torah. Indeed, it is not uncommon to see inscribed above the ark holding the Torah scrolls in synagogues around the world the words of Proverbs 3:18, "She is a Tree of Life to those who hold her close, and all who cling to Her find happiness." As we have noted, the text originally referred to Wisdom not Torah, but over time the two were conflated, and today the way of wisdom is the way of Torah.

To practice wisdom, then, is to practice Torah. But just what does this mean? Shall we equate Chochmah with the 613 *mitzvot* of rabbinic Judaism? To do so would be to ignore and indeed to undo the teachings of the Wisdom Literature we have just reviewed. So what is Torah? The answer can be found in the teaching of the first-century Jewish wisdom sage Hillel:

> It happened that a certain gentile came before Shammai [Hillel's chief rabbinic rival] and said to him, "I will convert to Judaism on condition that you teach me the whole Torah while I stand on one foot." Outraged by the insult [that the 613 commandments of Judaism could be reduced in this way], Shammai chased the man away, threatening to strike him with the builder's level that was in his hand [rabbis didn't earn a living from scholarship; Shammai earned his as a building contractor]. The gentile then went before Hillel and said, "I will convert to Judaism on condition that you teach me the whole Torah while I stand on one foot." Hillel replied, "What is hateful to you, do not do to your neighbor: that is the whole Torah, all the rest is commentary; go and learn it." (*Babylonian Talmud,* Tractate *Shabbat,* 31a)

Hillel's recasting of Torah as compassion is what makes him a wisdom sage. Like the authors of Proverbs, Job, and Ecclesiastes, Hillel makes no mention of mitzvot, prayer, or Temple sacrifice. For him, and I would say for them, wisdom is an understanding of reality that is lived out in acts of compassion. He is not denying the value of the mitzvot, he is only (!) saying that their essential purpose is to promote compassion. Compassion is how one lives Chochmah.

Compassion arises naturally when we realize two things: first, the post-conventional worldview rooted in Chochmah, that is, the interdependence and impermanence of all beings in the active be-ing of God; and second, the fact that most of us live in opposition to wisdom, craving independence and permanence in a world that allows for neither.

The Hebrew Bible has a name for this way of living: *achad,* alienation. Its opposite, the way of life arising from wisdom, is *echad,* unity or interdependence. When we live foolishly, that is, without wisdom, we live under the illusion of separate and competing selves. The point of wisdom is to reveal the true nature of reality as interdependent aspects of the singular God. As the nineteenth-century Hasidic sage Rabbi Aharon HaLevi wrote:

> God's only desire is to reveal unity through diversity. That is, to reveal that all reality is unique in all of its levels and in all of its details, and nevertheless united in a fundamental oneness (HaLevi, 1820).

One who realizes the nonduality of all things in, with, and as God, achieves a level of awareness that overcomes any sense of alienation. Speaking of such a person, the thirteenth-century Spanish kabbalist Abraham Abulafia wrote:

> For now he [the awakened individual] is no longer separated from God, and behold he is God and God is he; for he is so intimately adhering to God that he cannot by any means be separate from God, for he is God. See now that I, even I, am God. He is I and I am He (Abulafia, 1988).

The practical implications of this awakening come when we realize that the unity of "I and God" includes the unity of "I and everything else," as the eighteenth-century Hasidic sage Menachem Mendel of Kotzsk wrote:

If I am I, and you are you,
Then I am I and you are you.
But I am I because you are you,
Then I am not I and you are not you.
(Raz & Levin, 1995)

There is no alienated I in the world of the awakened wisdom sage. There is only the interdependence of all in All. As I read the Bible, albeit from my own transpersonal perspective, the root of this insight can be found in Book of Genesis. When God discovers that Adam has eaten from the Tree of Knowledge of Good and Evil, God says,

"Behold the man has become *achad mimenu,* knowing good and evil. Now he might reach out and take also from the Tree of Life, and eat it and gain immortality!" So HaShem God banished him from the Garden of Eden, to work the soil from which he was taken. And having driven out the man, He stationed at the east of the Garden of Eden the cherubim and the flame of the ever-turning sword, to guard the way to the Tree of Life. (Genesis 3:22–24)

To understand this myth we have to understand the Hebrew phrase *achad mimenu,* usually translated as "like one among us." The Hebrew, however, literally means "unique from us," or "one separate from us," or as the great nineteenth-century German scholar and Bible commentator Rabbi Samson Raphael Hirsch taught, *achad* always means the separation of one being from another being or from a group of beings (Hirsch, 1999).

Eating from the tree does not make Adam *like* God, as the serpent promised (Genesis 3:5); rather he becomes *alienated* from God, first psychologically and then physically. Becoming *achad* means that humanity can no longer see itself as a part of the divine whole. Instead, humanity imagines itself to be apart from rather than a part of both God and nature.

God is going to expel Adam from the Garden not simply because God fears Adam could eat from the Tree of Life and thereby gain immortality (God had actually never prohibited the first couple from eating of the Tree of Life or any other tree in the Garden, *except* for the Tree of Knowledge of Good and Evil), but that by eating from it without first overcoming this state of *achad,* alienation, Adam would be eternally cut off from God; he would be forever locked in a world of seeming separation and duality. Thus, the expulsion from the Garden is not so much a punishment as it is a prophylactic.

Chochmah is the cure for the disease of *achad*. Seeing through the illusory duality that is *achad* (imagined alienation from the whole that is God), we awake to *echad,* the unity of all things in, with, and as God, and with this awakening live the way of wisdom by loving our neighbor as our self (Leviticus 19:18) where "neighbor" is understood to be all things. Note the Torah doesn't say, "Love your neighbor as you love yourself," for that would imply a separation of self and neighbor that wisdom rejects. Rather, Torah says love your neighbor as yourself, as a part of the singular self that is the whole of reality.

But the question is how: How do we overcome the alienation that is *achad* and restore the truth of *echad* that is the hallmark of wisdom? The rabbis offer us a variety of ways, all of which are designed, as Rabbi Menachem Mendel Schneerson put it, "to go beyond our own mind" (Schneerson, 1995).

According to the Talmud, for example, the ancient rabbis used to "sit motionless one hour prior to each of the three prayer services, then pray for one hour, and afterwards be still again for one hour more" (*Berachot* 32b). While the Talmud says nothing more about this practice, the preeminent twelfth-century Jewish philosopher Moses Maimonides taught that they practiced sitting motionless "in order to settle their minds and quiet their thoughts" (*Mishneh Torah, Yesodai ha-Torah,* 7:4).

Abraham Abulafia taught a number of techniques for going beyond one's own mind, most of which, however, require a solid foundation in Hebrew. One method that doesn't require this is based on his notion that reality is essentially vibrational and experienced through primal sounds: "And God said . . ." (Genesis 1:3 for example). Abulafia identified these sounds as OH, AH, AY, EE, and UU, the vowels of the Hebrew alphabet. The recitation of these sounds was accompanied by movements of the head: OH—raise the head up and then return to center; AH—turn the head toward the left shoulder and then back to center; AY—turn the head toward the right shoulder and then back to center; EE—turn the head downward and then return to center; and UU—rock the head forward and back, and then return to center (Baer, 1982).

In the nineteenth century, Reb Nachman of Breslav, the great grandson of Hasidism's founder, Rabbi Israel Baal Shem Tov, taught a meditation technique he called *hitbodedut,* self-isolation. Reb Nachman encouraged people to go out into the fields away from other humans and to (among other things) practice "the silent scream":

> You can shout loudly in a "small still voice". . . . Anyone can
> do this. Just imagine the sound of such a scream in your mind.
> Depict the shout in your imagination exactly as it would sound.

Keep this up until you are literally screaming with this soundless "small still voice."

This is actually a scream and not mere imagination. Just as some vessels bring the sound from your lungs to your lips, others bring it to the brain. You can draw the sound through these nerves, literally bringing it into your head. When you do this, you are actually shouting inside your brain. (*Likutey Moharan* I, 52)

The inner scream eventually blots out any self-chatter and leaves one, paradoxically, absorbed in the Divine.

Perhaps the simplest and most widespread Jewish practice for going beyond the mind of achad is *hagah*, the contemplative practice of repeating single words or phrases over and over. "The mouth of the righteous utters (*hagah*) wisdom" (Psalm 37:30); "My tongue shall utter (*hagah*) Your righteousness" (Psalm 35:28).

The Book of Joshua also promotes *hagah*, "This book [perhaps the Torah] shall not depart from your mouth, and you shall meditate (*hagah*) on it day and night" (Joshua 1:9).

Rabbi Dov Ber taught *hagah* in the nineteenth century as a means of overcoming *achad* and achieving *echad*:

A person should be so absorbed in this practice that there is no longer awareness of self. There is nothing but the flow of life; all thoughts are with God. One who still knows how intensely goes the practice has not yet overcome the bonds of life. (Schneerson, 1995)

What word shall we say? There is no agreed upon term, but I follow the teaching of Rabbi Levi Yitzhak of Berditchev (1740–1810), author of the poem *Dudele*:

Where can I find You—and where can I not find You?
Above—only You;
Below—only You;
To the East—only You;
To the West—only You;
To the South—only You;
To the North—only You;
If it is good—it is You;
If it is not—also You;
It is You; It is only You.

Levi Yitzhak taught *hagah* as a means of realizing this poetic expression of the nonduality of God. The word he recommended was *HaRachaman,* the Compassionate One. The practice is simple. There is no formal sitting or walking practice; no melody to be learned, or specific time of day for practice. Simply repeat the word over and over throughout the day: "when sitting in your house when walking on your way, when lying down, and when rising up" (Deuteronomy 6:7).

The practice of *hagah* is a gentler way of experiencing the comfort and consolation Job found when he realized the all-encompassing reality of God. Over time (the rabbis say forty days of serious practice), you awaken to the interconnectedness of all things in, with, and as the One Thing, HaElohim, God. Compassion is the way the wise live out this realization. Or, to state it as clearly as I can: to live wisely is to love fully.

References

Abulafia, A. (1988). In Moshe Idel, *The mystical experience of Abraham Abulafia.* (pp. 126–127). Albany: State University of New York Press.

Baer, D. (1982). *Or Ha-Emet,* 2b, *Yhadut.* In A. Kaplan, *Meditation and Kabbalah.* (p. 302). York Beach, ME: Red Wheel/Weiser, LLC.

Cooper, D. (2005). *Ecstatic Kabbalah.* Denver: Sounds True. (For a solid introduction to Abulafia's methods).

Cordovero, M. (1881). *Eilima Rabati,* fol. 25a. Lvov.

HaLevi, A. (1820). *Sha'arei ha-Yihud ve'ha-Emunah,* IV, chapter 5. Shklov.

Hirsch, S. R. (1999). *The Pentateuch.* (p. 91). Gateshead: Judaica Press.

Jacq, C. (1999). *The living wisdom of ancient Egypt.* New York: Simon & Schuster.

Raz, S., & Levin, E. (1995). *The sayings of Menahem Mendel of Kotsk.* (p. 10). Northvale, New Jersey: Jason Aronson.

Schneerson, M. (1995). *Toward a meaningful life.* In Simon Jacobson, (Ed.). (p. 215). New York: William Morrow & Company.

von Rad, G. (2006). In James Limburg, *Encountering Ecclesiastes: a book for our time.* (p. 12). Grand Rapids, MI: Wm. B. Eerdmans Publishing.

Wilber, K. (2001). *Grace and grit.* (p. 228). Boston: Shambhala.

Zalman, S. (1979). *Likkutei Torah,* Shir ha Shirim, fol. 41a. Brooklyn, NY: Kehot Publication Society.

Bibliography

Bergman, Ozer. (2006). *Where earth and heaven kiss.* Jerusalem: Breslov Research Institute. Published by the Breslover Hasidim and yet written for those not familiar with Reb Nachman, the movement's founder, or *hitbodedut,* his core spiritual practice, *Where earth and heaven kiss* is a masterful introduction to this key Jewish contemplative practice.

Buxbaum, Yitzhak. (1999). *Jewish spiritual practices*. Northvale, NJ: Jason Aronson. This is the "bible" of Jewish contemplative practices, exploring more than two dozen practices from a variety of Jewish mystical and rabbinic schools throughout the millennia.

Cooper, David, *Ecstatic Kabbalah*. (1998). Denver: Sounds True, 2005. Building on his classic introduction to Jewish mysticism, *God is a Verb* (Riverhead Books), Rabbi Cooper focuses his attention on the life, teachings, and contemplative practices of Abraham Abulafia, one of the greatest kabbalists of all time. The book comes with a CD to augment the reader's understanding of Abulafia's sound-based meditative practices.

Raz, Simcha; Edward Levin. (1995). *The sayings of Menahem Mendel of Kotsk*. Northvale, NJ: Jason Aronson. Menahem Mendel was one of Hasidism's most innovative teachers and sages. This collection is a fine introduction to his thought and the greater field of Hasidic wisdom from which he draws.

Schneerson, Menachem Mendel, (1995). *Toward a meaningful life*, Simon Jacobson, ed. New York: William Morrow & Company. This selection of the core teachings of Rabbi Menachem Mendel Schneerson, the last rebbe of Chabad Hasidism, applies the wisdom of Hasidism to contemporary life in a nontechnical manner.

Shapiro, Rami, (2005). *The divine feminine in Biblical wisdom literature*, Woodstock, VT: Skylight Paths. This collection of readings from the entire body of Jewish Biblical Wisdom Literature is accompanied by explanatory notes and contemporary commentary that seek to bring the teachings of Chochmah/Wisdom alive in the life of the reader.

3

Wisdom in the Christian Tradition

LUKE DYSINGER

Christianity is the world's largest religion, with more than 2.1 billion adherents.[1] Christians are found on every continent and in every nation on earth, and the exact number of Christian cultures and subcultures is impossible to calculate. "Christian wisdom" cannot therefore be defined as a single intellectual or spiritual construct, since each Christian culture necessarily cherishes a unique constellation of values and practices that characterize the sage or practitioner of wisdom within that culture. Nevertheless, organized Christianity exists in three major branches: Eastern Orthodoxy, Roman Catholicism, and Protestantism.[2] Since these broadly represent the major historical epochs and cultural groupings that shaped Christianity they will be used in this chapter as reference points for different models of Christian wisdom.

The overwhelming majority of Christians from these three traditions would agree with a definition of wisdom proposed by Paul of Tarsus, also known as the apostle Paul (d.c. 65 CE), whose letters to new Christian communities are among the earliest texts in the New Testament. He succinctly writes, "God made Christ Jesus our wisdom."[3] In other words, for Christians wisdom is not primarily a philosophical concept or ideal, but rather a person—Jesus of Nazareth. Christians are thus considered to be "wise" to the extent that their words and actions reflect and conform to the teaching and practice of Jesus, whom they revere not only as a sage, but as the incarnate Word of God.[4]

Each of the three major branches of Christianity highlights unique aspects of the one wisdom that is Jesus Christ. It is possible to subdivide Christian wisdom into four traditional (although necessarily artificial) categories that reflect broad emphases in these three branches. Roman Catholicism is the Christian continuation into the present of the Latin-speaking western

29

portion of the ancient Roman Empire. Roman Catholicism emphasizes both moral and intellectual wisdom. Great emphasis is laid on a philosophically coherent and consistent system of ethical and theological teaching, based ultimately on the Bible, but informed as well by "tradition," centuries of theological reflection and debate, defined and promulgated by an official "teaching *magisterium*" led by the pope (the bishop of Rome) that also includes other bishops and approved theologians. But the Catholic sage is not always an intellectual or teacher. Those who serve others through social action or prayer are revered in the Catholic Church as exemplars of moral wisdom.

Protestant Christianity arose from Catholicism in the sixteenth century. It is characterized by profound reverence for the Christian sacred scriptures. This textual wisdom lays stress on the ability to memorize, cite, and apply biblical texts. The Bible is regarded as the principal, often the sole basis for doctrine, and the protestant sage is usually a preacher or teacher who can be trusted to correctly interpret the Christian scriptures.

Eastern Orthodoxy is the continuation into the present of the Greek-speaking, eastern half of the Roman Empire, and it particularly emphasizes mystical wisdom. Christian rituals and images are intended to evoke personal awareness of God's immediate presence. Worship is a foretaste of heaven: icons, chant, and ritual gestures invite contemplation of deeper realities that lie hidden beneath surface appearances. The Eastern Orthodox sage is often a mystic who experiences transforming union with God, and shares this gift with others through prayer or spiritual counsel. In what follows, these four categories of wisdom, textual, moral, intellectual (or theological), and mystical (or contemplative) will provide a framework for exploring the development and practice of Christian wisdom. However, it should be borne in mind that there is considerable overlap between them and that these four types of wisdom are deeply interconnected and interdependent.

The Nature of Wisdom:
The Historical Evolution of Christian Wisdom

Jewish Wisdom

Early Christianity inherited well-established wisdom traditions from both Judaism and Greek philosophy. In the Hebrew Scriptures (revered as the "Old Testament" by Christians) wisdom is both practical/moral and spiritual. At an early stage in the history of Judaism "wisdom" (*hokmah* in Hebrew) described both cleverness and rules of behavior. The early Jewish wisdom literature

(c. 1000 BCE) employed proverbs, short pithy sayings conveying advice, and admonitions for a variety of contexts including court etiquette, community interactions, and family dynamics. A principal goal of this literature was to encourage a shift from angry, primitive modes of reacting to a more educated, reflective approach, characterized by patience and self-possession.[5] While very widespread and popular, this approach was intermittently criticized both from within the wisdom tradition itself (particularly in the biblical books of Job and Ecclesiastes) and by the Jewish prophets, who warned that passive conformity to civic and social norms can encourage complacency and diminish awareness of the need for reform and renewal in accordance with the divine law. Later (c. 700–600 BCE), "wisdom" came also to be associated with the divine source of revelation and the divine principle that created and sustains the universe. The Jewish philosopher Philo (c.20 BCE–c.50 CE), who studied Hellenistic philosophy and wrote in Greek, exemplifies this more spiritual, contemplative identification of wisdom with the divine *logos* ("word," "meaning," or "principle"). Philo's biblical commentaries greatly influenced Christian authors of the third and fourth centuries CE.

By the time of Jesus these various understandings of wisdom had given rise to different models of the Jewish sage or practitioner of wisdom. First was the local rabbi or religious teacher, a scholar well educated in the sacred texts who was expected to live an exemplary lifestyle. Second was the enigmatic and generally unpopular, if revered, figure of the prophet, a person uniquely called by God to challenge the Jewish community and recall the faithful from complacency to faithful observance of the law. Third were Jewish martyrs, men and women whose heroic fidelity to their religious heritage had been prefigured to some extent by the often-rejected and suffering prophet. However, their example (the word *martyr* means "witness") became particularly prominent during the intermittent religious persecutions that characterized Greek and Roman domination of the Jewish nation (c. 320 BCE–140 CE). The Jewish martyrs were not generally teachers: it was their example of faithful endurance, rather than their words, that attested to a growing conviction that the final end of wisdom is attainable only after death in "the world to come."

Greek Philosophy

In the Greek philosophical tradition, "wisdom" (*sophia*), originally described adeptness at professional skills or crafts. In this sense it was closely allied to the term *ascesis,* which referred to the practice or exercise necessary to master a skill. In time *sophia* also came to be linked with the word *aretē,* or "virtue," which at this early stage (c. 600 BCE) referred chiefly to successful mastery of a skill or athletic endeavor. The Sophists (c. 450 BCE) identified wisdom with cleverness of speech, understood as a tool for acquiring expertise in practical living. Their approach was rejected and ridiculed by Socrates (c. 469–399 BCE) who maintained that *sophia* begins with an awareness both of one's own ignorance and of what cannot be known. For Socrates's pupil Plato (428–348 BCE), wisdom is concerned with the nature of being and with the archetypal ideas (also called "forms") of the Good, the True, and the Beautiful. True wisdom for Plato is something mystical and divine, ultimately proper to God alone, but which is sought and practiced by the philosopher as the highest in the tetrad of the four cardinal virtues: wisdom, courage, temperance, and justice.

Plato's student Aristotle (384–322 BCE) defined virtue as a "mean" or midpoint, a habitual balance between the vice of excess and the vice of deficiency.[6] He distinguished wisdom (*sophia*) from prudence (*phronēsis*). Prudence, he taught, is a practical or moral virtue, while wisdom is the most complete form of knowledge because it perceives and seeks out the underlying causes (*archai*) and significance of events and things.

The Greek philosophical sage was typically a teacher and a contemplative, that is, a schoolmaster who encouraged his students or disciples to begin their search for wisdom with the practice of virtue (*praktikē*) and the avoidance of vice. They were then to look both closely at and also mystically "within" or "beyond" the conventions of society and the appearances of persons, events, and things. This contemplative study (*theōria*) reinforced and expanded their practical study of personal and social virtue. Thus, the search for wisdom enabled the wise philosopher to ascend from ethical practice to contemplative knowledge and (for Plato) mystical vision.

Early Christian Wisdom

Early Christianity employed definitions and models of wisdom drawn from both Judaism and Greek philosophy. While the influence of classical philosophy was initially more subtle and took longer to become apparent, Christianity's inheritance from Judaism was obvious from the beginning. Jesus was regarded by his earliest disciples as having fulfilled in his own person the triple roles of rabbi, prophet, and martyr. Although he undoubtedly preached in Aramaic (a dialect of Hebrew), his teachings are extant only in Greek, the language of classical philosophy. He uses the words *wisdom* and *prudence* in ways that are compatible with both Jewish *hokmah* and the Greek ideals of *sophia* and *phronēsis*. His wisdom is eminently practical and moral, grounded on the classical Jewish proverb, "Do to others what you would have them do to you."[7] Jesus also exhorts his followers to an extraordinary level of compassion for those neglected by society and religion, including the poor, the sick, women, the defenseless, overt sinners, and the ritually impure. However, his understanding of wisdom is highly eschatological, that is, it emphasizes the nearness of eternal life with God in heaven as well as the presence of God in all human activities. Jesus was unique among his contemporaries in encouraging sinners to offer simple, frequent prayers to their "Abba," their divine "Father," whom Jesus portrayed as eager to hear even seemingly trivial prayers presented by those who are readily welcomed into his "kingdom."[8]

The followers of Jesus taught that he had been unjustly condemned to death and crucified, but that he had risen from death and ascended to heaven after commissioning his followers to continue his ministry of healing and teaching. Among these, some quickly identified Jesus with the divine *logos* or *sophia* that had created and was now healing the world. Others were less willing to employ these categories. In his letters, the apostle Paul reveals himself as skeptical of classical philosophy. Although he wrote in Greek and was thus forced to use words that were part of the technical vocabulary of philosophers, such as "wisdom," "prudence," and "vice," he seems to have deliberately avoided other key terms, such as "virtue." Paul wrote as a rabbi, employing a hortatory rather than a scientific style, assigning different shades of meaning to his terms depending on the context and intended audience. His hostility toward the categories of Plato and Aristotle is clear in passages where he polemically juxtaposes the doomed philosophical "wisdom of the world" with his own simpler message of salvation through faith in Jesus Christ.[9] With few exceptions, Paul's antagonism toward classical philosophy was shared to some degree by most Christian authors of the first and second centuries, largely due to increasing Christian hostility toward Gnosticism, an eclectic blend of Platonic philosophy with Mediterranean and Near Eastern religions that offered a form of salvation vaguely reminiscent of modern computer games. Initiates into Gnosticism were assured that after death they would be able to deploy esoteric "knowledge" (*gnosis*) as a means of ascending past watchful, sometimes malignant spiritual entities, into ever-higher celestial realms.

At this stage in the evolution of Christianity (around 180 CE), Christian wisdom was generally thought to consist of: first, faith in Jesus Christ as the Son of God and savior of the world; and second, a lifelong commitment to live according to Jesus's ethical precepts, which were largely those of Pharisaic Judaism. The ideal Christian sage or practitioner of wisdom was a "saint," a holy person whose words and example particularly inspired the growing Christian communities. Around the end of the first century Christianity was designated a proscribed (illegal) religion in the Roman Empire. During periods of persecution Roman officials often found it convenient to focus on Christian clergy in the hope that their defection or punishment would discourage conversions. Early Christian wisdom-figures or saints were thus often members of the clergy who had been imprisoned and executed by Roman officials, and who represent an amalgam of the older Jewish models of rabbi and martyr. The role of itinerant preachers such as the apostle Paul had been absorbed into an increasingly well-organized clergy, officially designated by "ordination," the ritual laying on of hands by a senior member of the clergy. Bishops (*episkopoi*—"overseers") were the leaders of local Christian communities who preached and presided at the most important religious ceremonies or "mysteries" (*sacramenta* / *mysteria*). These included baptism, ritual initiation by immersion in water; and the eucharist, a partial reenactment of Jesus's last Passover meal in which Christians experienced "communion" with the risen Christ who was regarded as mysteriously present in the bread and wine. Bishops were assisted by elders (*presbyteroi,* later called "priests") and by deacons, (*diakonoi,* literally "waiters, table-servants") who were concerned with the finances and social welfare of the community. Although there are examples from this period of revered sages and saints who were laypersons, the definition and models of Christian wisdom were generally shifting toward the clergy.

Christian Philosophers and Wise Monks

Toward the end of the second century Christian leaders became increasingly more receptive to the study of Greek philosophy and its application to Christian theology. Even Tertullian (c.160–c.225), an implacable foe of "pagan teaching" had to admit that he had been trained in the classics. The bishop Irenaeus of Lyons (c.120–c.202) opposed Gnosticism, not primarily by condemning the trivialized Platonism employed by the Gnostics, but rather by discussing Christian mysteries in a learned and philosophically respectable fashion. A few decades later in Alexandria, the commercial capital of Egypt, the Christian philosophers and teachers Clement (c.150–215) and Origen (c.185–254) employed Platonic notions of natural and divine contemplation to interpret the scriptures and explain Christian methods and states of prayer. Origen and Jerome (c.345–420) also stressed the importance of philological and textual study of the sacred scriptures in order to make available the most reliable version of the Bible.

It was in the deserts near Alexandria that the early Christian monastic movement arose and flourished.[10] Celibate communities of Christian women had existed since the first century; and by the end of the third century communities of both men and women began to appear in northern Egypt. The sayings and biographies of these "desert fathers and mothers" are an important genre of Christian wisdom literature that is still revered and studied. The earliest monks and nuns were Egyptians (Copts), but new recruits soon poured in from all over the empire, and Christian monasticism rapidly became culturally diverse. Three basic styles of monasticism quickly arose: large monasteries (*cenobia*) led by an abbot or abbess; hermits who lived in complete or semi-solitude; and small communities (*lavras*) that gathered regularly for prayer and the eucharist, but allowed members some degree of solitude.

Whatever their preferred mode of life, all monks and nuns emphasized the importance of practicing the virtues and of memorizing, pondering, and ritually chanting the Christian scriptures, particularly the Book of Psalms. However, their approaches to the acquisition of Christian wisdom varied widely. At one end of the spectrum were monks, often rustic Copts, who eschewed intellectual study: their hero was Antony the Great, the "Father of Monks," who had lived in holy solitude for many decades and who was reputed to have been illiterate. At the other end were those who encouraged reading and classical studies, such as the nun Melania, a highly literate student of Origen, and the monk Evagrius Ponticus (345–399), a classically trained theologian who brought his philosophical acumen with him into the Egyptian desert. As will be described, Evagrius employed Aristotle and the Stoics to analyze temptation and virtue, and Platonic metaphysics to understand Christian contemplation. Whether learned or not, the early monks and nuns were eagerly sought out as spiritual guides and teachers of wisdom, and their sayings or *apophthegmata* represent their attempts to distill into brief proverbs and commandments their personal methods of attaining Christian wisdom.

Later Developments in the Christian East and West

Mystical Wisdom

With the conversion of the emperor Constantine to Christianity and the Christianization of the Roman Empire during the fourth century, public religious rituals or "liturgical celebrations" came to play an increasingly important role as settings where Christian wisdom was taught. Bishops such as Ambrose of Milan (ca. 339–397) in the West and Cyril of Jerusalem

(c. 315–387) in the East encouraged the Christian faithful to meditate on the symbolic meaning of the rituals performed during baptism and the weekly Eucharist. In subsequent centuries, particularly in the East, the writings of Dionysius the Areopagite (c.500), Maximus Confessor (ca. 580–662), and Germanus of Constantinople (c.634–c.733) presented these rituals as potent means of teaching moral wisdom ("purification"), encouraging contemplation of the divine within creation ("illumination"), and even of wholly transforming the faithful through mystical "divinizing union."

Textual Wisdom

In the West, the mystical understanding of worship was supplemented by an ever-increasing emphasis on study of the Bible, both the Old and New Testaments, as principal sources of wisdom. Augustine of Hippo (354–430) produced extensive biblical commentaries and collections of sermons on biblical texts. The moral, theological, and mystical insights he transmitted to posterity in his famous *Confessions* and in his other theological treatises such as the *City of God* are all firmly based on his voluminous interpretations of sacred scripture. Medieval commentators such as Gregory the Great (c.540–604), Bede (c. 673–735), and Bernard of Clairvaux (1090–1153) helped create an intellectual climate in which the study of ancient languages, particularly Hebrew and Greek, would later be regarded as the key to unlocking the hidden treasures of biblical wisdom. This mindset paved the way for the Protestant Reformation of the sixteenth century whose founders, such as Luther (1483–1536) and Calvin (1509–1564), were often scripture scholars who bequeathed to their followers the principle of *sola scriptura,* a conviction that the whole of Christian wisdom, or at least all that is necessary for salvation, can be found solely in the Bible. This principle remains foundational for the majority of Protestant Christians today.

Intellectual Wisdom

A second characteristic of the Christian West was an enthusiasm for the application of Aristotle's analytical categories to the quest for wisdom. Theological terms were defined with increasing precision and employed in an attempt to understand and explain every conceivable theological question. "Summas," encyclopedic collections of systematic theological reflection, began to appear, culminating during the middle ages in the *Sentences* of Peter Lombard (c. 1100–1160), the *Summa Theologiae* of Thomas Aquinas (c.1225–1274), the commentaries of Bonaventure (c.1217–1274), and during the modern era in the *Church Dogmatics* of the Protestant theologian Karl Barth (1886–1968). During the medieval period women theologians such as Gertrude of Helfta (c.1256–1302), Catherine of Siena (1347–1389), and Julian of Norwich (1342–1413) generally employed the genre of personal visions and revelations to expound their theological insights. The limitations of these approaches were courteously but firmly pointed out by Meister Eckhart (c.1260–c.1328) and the anonymous author of the *Cloud of Unknowing,* who emphasized the importance of "apophatic" (transcendent, nonverbal) wisdom in understanding and approaching God.

Moral Wisdom

From the beginning, Christians have been expected to implement Jesus's ethical precepts of compassion toward all. Over time, the expression of this charity has increasingly taken on institutional forms. As has been mentioned, in the early church the clerical order of deacons was chiefly responsible for caring for the poor and vulnerable. In the Christian East, Basil of Caesarea (ca. 330–379) entrusted the care of the sick to monks. Throughout the Middle Ages, religious orders and lay societies were created that specialized in particular forms of social service, such as vocational and liberal education, nursing, and care of the poor. These orders and societies remain widespread and active in modern Catholicism, and many of them have lay equivalents in the Protestant denominations.

Stages of Wisdom

Biblical and Sacramental Stages

From Judaism, and especially from the tradition of Jewish prophecy, Christianity inherited a tradition of stages in the acquisition of wisdom that begins with the recognition of one's need for God. Awareness of sinfulness or failure to keep the divine law evokes repentance, a "change of heart" accompanied by a desire to abandon old ways and lead a new life. In Christianity this conversion is either preceded or followed by "faith in Jesus Christ," a conviction that Jesus is the Son of God and has both the authority and the desire to forgive sins. Acceptance of forgiveness leads to deepening trust in Jesus and a commitment to follow God more closely through prayer, study of the scriptures, and the imitation of Jesus Christ through good works. In early Christianity this rather simplistic twofold model of repentance and new life was associated with the sacraments of baptism and Eucharist. Conversion and forgiveness were experienced once and for all in baptism, and the weekly celebration of the Eucharist, with its annual cycle of readings from the Bible, instructed believers in the faith and afforded both training in Christian ethics and doctrine and a sense of communion with Christ.

The limitations of this model appeared quite early in the history of Christianity, as it became obvious that even committed, baptized Christians can commit serious sin. Slowly, from the second to the sixth centuries, a discipline and eventually a sacrament of "restoration of the lapsed," later called "penance and reconciliation," evolved that permitted baptized Christians guilty of serious failings to again formally confess, repent, and experience forgiveness. The older twofold model of spiritual progress thus slowly expanded into something more complex that acknowledged a lifelong process of growth in Christian wisdom.

Monastic Models

The desert father Evagrius Ponticus employed the vocabulary of Plato, Aristotle, and the Stoics to elaborate a more detailed model of spiritual progress. He described the first stage of the journey toward Christian wisdom as *praktikē*, moral/ascetical practice. This consists largely of an inner struggle against temptations and compulsions (which he called "passions") in order to attain both *apatheia,* inner tranquility and freedom, and *agape,* the capacity to love unselfishly. The arena for this first stage in the spiritual journey is primarily the psychological world of thoughts, distractions, and obsessions; but progress may also be gauged by the extent to which one is able to show compassion and empathy in one's daily tasks and interactions with others. Evagrius borrowed the Platonic tripartite model of the soul to classify temptations and virtues in a systematic way. He described eight principal "tempting thoughts" (*logismoi*) that later became the "seven deadly sins" of the medieval West. Although Evagrius described in broad outline how the *praktikē* usually unfolds, he also stressed that important aspects of this movement are always unique to the individual, and that a vital part of the discipline consists of carefully noting the sequence and circumstances of each temptation so as to discover one's own pattern of susceptibilities and strengths.

Progress in virtue enables the soul to engage in contemplation, to intuitively perceive more clearly the inner meanings and purposes of events, persons, and things. For Evagrius, this contemplation of God in creation (*theoria physikē*) has as its principal objects both the created world and the Christian scriptures. He regarded the Christian sage as an adept contemplative and teacher who is able to interpret both human experiences and the Bible at multiple levels, and to employ biblical verses as healing remedies and meditative gateways to deeper wisdom. He used the term *theology* to describe the highest form of contemplative wisdom: understanding of the divine nature associated with "pure prayer," unmediated communion with God beyond words and without the need for mental images. His recommendation of setting aside mental images and concepts during "pure prayer" would be echoed in later centuries in the apophatic theology of Dionysius the Areopagite, the author of the *Cloud of Unknowing,* and John of the Cross (see below).

Evagrius thus articulated a threefold model of spiritual progress toward Christian wisdom consisting of: (1) *praktikē,* asceticism and the cultivation of virtue; (2) *physikē,* the contemplation of God in creation and sacred scripture; (3) *theologikē,* contemplation of the divine nature. However, he was careful to point out that this model must not be taken too literally as a simple stepwise progression. For each individual certain struggles will persist until death, such as the species of anger that avoids responsibility by projecting blame on one's neighbor:[11] thus, the practice of asceticism is never transcended. Evagrius's "stages" more properly describe three broad categories of spiritual tools that are employed in various combinations throughout life as circumstances require.

John Cassian, Evagrius's disciple, transmitted his master's teaching to the Latin-speaking West by reformulating the wisdom of the Egyptian desert fathers as *Institutes,* an early attempt at monastic legislation, and *Conferences,* essays on spiritual progress, prayer, and contemplation. Cassian emphasized the interrelationship between models of spiritual growth and methods of biblical interpretation. He encouraged a four-stage quest for hidden wisdom that adapts Evagrius's reworking of categories found in Plato, Philo, and Origen. One begins with the literal or historical sense of a text and then searches for three underlying spiritual "senses" or meanings. Beneath the historical letter of the text the skilled contemplative will discover, first the moral or "tropological" sense that invites inner ethical renewal and external acts of compassion. At a deeper level lies the allegorical sense that presents Christian doctrine in veiled, symbolic metaphors. The deepest or highest level is the "anagogical" sense that transcends time and invites an awareness of the eternal "world to come."[12] This technique of searching for hidden wisdom in sacred texts became the standard method of interpreting the Bible in the West, and it was specifically recommended by Dante Alighieri (1265–1321) as the proper way to interpret his *Divine Comedy,* a detailed poetic allegory of the search for divine wisdom.[13] The popularity of this method began to fade during the sixteenth century, when biblical scholarship began to definitively assert the superiority of the literal, historical sense over mystical, allegorical interpretations.[14]

Liturgical Models of Spiritual Ascent

In the Christian East, Evagrius's model of progress from *pratikē* through *physikē* into *theologikē* was applied to Christian worship and sacraments by the sixth-century author who wrote under the pseudonym of Dionysius the Areopagite. Dionysius employed both Evagrius's teachings and the Neoplatonism of the pagan philosopher Proclus to describe a threefold "movement" of God that invites a threefold Christian response. When the universe that God created falls away from divine union, God redeems the fallen world through acts of "procession" or self-outpouring into the universe. God then "indwells" or abides within the created world. Finally, he restores fallen creation by reuniting it to himself. This threefold divine action is mirrored in human spiritual progress and Christian sacramental worship in three movements or stages: purification, illumination, and union. Through prayer, ascetical practice, and God's grace in the sacraments of initiation the worshiper is freed from sin and vice (purification). Growth in virtue, love of God, and contemplation enable the Christian to perceive God abiding in all of creation (illumination). Finally, through private and sacramental worship, especially in eucharistic communion, the believer experiences an increasing sense of intimacy with God (union). Dionysius used this threefold model to describe everything imaginable: God, in *The Divine Names*; the angelic ranks in *The Celestial Hierarchies*; and Christian sacraments and clerical orders in *The Ecclesiastical Hierarchies*. His approach was expanded by Maximus Confessor (ca. 580–662), and Germanus of Constantinople (c.634–c.733) who assigned mystical meanings to each part of the eucharistic celebration using Dionysius's three stages. Thus, the spiritual life of the individual was reflected in the experience of worship: liturgy became a training ground for self-knowledge, contemplation, and the vision of heaven.

Apophatic Correctives and Spiritual Exercises

In the Christian West, Dionysius's threefold ascent from purgation through illumination into union was employed chiefly in models of spiritual progress. Bernard and Bonaventure made use of it to describe the soul's gradual ascent toward God. As has been noted, Meister Eckhart and the anonymous author of the *Cloud of Unknowing* corrected an overly optimistic dependence on this model by emphasizing the place of inner dryness, emptiness, and even darkness, as important modes of God's presence and stages in the acquisition of both moral and mystical wisdom.

The fourteenth through the sixteenth centuries saw the evolution of formal "spiritual exercises" intended to guide the soul on the path of Christian wisdom and to highlight the inner work yet to be undertaken. Gertrude of Helfta, Cisneros of Montserrat (1455–1510), and, most famously, Ignatius of Loyola (1491–1556) wrote books of "exercises" that laid out specific prayers and meditations to be undertaken during a set period of days or weeks in order to revive spiritual fervor or aid in discerning correct choices. The sixteenth-century Carmelites Teresa of Avila (1515–1582) and John of the Cross (1542–1591) described their own spiritual journeys in ways that later generations interpreted as ratifying the tradition of a fixed spiritual ascent through successive purgative, illuminative, and unitive "ways." In the purgative way the primary task is recognition of sin and the correction of vice. After an indeterminate number of years of spiritual struggle one undertakes "acquired contemplation" in the relative calm bestowed by acquisition of the virtues. Finally, generally toward the end of life, one may be rewarded with the gift of "infused" or passive contemplation and an awareness of union with God.

Modern Reassessment of the Stages

From the seventeenth through the mid-twentieth centuries this model of a three-tiered spiritual ascent prevailed in Roman Catholic communities. Manuals and textbooks were produced that purported to describe the characteristic signs and symptoms of each "way" and to recommend appropriate spiritual practices and exercises for Christians at each stage. During the last sixty years it has become generally accepted that, although not without great value, this traditional model is in need of substantial revision. While it is generally true that struggle with certain sins is most acute in youth, and that years of spiritual practice can yield some degree of calm and balance, it seems more accurate to describe the three ways as facets or aspects, rather than stages. Contemplative insight often provides a motive for ascetical training, and is not always experienced as its consequence. Rather than describing the journey toward Christian wisdom as a stepwise ascent, it may be more accurate to envision it as a helix, a geometrical form that combines both linear direction and circular movement. The movement of progress or ascent toward God contains within it a "circular" movement between the poles or facets of asceticism and contemplation. Thus, when late in the spiritual journey the sages finds themselves incomprehensibly struggling with issues thought to have been resolved long ago, this is not necessarily regression or backsliding, but rather an opportunity to consecrate yet deeper levels of the self by reengaging ascetical struggle within a dynamic movement that leads toward God.

The Cultivation of Wisdom

The cultivation of wisdom in all three major branches of Christianity begins in the local church or parish where the Christian is baptized and receives instruction in the faith. There are a few examples of founders and reformers of religious movements within Christianity who received only initial instruction in their youth; later, with only their conscience and sense of God's will to guide them, they experimented with new modes of life. Such founders include: Antony of Egypt (c.251–356) one of the first desert hermits; Benedict of Nursia (c.480–c.540), the father and principal legislator of Western monasticism; and Francis of Assisi (1181–1226), devotee of poverty and founder of the Franciscan Order. Such informal training in asceticism and spirituality is the rare exception, however: for the majority of Christians the cultivation of wisdom takes place within an organized community according to established models, usually with instruction in groups, and less commonly in a one-to-one relationship with an individual teacher.

The Evolution of Spiritual Practices
and the Formation of the Sage

Textual Wisdom

Christianity inherited from Judaism both a sacred text and the tradition of a "lectionary," a cycle of biblical readings that are solemnly proclaimed and interpreted during public worship. In early Christianity this ensured familiarity with the sacred scriptures even by the illiterate, since the ability to memorize large blocks of text was extremely widespread if not universal in antiquity. Such memorization facilitated the private practice of *lectio divina,* a slow repetitive recitation and pondering of sacred text that encourages prayer and leads the practitioner into a sense of the presence of God. This meditative technique had been practiced in Judaism before the birth of Jesus.[15] It was described and recommended by early Christian leaders[16] and has remained an essential part of the daily spiritual practice of Christian monks and nuns from the fourth century to the present (see below). Today, both the private practice of *lectio divina* and more formal study of the Bible in groups are common in most Christian denominations. While *lectio divina* is oriented toward prayer, "Bible study" usually examines sacred scripture as the basis for ethical and theological doctrine. In Roman Catholic and Eastern Orthodox contexts particular emphasis is placed on the relationship between the Bible and sacramental worship.

Advanced training in biblical studies, including biblical languages, philology, and ancient history, is available both in seminaries intended for the training of clergy and in colleges and universities that offer advanced academic degrees. While not a prerequisite for ordination in the early church, advanced biblical studies have become normative for Protestant and Catholic seminarians since the sixteenth century and for most Eastern Orthodox candidates for ordination since the beginning of the twentieth century.

Textual wisdom finds its highest expression in the ability to correctly interpret and apply the Bible in ever-changing circumstances. This is done formally during the sermon or homily, the explanation and application of a biblical text during public worship. Christians believe both that the Bible is divinely inspired and that the many individuals who produced it did so from within the framework of their language, culture, and historical context. Thus, the task of the minister or priest who preaches is to employ textual expertise to enable the Christian faithful to both rekindle the experience of God that inspired the author to write the sacred text, and to apply that experience in a wholly new setting.

Intellectual Wisdom

Intellectual wisdom or "theology" understood in its broadest sense attempts to use language and philosophy to understand and interpret divine revelation. While the scriptures are foundational for Christian theology, this discipline also looks to human history, science, and the arts to consider questions not addressed in the Bible. Most Christian churches divide the search for intellectual wisdom into various subdisciplines. The place of biblical studies, including ancient languages, has been mentioned. Also important is church history and historical theology, the study of the development of Christian doctrine and practice over the centuries. The field of systematic theology includes doctrine concerning the Divine Nature and the person of Christ, the church, the saints, the sacraments, eternal life and the end of time. Moral theology includes Christian personal and social ethics. Spiritual theology (formerly called ascetical/mystical theology) concerns the search for holiness through ascetical practice, prayer, and contemplation. Pastoral theology teaches the skills necessary to lead, instruct, and counsel the Christian faithful, including the art of preaching, or homiletics. Intellectual wisdom is usually taught in formal academic settings, most commonly through lectures and seminars and occasionally in individual tutorials. However, it is important to emphasize that theological scholarship does not always produce a wise scholar. The goal of intellectual wisdom is to describe and reflect on the various ways Christian faith touches all human endeavors and experiences. As has been described, it is only to the extent that knowledge and study enable a Christian to teach and exemplify the love and compassion of Jesus Christ that "theology" becomes "wisdom."

Moral Wisdom

Moral wisdom is initially inculcated by means of ethical precepts taught both at home and in the church. Ethical exhortation is usually part of the sermon or homily preached at public worship, and it is thus closely linked to textual wisdom. In Roman Catholicism and Eastern Orthodoxy there also exists a requirement for private, individual moral instruction through the sacrament of penance and reconciliation. Catholic and Orthodox Christians are expected at least annually to confess their sins and seek the advice of a "confessor" who is usually, but not always, a priest or bishop.[17] Many Christians receive this sacrament on a regular basis and use it as an opportunity for acquiring deeper self-knowledge and guidance in the quest for virtue.

In most Christian churches there exists the option of formal, public commitment to a lifestyle particularly devoted to the social dimensions of moral wisdom. As has been described, the ancient clerical order of deacons was originally concerned with the welfare of the poor and vulnerable. Monastic orders and religious organizations arose that were, and still remain, committed to particular forms of social service. Vincent de Paul (1581–1660) founded an order of priests and an order of nuns to educate and care for the poor. In the nineteenth century, Florence Nightingale (1820–1910), an English Protestant, adapted the training methods and practices of a German Lutheran nursing order to effectively create the secular profession of nursing. Other modern examples of public commitment to moral wisdom include Albert Schweizer (1875–1965), a Protestant biblical scholar and missionary physician in Gabon, Africa; and Mother Teresa of Calcutta (1910–1997), foundress of the Missionary Daughters and Missionary Brothers of Charity, Catholic religious orders dedicated to the care of the homeless and the dying. The Christian organizations founded or inspired by such individuals generally offer a variety of options for membership ranging from lifetime commitment in religious vows to part-time assistance as affiliates of the organization. Training in the different forms of moral wisdom practiced by these organizations is usually provided by the institution itself, although specialized skills or professional qualifications may need to be obtained elsewhere.

Mystical or Contemplative Wisdom

The tradition of seeking instruction in prayer and contemplation from an *amma* or *abba,* a spiritual mother or father, arose together with Christian monasticism in the fourth century, and has been constantly practiced since that time, particularly in the Orthodox churches. While this practice is nearly universal in monasteries of the Christian East and West, the laity, too, often make regular "pilgrimages" to monasteries for this purpose, especially in Egypt, Greece, and Russia.

In Eastern Orthodoxy, training to become an *abba* or sage consists chiefly in faithful observance of monastic practices together with obedience to a chosen *abba* over many years or even decades. However, the spiritual father does not necessarily impart a technique or method of counseling that, in itself, qualifies the disciple to eventually undertake this role. In the East the spiritual father or mother is generally expected to acquire the "gift of discernment," the ability to spiritually intuit the struggles and needs of the person who seeks advice. This ability is regarded as "charismatic," that is, a gift of God that is not learned through any technique or formal training other than commitment to prayer, contemplation, and faithful monastic practice. In the Christian West the role of "spiritual director" was often assumed in monasteries by the abbot or abbess, the elected or appointed superior of the community. For the majority of the Christian laity the parish priest to whom one confessed, and who offered moral exhortation was the same individual who provided advice on prayer and contemplation. In the fifteenth and sixteenth centuries, increasing emphasis was placed on the value of a trained spiritual director whose qualifications derived principally from holiness and experience, rather than hierarchical status. Until recently the majority of spiritual directors in Western Christianity were priests, and the art of spiritual direction was part of the regular curriculum in Catholic seminaries. Since the mid-twentieth century training programs for both lay and ordained spiritual directors have been established by Catholic and Protestant authorities, chiefly in North America and Europe. Training is usually in groups by means of lectures, seminars, and retreats.

Practices

Prayer

For all Christians the most fundamental and important spiritual practice is prayer. As was described above, it was in his teaching concerning prayer that Jesus differed most notably from his contemporaries. He insisted that access to God through prayer is solely dependent on God's love for humanity: there is no prerequisite of personal holiness, social status, formal religious instruction, or the use of any intermediary. His followers took this teaching concerning prayer very seriously and in their turn encouraged frequent, even constant prayer.[18] The significance and potential of frequent prayer was described by the desert father Evagrius Ponticus (d. 399), who linked prayer with the highest Christian wisdom, which he called "theology": "If you are a theologian, you will pray truly; if you pray truly, you will be a theologian."[19]

According to a popular early Christian definition prayer is "a conversation of the innermost self with God."[20] This "conversation" can take many different forms. Petitionary prayer makes requests; intercessory prayer is offered on behalf of other persons. Although Jesus emphasized approaching God directly, Christians often ask others to pray or intercede for them in what is called "the communion of saints," a metaphysical interconnection that is believed to transcend death. Thus, it is very common for Roman Catholic and Eastern Orthodox Christians to pray for the dead or to request the intercession of those who have died, especially saints. Other forms of prayer include thanksgiving, repentance, and benedictions or "consecration," the invocation of God's blessing on persons or things. Silent, wordless enjoyment of God is often called contemplative prayer; it will be described in more detail below. Prayer may be offered privately or in community; it may be spontaneous or "liturgical," that is, offered according to a set form, often a series of responses by different individuals in a group. Prayer is most often offered in the "vernacular," the language employed in everyday usage by the one praying, or it may be offered in traditional archaic forms, sometimes in languages only partially familiar to the one who prays.

"Monologistic" or short formulaic prayer employing a frequently repeated phrase is widely practiced in Roman Catholicism and Eastern Orthodoxy. In Eastern Christianity the practice of the "Jesus Prayer," also called *hesychasm* (from the Greek *hesychia*, "stillness"), is especially common among Orthodox monks and nuns. It consists of the constant repetition of some variant of the prayer, "Lord Jesus Christ, Son of God, have mercy on me, a sinner." It is prayed in the vernacular and is non-iconic: that is, the goal is not to meditate on some religious doctrine or mystery, but rather to empty the mind of distractions and allow the *nous* or mind (literally the "innermost self") to "descend into the heart." This is understood as a deliberate interior movement of conscious prayer from the head, the place of thought, down into the heart, the traditional center of feeling. Throughout this process the prayer is continuously repeated without interruption, often linked to the rhythm of breathing. This inward "descent" is not regarded primarily as a rejection of the world of conscious thought, but rather as a consecration of the center of feeling and passion by the *nous,* the image of God within the soul. This practice is intended to evoke *penthos,* repentance, and to facilitate an imageless, wordless sense of God's presence, sometimes perceptible as warmth or light in the region of the heart.

In Roman Catholicism the most common form of monologistic prayer is the Rosary, repetition of a sequence and set number of brief prayers including the "Hail Mary,"[21] the Lord's prayer, the Apostle's Creed, and the "Glory be." Unlike the Jesus Prayer, the prayers said during the Rosary are intended to be accompanied by meditation on fixed cycles of "mysteries," significant and symbolic events in the lives of Jesus and Mary. A circle of beads is very often used to keep track of the number of times the prayers are recited and as an indicator of when it is time to move on to the next mystery.

Contemplation

The Latin word *contemplatio* and its Greek equivalent, *theōria,* both mean "vision." Contemplation or contemplative prayer is the Christian appropriation of the ancient Platonic belief in the ability of the *nous,* the innermost self, to see beneath surface appearances into underlying divine patterns, and even in some sense to behold God. Contemplation may be *kataphatic* (image-filled, the "way of affirmation") or *apophatic* (imageless, the "way of negation").[22] Kataphatic contemplation perceives the divine presence and purposes in the complexity and interconnectedness of creation. God is celebrated in the ever-changing patterns of nature, art, poetry, music, and history. In apophatic contemplation. God is experienced beyond words, images, and concepts in silence and simplicity. The majority of Christian spiritual practices facilitate kataphatic contemplation, but a few, like the Jesus Prayer described above, encourage silence and the setting aside of thoughts.

A form of Christian contemplation that encourages a dynamic, alternating rhythm between apophatic and kataphatic experience is the practice of *lectio divina,* or "sacred reading" of the Christian scriptures. Although there is a growing enthusiasm for the practice of lectio divina in groups, it has traditionally been a private spiritual exercise.[23] A biblical text is chosen, then after a period of silent preparation, the text is slowly read, silently or aloud (*lectio*). The practitioner "listens" inwardly for any word or phrase that seems to invite or attract; then the text is memorized and repeated, pondered (*meditatio*). During this period of meditation, ideas, memories, and images often arise; the goal is not necessarily to ignore or bypass them, but rather to consecrate, to bless them with the gently repeated text.[24] This "consecration prayer" (*oratio*) naturally leads into conversation with God—prayer in the more familiar sense. At intervals the practitioner will cease using words and simply rest silently in the presence of God (*contemplatio*). Although these four phases (*lectio, meditatio, oratio,* and *contemplatio*) have traditionally been called "steps" or "stages," in reality they interweave and give way to one another in a pleasantly unpredictable fashion. Like the "stages" of spiritual progress described above, they could more properly be compared to recurring notes in a constantly changing melody.

Ascetical Practices

The Greek work *askesis* means "exercise" or "training." For Christians the term *asceticism* refers to practices that train one to more effectively fulfill Jesus's summary of the Jewish law: "You shall love the Lord your God with all your heart, with all your mind, and all your strength; and you shall love your neighbor as yourself."[25] Jesus particularly recommended the ascetical practices of fasting, almsgiving, and prayer.[26] Fasting in early Christianity meant eating little or no food until late afternoon or sunset; today, it usually entails temporary abstinence from certain kinds of food such as meat or dairy products on particular days or during ritual seasons such as Lent, the forty-six days preceding the annual Easter commemoration of Jesus's resurrection. Almsgiving broadly includes all forms of service toward others, especially financial support of the poor and sick. Also traditional in Christianity is *nepsis,* interior vigilance with regard to thoughts and fantasies. Jesus reiterated that abusive and destructive actions begin in the mind and the will, and it is there that they must be most vigorously confronted.[27] Other forms of asceticism include setting aside time for private ritual prayer and spiritual exercises, mentioned above. Periods of several days or weeks may be set aside for formal ascetical training during retreats or pilgrimage to religious sites: these include the popular and widely practiced thirty-day *Spiritual Exercises* of Ignatius of Loyola (1491–1556) and walking pilgrimages to traditional shrines, such as the tombs of the apostles James in Compostela, Spain, and Matthias in Trier, Germany.

Challenges and Obstacles

In the United States and Europe today there exists an apparently insatiable hunger for novelty and stimulation, together with a dread of regularity and boredom. In such cultures it is easy for the pursuit of Christian wisdom—or wisdom of any kind—to become yet another pastime, a pleasant but temporary hobby to be taken up when the world seems grey and empty and then neglected when more intriguing pastimes beckon. The four kinds of wisdom described in this chapter all presuppose dedication, study, and practice over the course of a lifetime. Textual wisdom requires years of linguistic and historical study as well as ongoing attention to contemporary values and modes of expression so that the scriptures can be effectively preached and understood. Intellectual wisdom similarly requires detailed study of a complex tradition that developed over millennia and is still evolving. Articulating and applying this tradition requires integration of insights from a variety of disciplines and commitment to ongoing collaboration with experts, since no single individual can possess competence in all fields of theology. Moral wisdom requires daily recommitment to a deepened sense of humility based in constant attention to one's strengths, limitations, motives, and goals, so that beneficial actions are motivated by genuine concern for others, rather than by elaborately disguised self-interest. Contemplation of the mystery of God, whether in simplicity or complexity, has as an absolute precondition a willingness to regularly spend time in silent prayer and meditation; and in an age bombarded by intrusive, unsolicited opinions expressed in new and constantly metastasizing forms of media, silence is often feared and deliberately suppressed. Christian wisdom of every type has as its prerequisite the practice of virtue, the constant recovery of balance and clarity in light of the *telos* or final goal of existence: eternal union with God. In other words, the pursuit of Christian wisdom requires an environment, a mindset, and a level of commitment that are both difficult to maintain and increasingly countercultural.

Social Implications

The benefits of Christian wisdom for human society are clear. Textual and theological wisdom teach reverence for human philosophy and history, and promote both the search for meaning in all human activity and the conviction that human existence has a purpose and goal. Christian moral and contemplative wisdom encourage respect and compassion toward the weak and vulnerable by inviting human beings to see in each other reflections of

God's image. Christian social teachings are robust and adaptable since they are not tied to any particular political ideology or cultural ethos. The pursuit of Christian wisdom has progressed, sometimes tolerated but often persecuted, in republics, monarchies, dictatorships, oligarchies, and democracies. Since Christians do not believe that the world or its political structures are eternal there can be only provisional Christian political and social agendas, their value and effectiveness judged solely by the extent to which they mirror the ethics of Jesus in promoting solidarity with the poorest and most vulnerable members of society.

Summary and Conclusions

In this chapter, Christian wisdom has been subdivided into four categories: textual, moral, intellectual, and mystical. This division adapts two related models: the Platonic ideal forms of the Good, the True, and the Beautiful; and John Cassian's fourfold division of Christian knowledge into literal, moral, allegorical, and anagogical "senses." These subdivisions reflect emphases within the three major branches of Christianity, and there are numerous examples of Christian saints and institutions that reflect the possibility of specializing in one or another of these subdivisions. However, it should be strongly emphasized that Christian textual, moral, intellectual, and mystical wisdom are all deeply interconnected and interdependent. Sages have frequently described a progression through these four divisions that mirrors the lifelong movement of the soul toward God and that also provides a model of "spiritual exercise," a means of perceiving the events of daily life as part of sacred history.

Endnotes

1. This is a conservative estimate. Most sources estimate the actual number in 2010 as somewhere between 2.14 and 2.2 billion.

2. The number of adherents is roughly as follows: Roman Catholicism—1.1 billion; Protestantism—800 million; Eastern Orthodoxy—200 million.

3. The Bible, 1 Corinthians 1:30–31: "He is the source of your life in Christ Jesus, whom God made our wisdom, our righteousness and sanctification and redemption; therefore, as it is written, 'Let him who boasts, boast of the Lord'" (Revised Standard Version, RSV).

4. In the Nicene Creed, to which the overwhelming majority of Christians belonging to all three major branches subscribe, Jesus is the Second Person of the

one triune God: Jesus is "God from God, light from light, very God of very God, of the same nature as the Father." In the Nicene Creed and in the Gospel of John (1:3), Jesus is also the creator of the universe, "by whom all things were made" (RSV).

5. Proverbs 14 & 17.

6. Aristotle, *The Nichomachean Ethics,* books 2–5.

7. Matthew 7:12.

8. A balanced comparison of Jesus's teaching with that of his rabbinic contemporaries may be found in Geza Vermes's *Jesus the Jew:* see esp. pp. 119, 210, 224.

9. Romans 1:22; 1 Corinthians 1:20, 3:19.

10. Celibate communities of men and women, the "Sons and Daughters of the Covenant" also arose independently in late-third-century Syria, but their unique mode of life did not endure and was rapidly replaced by models drawn from Egyptian monasticism.

11. Evagrius, *Praktikos* 36; *Gnostikos* 10, 31, 32.

12. John Cassian, *Conferences* 14, "The First Conference of Abba Nesteros."

13. Dante Alighieri, *Letter to Can Grande,* 7–33.

14. This approach had been foreshadowed much earlier. In the fourteenth century, Thomas Aquinas cited a fifth-century letter of Augustine (*Letter* 93.8, *to Vincent the Donatist*) in support of his assertion that only the literal sense of the scriptures may be used to formulate doctrine (*Summa Theologiae* 1a.1,10). However, unlike Renaissance and modern biblical scholars, both Augustine and Aquinas believed in the spiritual value of allegorical interpretation.

15. Philo of Alexandria, the Jewish philosopher and Egyptian contemporary of Jesus, recommends this practice in his writings (*That Every Good Man is Free,* 80–81; *On the Contemplative Life*).

16. Cyprian, bishop of Carthage (d.258) described and encouraged the practice of *lectio divina* in his *Letter to Donatus*. The classical descriptions of this practice are found in medieval texts, particularly *Didascalion* 5.9. by Hugh of St. Victor (c.1090–1142) and the *Ladder of Monks* by Guigo II (1140–1193).

17. In some Eastern Orthodox churches, confession is sometimes made to, and counsel is received from, a non-priest, usually a monk who may not be ordained; however, sacramental absolution, the ritual pronouncement of forgiveness, can only be provided by an ordained priest or bishop.

18. 1 Thessalonians 5:17; Romans 12:12; Ephesians 6:18.

19. Evagrius Ponticus, *On Prayer* 61.

20. Evagrius Ponticus, *On Prayer* 3; probably based on Clement of Alexandria *Stromateis,* VII.12.73,1.

21. Based on the brief angelic salutation of Luke 1:28, the "Hail Mary" progressively expanded throughout the middle ages into its present form: "Hail Mary, full of Grace, the Lord is with you. Blessed are you among women and blessed is the fruit of your womb, Jesus. Holy Mary, Mother of God, pray for us sinners now and at the hour of our death, Amen."

22. The terms *apophatic* and *kataphatic* were first introduced in Christian spiritual theology by Dionysius the Areopagite (c.500) in his texts *The Divine Names* and *The Mystical Theology*.

23. For more detailed descriptions and introductions to *lectio divina*, see below.

24. The concepts and images that arise during *lectio divina* are clearly the basis for much of the mystical and allegorical exegesis that characterized Christian commentaries on the Bible until the sixteenth century (note 14).

25. Mark 12:29–31; Matthew 22:37–39.

26. Matthew 6:1–18.

27. Matthew 5:21–28; 15:10–20.

References

Alighieri, D. *Letter to Cangrande*.

Aristotle. (1934). *Nichomachean ethics*. Loeb Classical Library, *Aristotle*, XIX. Cambridge: Harvard University Press.

Barth, K. (2010). *Church dogmatics*. T & T Clark International.

The Bible, Revised Standard Version (RSV). (1977). *The New Oxford Annotated Bible with the Apocrypha*, Revised Standard Version, Expanded Edition. Oxford: Oxford University Press.

Cassian, J. (1886). *Conferences (Conlationes XXIIII)*. M. Petschenig (Ed.), Corpus Scriptorum Ecclesiasticorum Latinorum 13. Vienna.

———. (1965). *Institutes (De institutis coenobiorum et de octo principalium vitiorum remediis)*. J-C. Guy (Ed. & Trans.). *Jean Cassien Institutions Cénobitiques*, SC 109. Paris: Cerf.

Dionysius the Areopagite. (1987). *Pseudo Dionysius: The complete works*. P. Rorem (Trans.). Classics of Western Spirituality. (Paulist Press, 1987).

———. (1990). *Corpus Dionysiacum*. Berlin: Walter de Gruyter.

Evagrius Ponticus. (1971). *Praktikos* and *On Prayer. Praktikos* A. & C. Guillaumont (Eds. & Trans.). *Évagre le Pontique Traité Pratique ou Le Moine*. Sources Chrétiennes. Paris: Cerf.

———. (1987). *Evagrius Ponticus: Praktikos and De oratione*. S. Tugwell (Trans.). Oxford: Faculty of Theology.

———. (1981). *De oratione (De oratione capitula)*. S. Tugwell (Ed.). Oxford: Faculty of Theology.

Schweitzer A. (1998). *Out of my life and thought: An autobiography*. Baltimore: Johns Hopkins University Press.

———. (1931). *Aus Meinem Leben und Denken*. Leipzig: Felix Meiner Verlag.

Vermes, G. (1973). *Jesus the Jew*. New York: HarperCollins; repr. Fortress Press, 1981.

Further Resources

Bibliography

The Holy Bible. Many translations are available: one of the most accurate and widely used is the Revised Standard Version (RSV) available from many publishers and on the Internet (see below).

The *Praktikos, Chapters on Prayers,* and *On Tempting Thoughts* of Evagrius Ponticus. *The Praktikos and Chapters on Prayer,* J. E. Bamberger (Trans.). Cistercian Publications, 1980; *The Philokalia* vol. 1, Palmer, Sherrard, and Ware (Eds. & Trans.). London: 1979.

The *Institutes* and *Conferences* of John Cassian. *The Nicene and Post-Nicene fathers,* vol. 11, (Edinburgh, 1894) available on the Internet at CCEL (see below). A more recent translation by Boniface Ramsey is available in the Ancient Christian Writers series. Paulist Press, 2000.

The *Lives* and *Sayings* of the Desert Fathers: Cistercian Studies series: *Lives* § 34; *Sayings* § 59. Cistercian Publications.

Dionysius the Areopagite, *Pseudo Dionysius: The Complete Works,* P. Rorem (Trans.), Classics of Western Spirituality. Paulist, 1987.

The Writings of St. John of the Cross: *Ascent of Mount Carmel, Dark Night of the Soul,* and *Living Flame of Love* (see below).

The Catechism of the Catholic Church (see below).

The Philokalia vol. 1–4, Palmer, Sherrard, and Ware (Ed. & Trans.). London: Faber & Faber, 1979–1999.

The Book of Common Prayer (various printed and online editions).

The *Large Catechism* and *Small Catechism* of Martin Luther (see below).

Internet Resources

The Bible. RSV translation (recommended): http://quod.lib.umich.edu/r/rsv/browse. html; other translations.

The Christian Classics Ethereal Library (CCEL). A library of Christian primary sources, including most of the authors mentioned in this article. http://www. ccel.org.

(Roman Catholic) The Holy See, including especially, The *Catechism of the Catholic Church* and The Documents of Vatican II. http://www.vatican.va.

(Eastern Orthodox) St. Pachomius Library. An extensive reference library of Eastern Orthodox sources. http://www.voskrese.info/spl/index.html.

Ignatian Spiritual Exercises. http://www.jesuit.org.

(Protestant-Lutheran) The *Large* and *Small Catechisms* of Martin Luther, the *Augsbug Confession,* and the Lutheran *Book of Concord.* http://bookofconcord.org.

(Protestant-Anglican/Episcopalian) *The Book of Common Prayer.* http://justus.anglican. org/resources/bcp/index.html.

(Protestant-Evangelical) The theology of Karl Barth. http://www.tyndale.ca/seminary/ mtsmodular/reading-rooms/theology/barth.

Dante Aligheri, *Letter to Cangrande.* J. Marchand (Trans.). http://www.english.udel. edu/dean/cangrand.html.

The practice of *lectio divina.* http://www.valyermo.com/ld-art.html; http://www. lectio-divina.org/index.cfm; http://www.osb.org/lectio/.

4

The Wisdom of Gratitude in Islam

Reza Shah-Kazemi

Introduction

"A word of wisdom is the lost property of the believer," the Prophet said, "wherever he finds it, he has the greatest right to it."[1] This "word of wisdom" might well be identified with the "good word" mentioned in the following Qur'anic image: "Do you not see how God coins a similitude: A good word is as a good tree, its root firm, and its branches reaching into heaven; giving its fruit at every season by permission of its Lord? God coins similitudes for mankind in order that they may reflect" (Qur'an, 14:24–25).

Reflecting upon the image of wisdom as a tree helps us to see some key aspects of the nature of wisdom in the Islamic tradition, which we hope to address in what follows. First, and most importantly, is what the Qur'anic verse does not mention: the seed of the tree. The seed of the tree of wisdom is planted by God in the "soil" of the human heart. Second, the tree cannot grow unless it receives sunlight and rain from heaven: the seed of wisdom cannot realize its potential without the grace of divine revelation. Third, the tree needs nourishment from the soil: the truly wise human being needs to be rooted in humility,[2] an awareness that wisdom is a divine gift, both as regards its origin—the "seed" planted by God—and as regards its consummation through the enlightenment granted by divine revelation. "He gives wisdom unto whom He will, and he unto whom wisdom is given, he truly has received abundant good. But none are reminded except those of spiritual substance" (2:269).

The final sentence of verse 2:269 refers to those of spiritual substance who are "reminded" by the Qur'an, which is itself referred to as the reminder (*dhikrā*) and as the remembrance (*dhikr*).[3] This takes us to another level of the symbolism of the word as a tree. For the humble awareness of one's total dependence on God needs to be complemented by transformative activity; and no activity is more transformative or more enlightening than the remembrance or invocation of God, *dhikr Allāh*. The "good word" can also be seen to refer to the Name of God that is invoked by the wise, those whose spiritual substance is brought to light by the invocation. Referring to verses 14:24–25, the great scholar of Sufism[4] Martin Lings (d. 2005) writes: "This may be interpreted: an invocation, and above all the Supreme Name which is the best of good words, is not a flat utterance which spreads horizontally outwards in this world to be lost in thin air, but a vertical continuity of repercussions throughout all the states of being."[5]

In what follows, we hope to reveal the way in which wisdom in the Islamic tradition can be viewed as a seed:

- implanted in the heart by the Breath of God: spiritual inspiration;

- enlivened thereafter by the Qur'an and the Prophet: divine Revelation;

- nurtured by faith, humility, gratitude, and love: human purification;

- nourished by meditative thought: intellectual contemplation;

- brought to fruition by the graces inherent in worship: heartfelt invocation.

The Wisdom of Revelation

Human wisdom in the Islamic tradition is inseparable from the enlightenment bestowed by Divine Revelation.[6] By the word *revelation* is to be understood not just the various revealed scriptures and prophetic revelations by means of which God has disclosed Himself[7] to human beings. By "revelation," we must also understand the human being as such. For the human soul is itself a revelation. Indeed, according to the mystics of Islam, the human being is the most revealing of all the signs of God. In Arabic the word for a verse of scripture is the same as that for a sign of God, *āya* (plural, *āyāt*): "We shall show them Our signs/verses on the horizons [around them] and in their own souls, such that it be clear to them that He is the Real" (41:53).[8] Similarly,

"Have they not reflected upon their own souls?" (30:8). Imam 'Alī[9] expresses the cosmic significance of the human being in the following lines of poetry:

> Although you see yourself as an insignificant speck, within you the entire universe is contained; you are thus yourself the *meaningful book*[10] whose letters make clear what is concealed.[11]

Those human beings are wise who most fully conform to the essential nature of humanity, *al-fiṭra*. This primordial human nature is in perfect harmony with God, it is the intrinsic spiritual constitution of humanity, according to which all souls are created by God (30:30); and it is, moreover, immutable: "The creation of God cannot be changed." This verse then comes to a close with an affirmation that what is configured within the *fiṭra* is the "eternally subsistent religion" (*al-dīn al-qayyim*): the immutable quintessence of religion is thus inscribed within human nature. This is religion as such, as opposed to such and such a religion. All subsequent formal revelations from God through such and such a religion do not therefore teach the human being something fundamentally new; rather, they bring to fruition the seeds of that quintessence of religion, which is spiritual certainty, already present within the soul. The Latin root of the very word *religion* expresses this function precisely: *re-ligare* is to "re-bind" that which has been loosened, the relationship between the Creator and the creature, Heaven and earth, the Truth on high and the Truth within.

The Prophets of God are those in whom there is a perfect concordance between what God reveals and what they themselves *are*: their *fiṭra* being fully realized, the message they are charged to deliver radiates both from their teachings and their very being. The Prophets of God are thus themselves "revealed signs." Again, from the mystical point of view, the Prophet Muhammad is regarded as being the "greatest of all signs" (*al-āyat al-kubrā*). Such is how the Imam Būṣīrī addresses the Prophet in his famous poem, the *Burda*: "O greatest sign for those who seek to learn."[12] There is a clear allusion here to the verse of the Qur'an describing the Prophet's own vision at the climax of his celestial ascent (*mi'rāj*): "And indeed he saw, among the signs of his Lord, the greatest" (53:18).

On the one hand, the meaning here is that the Prophet saw the most exalted form of divine Self-disclosure—whether this be a "vision" of the eyes, the heart, or both, for the verses in question refer both to his eyes and his heart. On the other hand, esoterically, the meaning is that the Prophet saw the essence of his own soul, which is the most perfect image of God. For, as

in Genesis, the human being is described by the Prophet as being made in
the "form of God";[13] and the Prophet, as Perfect Man (al-Insān al-Kāmil), is
the most perfect image of God. This esoteric interpretation is reinforced by
one of the most mystically fecund sayings of the Prophet: "He who knows
himself knows his Lord."[14] This is also the lesson of the classical Persian Sufi
poem *Conference of the Birds,* in which the spiritual quest of the *sī morgh*
(thirty birds) is fulfilled by their vision of their own selves, transformed by
"the celestial and ever-living Light" into the mythical *Sīmorgh,* the goal of
their quest:

> Their life came from that close, insistent sun
> And in its vivid rays they shone as one.
> There, in the Sīmorgh's radiant face they saw
> Themselves, the Sīmorgh of the world—with awe
> They gazed, and dared at last to comprehend
> They were the Sīmorgh and the journey's end.
> And silently their shining Lord replies:
> "I am a mirror set before your eyes,
> And all who come before My splendour see
> Themselves, their own unique reality."[15]

In the Islamic worldview, all the Prophets possess that wisdom which
is the fruit of self-realization in God. It is the primary purpose of prophetic revelation to impart the light of divine wisdom, and indeed one
finds the two elements, scripture and wisdom, repeatedly linked together
in the Qur'an as complementary aspects of divine Self-disclosure. It is "the
scripture and wisdom" (al-kitāb wa'l-hikma) that the Prophet is given, and it
is by means of these two principles that he "purifies" the believers (3:164;
62:2). Abraham likewise prays to God for the community that was to spring
from his son Ismail: "Our Lord, raise up in their midst a Messenger from
among them who shall recite unto them Thy revelations, and instruct them
in the Scripture and in wisdom and shall purify them" (2:129). Also, the
Qur'an tells us that God entered into a pre-terrestrial covenant with all of
the Prophets, bestowing upon them "scripture and wisdom" and receiving
in return the promise that they will believe in and help the final Prophet,
Muhammad (3:81). This covenant with the Prophets evokes another primordial pact, known as the covenant of *Alast*: that which was made between
God and every single human soul before the manifestation of the material
world. At the very dawn of creation, all of the "children of Adam" are sum-
moned, as particles of consciousness and are asked: "Am I not your Lord

(*Alastu bi-rabbikum*)?" Following the affirmation of all the souls, God says: "This is lest you say, on the Day of Judgment we had no knowledge of this" (7:172).

The Light of Inspiration

All souls, then, have innate knowledge of God, and it is this innate knowledge that rises from a state of potentiality to virtuality to actuality by the leavening power of divine revelation. Hence, in the words of Imam 'Alī, one of the primary purposes of revelation is to "unearth the buried treasures of the intellect."[16] If divine wisdom is the essential content of the message of Revelation, it can only be that same wisdom that allows one to recognize this message as being truly revealed by God. The wisdom revealed through the Prophets is thus of one substance with the wisdom already within the soul: the merging of the wisdom inseminated by God from within and the wisdom bestowed by God from on high is thus akin to "light upon light," in the words of the famous verse of Light:

> God is the light of the heavens and the earth. A similitude of His light is a niche wherein is a lamp; the lamp is enclosed in a glass; the glass is as it were a shining star. [The lamp] is lit [by the oil of] a blessed olive tree, neither of the East nor of the West. The oil well-nigh shines forth, through fire touches it not. Light upon light! God guides to His light whom He will; and God strikes similitudes for mankind; and God knows all things (24:35).

Here light is given as the supreme symbol of consciousness, which is one in essence, but diversified in its modes, degrees, and manifestations: whether it be that of a plant, a human being, or an angel, consciousness is consciousness and nothing else. Likewise, whether it be the light of a candle, a lamp, or the sun, light is light and nothing else. It is light that illumines all things, needing nothing to illuminate it; it is consciousness that bestows awareness on all conscious beings, needing nothing to render it conscious. Light, then, is one of the best symbols for conveying the meaning of wisdom in the context of Islamic revelation: wisdom is "enlightenment," and this entails not just the illumination of the mind by the Light of God, but a wholehearted participation in divine luminosity—a total engagement of all dimensions of the soul with the Light of God. To quote the words of a contemporary Muslim scholar and sage, Seyyed Hossein Nasr: "As the

Prophet said, 'Knowledge is light' (*al-'ilm nūr*), and realized knowledge cannot but be the realization of that light which not only illuminates the mind but also beautifies the soul and irradiates the body . . ."[17]

The innate luminous knowledge of which the *fitra* is compounded is not to be understood simply as a kind of foreshadowing of the purely empirical datum that "God is our Lord." Rather, one can understand the meaning of the "lordship" of God both exoterically, in terms of the unique source of divinity, and also esoterically, in terms of the unique source of reality—a reality at once exclusive of all relativity by virtue of its inassociable transcendence, and inclusive of all reality by virtue of its inalienable immanence. On the one hand, in terms of transcendence, knowledge of the Real implies metaphysical discernment, the capacity to distinguish the relative from the Absolute: "There is nothing like Him" (42:11). On the other hand, in terms of immanence, knowledge of the Real implies that contemplative vision which can witness God in and through all things: "Wherever you turn, there is the Face of God" (2:115). There is no authentic wisdom without this synthesis between discernment and contemplation; and such a synthesis cannot come about simply as a result of passively registering the data of Revelation: the Scripture, descending upon us as revelation from above, can do nothing without the *fitra,* the preexisting revelation already present within each human soul. Wisdom revealed outwardly by God brings to fruition—but does not "create"—the seeds of wisdom already embedded within the soul.

Jalāl al-Dīn Rūmī (d. 1273) expresses beautifully the identity between prophetic revelation from without and primordial revelation from within:

> In the composition of man all forms of knowledge were originally commingled so that his spirit might show forth all hidden things, as limpid water shows forth all that is under it . . . and all that is above it, reflected in the substance of water. Such is its nature, without treatment or training. But when it was mingled with earth or other colours, that property and that knowledge was parted from it and forgotten by it. Then God Most High sent forth prophets and saints, like a great, limpid water such as delivers out of darkness and accidental colouration every mean and dark water that enters into it. Then it remembers; when the soul of man sees itself unsullied, it knows for sure that so it was in the beginning, pure, and it knows that those shadows and colours were mere accidents. Remembering its state before those accidents supervened, it says, *This is that sustenance which we were provided with before.*[18] The prophets and the saints therefore remind

him of his former state; they do not implant anything new in his substance. Now every dark water that recognises that great water, saying, "I come from this and I belong to this." mingles with that water. . . . It was on this account that God declared: *Truly there hath come unto you a Prophet from yourselves.*[19]

'Abd al-Hakīm: Servant of the Wise

To speak of the human soul, therefore, is to speak by definition of divine "inspiration," not just in the sense of the "inner Prophet," but also in the literal sense of the word, "in-spire." On the one hand, the Prophet is referred to as a "beautiful model," *uswa hasana* (33:21); on the other, the believers are told that they should understand: you have within yourselves the Messenger of God (49:7).[20] As regards the deeper meaning of inspire: God "breathed into" the human substance nothing but His very Spirit (38:71–72).[21] It is this spirit of God, by which we as human souls are by definition "in-spired," that enables us to know God above and beyond us; it is also this spirit that accounts for the fact that the angels prostrate before Adam, in obedience to God's order.[22] This act can be understood not only as an act of obedience to the divine command, but also as a recognition and acknowledgment of the unique human capacity to know God in His totality, the angels knowing God only in part. The act of prostration by the angels can also be seen as an act of devotion to God: for in prostrating to Adam, the angels deepen the mystery that only in the human soul is to be found the reflection of all of God's Names and Qualities. They thus prostrate to God, alone, retracing the image back to its source. Adam was, according to the Qur'an, taught all of the divine Names, and it is important to note that, when the angels confess their ignorance of the Names, they say to God, "Truly You, You are the Knowing, the Wise" (*al-'Alīm, al-Hakīm*; 2:32). Adam, by virtue of this knowledge of the Names—which can be understood as the ultimate divine archetypes of all possible knowledge—is therefore the sole created being capable of being fully qualified by the qualities of knowledge and wisdom. Being a reflected image of the divine totality, the Adamic reality is the chief means by which the very purpose of creation is consummated: "I was a hidden treasure," God declares, "and I loved to be known."[23]

Ibn al-'Arabī (d.1240) in his celebrated work entitled "Ringstones of Wisdom" (*Fusūs al-hikam*) refers implicitly to this principle in the opening passage of his first chapter, "The Wisdom of Divinity in the Word of Adam": "The Real willed, in virtue of His Beautiful Names, which are innumerable,

to see their identities—if you so wish, you can say: to see His Identity—
in a comprehensive being that comprises the whole affair [the totality of
being]. . . . For the vision a thing has of itself in itself is not like the vision
a thing has of itself in another thing, which will be like a mirror for it."[24]

So Adam, in his very being, manifests "the wisdom of divinity," the
only wisdom there is. To fully understand the reality of man is to understand the purpose of life and to realize something of the profound mystery
of God, whence the principle: "He who knows himself, knows his Lord."[25]
The Lord is al-Hakīm, "The Wise," and the servant attains wisdom to the
extent that he is aware of himself as 'Abd al-Hakīm, "servant of the Wise."
Likewise, the Qur'an refers to itself as "the Wise Qur'an" (36:2). And we are
instructed: "Invite people to enter upon the path of God with wisdom and
fine exhortation" (16:125). But if we ask where and how the Qur'an defines
this wisdom, we will find that it is only by hints and allusions, not explicit
definitions, that wisdom is referred to. We may come closer to understanding why wisdom is left undefined if we take cognizance of the fact that
the Qur'an refers to itself in several places as a "reminder" (dhikrā), and a
"remembrance" (dhikr),[26] and describes the Prophet as "one who reminds"
(mudhakkir).

What we are reminded of, ultimately, is that innate wisdom which is
indefinable in its essence. Wisdom eludes simple definition, and surpasses all
description, and yet it is immediately recognizable to those who are searching
for it. It is recognizable because it is "re-cognized," the re-cognition being
a knowing of something already known, but partially forgotten. As noted
above, the Prophet referred to wisdom in terms of "the lost property of the
believer"; he then added: "Wherever he finds it, he has the greatest right to
it."[27] Wisdom is immediately recognizable, whatever be the outward form
in which it is expressed, for it resonates with the wisdom within; the depth
of this resonance will depend, however, on the degree to which this inner
wisdom is being enlivened by faith: "A word of wisdom is the lost property
of the believer." The believer whose faith is heartfelt and not merely notional
will feel "at home" in wisdom. So the encounter with wisdom is akin to a
homecoming, the home in question being the heart within which God Himself resides. The divine presence within the heart will be felt according to the
depth of one's faith: "My earth cannot contain Me," God says, "My heaven
cannot contain Me, but the Heart of My believing servant contains Me."[28]

The Prophet's description of wisdom as the "lost property of the believer" helps us to see the illogicality of chauvinism of any sort in relation to
wisdom: wisdom is universal, it cannot be monopolized by any particular
culture or religion, time or place. Wherever wisdom is manifested, it remains

wisdom, and as such "belongs" to every true believer; every person, that is, who believes in the Absolute, with gratitude, trust, humility, and the other virtues contained within piety, and who thereby cultivates a transformative relationship with the Absolute. Wherever this kind of believer encounters wisdom, it belongs to him, not in any exclusive sense; rather, in the sense that wherever the word of wisdom comes from, it is an echo of what he already knows, this knowledge being one with his very being, not alien to it, nor extrinsic to it. It may be indefinable but it is nonetheless immediately identifiable, precisely because it is not other than what one is, in one's heart of hearts. This indefinable quality of wisdom goes hand in hand with its universality: it belongs to all, by virtue of being woven into the very substance of the human soul, the soul as such. It cannot then be appropriated by such and such a soul.

This kind of knowledge does not lend itself to definitions, and that is why wisdom cannot be spelled out like a set of regulations; such injunctions and prohibitions address the will, not the intelligence. Nor is wisdom simply the sum of virtues and inner attitudes infusing the intelligence or being generated by it; rather, it is from wisdom that both intelligence and virtue acquire their dimension of depth. Nor can wisdom be equated with a particular mode of thought; for wisdom is a synthesis of rational discernment and spiritual contemplation—and, at the deepest level, a synthesis of consciousness and being, from which wise thought, actions and deeds all arise spontaneously. Hence, any attempt to define wisdom cannot but reduce it to one or another of its dimensions. Wisdom is best broached, then, not as if it were a set of teachings addressed to the mind, but through a series of evocations, addressed to the heart. "Truly in this there is a reminder for one who has a heart" (50:37).

Wisdom is evoked in the Qur'an by association with particular virtues. For example, after presenting a series of teachings pertaining to diverse moral traits—ranging from obedience to one's parents, being generous to all, avoiding miserliness, extravagance, and pride—the Qur'an declares: "This is part of the wisdom that your Lord has revealed to you" (17:39). We are invited here to go from the "part" which is disclosed to the "whole" that is hidden, a whole that is not going to be spelled out for us: we have to discover it within ourselves, on the basis of the "reminders" granted by Revelation, and on the basis of living a life fashioned by Revelation.

This is altogether typical of the way the Qur'anic discourse works: addressing, through the mind, the deeper dimensions of the intelligence—speculative reflection, creative imagination, contemplative intuition—thereby penetrating the heart and spirit of the listener. Rich in such rhetorical devices

as ellipsis (*hadhf*), metaphor (*majāz, isti'āra*), allusion (*ishāra, ta'rīd*), and implication (*tadmīn*); it also frequently resorts to *kināya* metonymy or concealment:
the mention of an attribute or part of a thing in order to refer symbolically
to the whole thing itself.[29] In other words, the literary style of the Qur'an
itself calls for and enlivens a certain kind of wisdom, an ability to intuit
the "whole"—which remains undisclosed—on the basis of a "part," which
is disclosed. Revelation helps us to embark on the inner journey, starting
from what is revealed, and moving toward that which is concealed. Arabic
rhetoric—based in large part on the Qur'anic model, deemed "inimitable" in
its eloquence[30]—is most effective when it draws forth from the listener/reader
the meanings that are hidden or implicit in that which is stated explicitly.

The levels of wisdom hidden in the Qur'an are thus revealed in accordance with the depth of the wisdom of the listener. The Prophet asserted that
each verse of the Qur'an has seven modes (*ahruf*), and that each mode has an
inner and an outer sense, a limit and a point of ascent. While the exoteric
scholars focus on the outer sense and the limit, Sufis stress the inner sense and
the point of ascent. According to one of the greatest medieval Sufi exegetes,
Rūzbihān Baqlī (d. 1209), God reveals the secrets of the Qur'an to "the best
of His people": "He showed them the unseen mysteries of the brides of different kinds of wisdom and knowledge, and the meanings of the innermost
understanding and innermost secret, the exoteric sense (*zāhir*) . . . and inner
sense (*bātin*), of which is an allusion (*ishāra*) and unveiling (*kashf*) which God
reserves for His purified ones and His friends (*awliyā'*)."[31] In other words,
one can only grasp the inner depths of the Qur'anic message in the measure
that one has been "purified" from the impurities of error, ignorance, vice,
and sin: "This is indeed a noble Qur'an, in a concealed book, which none
touch except the purified" (56:77–79). The Qur'anic discourse comprises
an inner text, a register of meaning, which will be understood by each in
accordance with the receptivity fashioned by purity of soul, spiritual aspiration, and the imponderables of Grace.

The Wisdom of Gratitude

The Qur'an invites us to consider wisdom through understanding the virtues
as wise "ways of being"—inasmuch as virtuous action is the outward embodiment of a particular mode of wisdom. By presenting wisdom in association
with virtues, at the same time as refusing to define wisdom per se, the
Qur'anic discourse does not allow us to think of the virtues solely in terms
of their immediate meaning, as constituting the good intentions underlying

outward deeds. Rather, we are invited to probe the spiritual repercussions and reflect upon the intellectual implications of the virtues, thereby rising from the diversity of human virtues to the unity of their divine source, each virtue being a reflection of a divine quality. This effort to relate the diversity of human virtues to the unity of God can be seen as one of the applications of the principle of *tawhīd,* the foremost theological axiom of Islam.

Tawhīd is often translated simply as "oneness," or "declaring divine unity," doing so through the affirmation that "there is no divinity but God" (*lā ilāha illa'Llāh*). A more subtle understanding of *tawhīd* emerges when one notes that the word is a verbal noun, the basic meaning of which is "to make one," hence "to integrate," and at the deepest level, "to realize" unity, doing so with utter sincerity, *ikhlās,* which can also be translated as "purity." To be pure or sincere in one's belief in divine unity not only implies that one worships God alone, eschewing all worship of idols (*shirk*); it is also to be inwardly purified of the hidden idolatry (*al-shirk al-khafī*) constituted by egotistic desire (*hawā'*): "Have you seen him who makes his desire his god?" (25:43; almost identical at 45:23). Wisdom presupposes a recognition of this subtle idolatry within oneself, and negating it through remorseless self-examination (*muhāsaba*), self-dominion through spiritual struggle (*mujāhada*), self-realization through integration, and finally self-transcendence through the graces that are attracted to the soul through heartfelt prayer. The result of this mastery of desire, achieved through orientation to the divine reality, is nothing short of Paradise in the Hereafter, and a paradisal state in the here below: "As for him who fears the rank of his Lord, and restrains his soul from its desire, verily the Garden will be his abode" (79:40–41).

Imam 'Alī alerts us to the relationship between asserting the oneness of God and the realization of unity within oneself: "He who knows God integrates himself [*man 'arafa'Llāh tawahhad*]."[32] *Tawhīd* is therefore a process of inner spiritual integration and is for this reason inseparable from the cultivation of wisdom. If the message conveyed by the Prophet is *tawhīd,* understood as the essence of monotheism, then the Prophetic soul should itself be regarded as the perfect consummation of *tawhīd* conceived as a spiritually transformative process. As mentioned earlier, the Prophet is the "beautiful model," *uswa hasana* (33:21). To contemplate the perfected soul of the Prophet is to open oneself up to a mode of being that is both fashioned by Revelation and is itself a prolongation of Revelation; and as already noted, he is himself regarded as the greatest "sign/verse" of Revelation.[33] Studying the life and sayings of the Prophet thus teaches one about wisdom in prac- tice: he showed us how wisdom manifests in his specific context. From this study one can glean something of the meaning of the essence or principle of wisdom, and how to apply that principle in our own lives. But one cannot simply imitate his outward actions, which were manifestations of wisdom in the particular conditions of his time and place. Again, one has to go from the outward expression of wisdom to its inner principle.

The virtues of the Prophet are the most explicit indicators of the existential nature of wisdom. He referred to his entire mission as being an effort to teach virtue: "I was only sent," he declared, "for the sake of perfecting the most noble virtues [makārim al-akhlāq]."[34] This means that the virtues must express something more than just moral wisdom, they must relate to the highest wisdom, which grants not just salvation in the Hereafter but also liberation in this life. In other words, the virtues in question must be connected with that wisdom which engages with the very heart of the prophetic message: no divinity but God. For it is this message, surely, that the Prophet came to deliver, and which in turn delivers souls from the bondage of sin and ignorance. This message, indeed, is the quintessence of all scriptural revelation: "We sent no Messenger before you without revealing to him: there is no God but Me so worship Me" (21:25). Knowledge of the oneness of God is thus conjoined to worship; such metaphysical knowledge and spiritual praxis, in turn, cannot be separated from the perfection of the virtues.

The subtle relationships between wisdom, virtue, and worship are alluded to in the chapter entitled "Luqmān"—a sage or prophet of antiquity: "We verily gave wisdom to Luqmān: be grateful to God. Whoever is grateful is indeed grateful to his own benefit; and whoever expresses ingratitude [or: disbelief][35]—God is truly Independent, Praised" (31:12). The importance of this verse, as far as wisdom is concerned, is reinforced by the fact that the opening verse of this chapter tells us: "These are the verses of the Wise Book (al-Kitāb al-hakīm)." It continues: "A guidance and a mercy for the virtuous—those who maintain prayer, and give charity, and are certain of the Hereafter" (31:2–4). The Book will be a source of wisdom, mercy, and guidance to those who are already, to some degree at least, "virtuous." What is brought to perfection by revelation must already be prefigured in the soul, and striving for virtue is just such a prefiguration. The outer revelation will awaken that innate wisdom of the fitra to the extent that virtue is already being intended, and, to some extent at least, practiced. Vice, heedlessness, and forgetfulness, on the contrary, are so many veils preventing the outer light of revelation from penetrating the heart and uniting with the immanent light therein: "Nay but what they have done has become rust over their hearts" (83:15).

One of the key virtues required for receptivity to the transformative power of divine revelation is gratitude, which verse 31:12 practically identifies with wisdom. Gratitude to God is, first of all, a mode of faith, and indeed may be seen as identical to faith, given that the antonym of both faith and gratitude is *kufr,* which can thus be translated either as disbelief or as ingratitude. The root meaning of the word *kufr* is "to cover over." To be a disbeliever (*kāfir*) is to "cover over" the fact that one owes one's existence to God; to "cover over" the blessings of the Lord, hence, to manifest ingratitude to Him. This ingratitude is the root of unbelief, for, as we have noted above, each human soul in its innermost depths is aware of God as its Lord. The overt declaration of atheism is thus only the mental affirmation of a fundamental spiritual malaise, that of ingratitude to the source of one's being, that is, to one's Creator, the Lord that one knows, deep down, to be real. Whence arises this obfuscation of reality that produces ingratitude and unbelief? From our own actions, their fundamental motivations, together with their inward repercussion, for, "What they have done has rusted over their hearts" (83:14). It is not the eyes that are blind, the Qur'ān tells us, "rather, blind are the hearts that are in the breasts" (22:46).

One knows of the reality of God with one's heart, and it is from the heart that springs the natural attitude of faith winged with gratitude. It is gratitude that lends to a possibly abstract or nominal faith that quality of love and devotion which deepens the relationship between God and the soul. "If you are grateful," God tells us, "I will give you more" (14:7). The more He gives, the more grateful we are, and the more grateful we are, the more He gives, in a never-ending virtuous circle. To manifest gratitude to God presupposes faith in God, and the most direct means of expressing this gratitude to God is heartfelt worship. To worship God is to do what most benefits the soul: "Whoever is grateful is indeed grateful to his own benefit." God is "Independent" (*ghanī*), the One who receives praise, hence "Praised" (*hamīd*) (31:12). God does not need our praise or our gratitude, it is we who need to worship Him with praise and gratitude. In return for this, He grants us "more."

This "more" can be understood to mean: more grace, consisting of such gifts as good character, love of beauty, deep spiritual orientations, interiorizing contemplative intuitions, beatific "tastes" of the divine reality. To be fully grateful to God thus engages or enlivens all other virtues, to the extent that one's aspiration toward virtue is sustained by prayerful focus on God as the source of all possible virtue. One not only receives spiritual sustenance from that upon which one focuses with loving aspiration; one is inwardly transformed into that upon which one is focused. Imam 'Alī describes this "alchemical" transformation in terms of a special "wine" God gives to His "friends" (*awliyā',* that is, the saints):

Truly, God has a drink for His friends [awliyā'ihi]. When they
drink it, they are intoxicated; and when they are intoxicated, they
are enraptured; and when they are enraptured, they are blessed;
and when they are blessed they dissolve; and when they dissolve,
they are free; and when they are free, they are pure; and when
they are pure, they seek [talabū]; and when they seek, they find;
and when they find, they arrive; and when they arrive, they are
at one: there is no difference between them and their Beloved.[36]

This evokes the saying of the great medieval German mystic, Meister Eckhart: "The bodily food we take is changed into us, but the spiritual food
we receive changes us into itself."[37]

To be grateful to God, then, means that one's faith in God is enlivened by the worship that flows forth from the grateful gift of oneself to
the source of one's existence, the goal of one's aspirations. Gratitude might
be described as faith imbued with love; the grateful believer is transformed
by his gratitude into a lover of God. For faith, without gratitude, can be
abstract or merely notional. But grateful orientation to the God in whom
one believes cannot but be infused with that love which gives wings to faith,
moving the soul to express loving thanks to God in total gift of self. To be
fully grateful to God logically implies that one serve God with all that one
is, according to the "two great commandments" of Jesus: "And thou shalt
love the Lord thy God with all thy heart, and with all thy soul, and with
all thy mind, and with all thy strength: this is the first commandment. And
the second is like, namely this, Thou shalt love thy neighbor as thyself" (St
Mark 12: 30–31). Through this total gift of self to God in love, one cannot
but give oneself likewise to the neighbor, doing so through all the other
fundamental virtues—such as kindness, generosity, charity, and fidelity, which
in turn calls for such virtues as courage, strength, and perseverance. Wisdom
shines through the soul into which these virtues have been woven.

All of these virtues can be conceived as the human reflection of divine
Names and Qualities, which in turn are rooted in the undifferentiated oneness of the divine Essence. The apparent equation made between gratitude
and wisdom should thus be viewed as an ellipsis: gratitude is at one with
wisdom in the same way that, in the divine nature, al-Shakūr, "the Grateful,"
is identical in essence with al-Hakīm, "the Wise." The two are outwardly differentiated in terms of their specific meaning (ma'nā) and mode of manifestation, their way of rendering explicit some aspect of the "hidden treasure," the
divine Essence. This Essence is both absolute and infinite, hence it comprises
infinite modes of perfection. But the two Names, "the Grateful" and "the

Wise"—together with all the divine Names—are inwardly identical by virtue of the oneness of their ontological substance: it is one and the same God that is "qualified" (*mawṣūf*) or described by these specific qualities (*ṣifāt*). Each of the ninety-nine Names or Qualities of God—"the Compassionate," "the Loving," "the Just," "the Powerful," etc.—is identical with all of the others. In other words, there are not ninety-nine "gods," there is one God, qualified by all of these Names. Given the unity and simplicity (non-compoundedness) of the divine nature, each Quality is inseparable from all of the others: in the Essence all the Names and Qualities are absolutely undifferentiated.

One sees the possibility of something analogous being established on the human plane. That which is true on the level of divine reality can also become true, *mutatis mutandis,* within the human soul: the virtue of gratitude can be rendered identical to wisdom in the measure that all the different qualities and faculties of the soul are rendered "unanimous"—literally: "of one spirit"; or integrated—literally: "made one."[38] Again, according to the sentence quoted above, from Imam 'Alī: "He who knows God integrates himself [*man 'arafa'Llāh tawahhad*]."

If knowledge of God leads to self-integration, it also ineluctably produces gratitude. The more one knows God as the source of all being, the more grateful one is to that source for the blessings inherent in being. The result of this gratitude is a special kind of worship. Imam 'Alī refers to three groups of worshipers:

> Indeed there is a group who worship God out of desire; and this is the worship of traders. And there is a group who worship God out of fear; and this is the worship of slaves. And there is a group who worship God out of gratitude, and this is the worship of the liberated.[39]

Those liberated from desire and fear are those liberated from ignorance. They are the wise, the defining feature of whose worship is gratitude. They express gratitude to their Lord not only for the fact of their creation but also for all the celestial graces already bestowed, here and now, such that they do not have to wait for Paradise to be inwardly "liberated" from the imprisoning limitations of the earthly condition. The hearts of the highest sages, Imam 'Alī tells us, are already in Paradise; their bodies, alone, are acting in this world.[40] "Truly We have given you [the Paradisal fountain called] al-Kawthar,"[41] the Prophet is told in the Qur'an, "so pray to your Lord . . ." (108:1–2).

The Prophet exemplified to perfection this wisdom which is expressed through grateful worship. He spent much of the night, every night, in prayer—"Truly your Lord knows that you stand in prayer close to two-thirds of the night, and half of it, and a third of it—you and a group of those with you . . ." (73: 20). He also made it beautifully clear, in the following incident, what it was that motivated these extraordinary night vigils, which are most often associated only with the most ascetic kind of monks or hermits. It is related that one night, he stood in prayer for so many hours that his feet became swollen. His wife, ʿĀʾisha, asked him why he was praying so much, reminding him that God had forgiven him whatever "sins" he had committed or might yet commit (referring to 48:1–2). "Am I not a grateful servant?" came the disarming reply.[42] The truly grateful soul is intense in its expression of gratitude; the quality of gratitude is thus dynamic, active, and actualizing: it does not remain a mere sentiment. Gratitude galvanizes the soul, precipitating it into a state of loving adoration of the One to whom it is grateful. Al-Ghazālī (d.1111), in his monumental work "Revival of the Sciences of Religion" (Ihyāʾ ʿulūm al-dīn), states that "God has paired gratitude to remembrance in His Book," namely, the Qurʾān. He cites, among others, the following verse to illustrate this "pairing": "So remember Me," God says, "I will remember you; and be grateful to Me, be not ungrateful/disbelieving (lā takfurūn)" (2:152).[43] Again, one notes that the opposite to gratitude, kufr, is both ingratitude and disbelief.

The relationship between gratitude and wisdom is thus mediated by loving adoration, by prolonged worship, contemplation of the beloved object of gratitude. For it is by means of this kind of worship that the heart, rather than just the mind, attains enlightenment. In the deepest degree of worship, the mind sleeps and the heart awakens: "My eyes are sleep but my heart is awake," said the Prophet,[44] echoing the Song of Solomon (5:2). The mind is eclipsed in deep worship by the light of the heart, or rather, by the light of God reflected by the heart. Human knowledge is displaced and then replaced by divine wisdom, in the very measure that the act of worship effaces the mind and awakens the heart. Gratitude, then, leads to worship, and worship leads to the wisdom of the heart: "So hymn your Lord's praise and be among those who prostrate [to Him]; and worship your Lord until certainty comes to you" (15:98–99). Commentators of this verse debate whether the phrase al-yaqīn, literally, "the certain," means certainty, or death, "that which is certain." The two meanings are complementary, however: for spiritual death—the death of egotism—is precisely what gives rise to absolute certainty, which is nothing other than certainty of the Absolute. And this certainty is the very substance of wisdom.[45] Unshakable certainty of the Absolute brings with it an implacable discernment between the Absolute and the relative, the Infinite and the finite, the True and the false. Wisdom flows naturally from the consequences, implications, and repercussions of this proper sense of spiritual proportions.[46]

Worship leads to wisdom, at least in principle. According to the Prophet, the remembrance of God, *dhikr Allāh,* is the most efficacious of all modes of worship. *Dhikr* refers to the principle of remembrance, or consciousness of God, and is thus the aim of all forms of prayer: "Establish the canonical prayer [*al-salāt*] for the sake of remembering Me" (20:14). It also refers to the methodic discipline of invocation, the repetition, silently or aloud, of the Name (or Names) of God: "And invoke the Name of your Lord devoting yourself to it with utter dedication" (73:8). The invocation is therefore presented as the practice that most effectively generates consciousness of God. Insofar as *dhikr Allāh* is nothing but the pure consciousness of God, it is the source of all possible wisdom.

Remembrance: Enlightenment of the Heart

Many sayings of the Prophet affirm that the quintessence of worship is the invocation of the Name of God. For example:

> "Shall I not tell you about the best and purest of your works for your Lord?" The people addressed by him said: "What is that, O Messenger of God?" He said, "The perpetual invocation of God."[47]

Likewise, the Qur'an states explicitly that, while the canonical prayer (*al-salāt*) keeps one from evil, the remembrance of God is "greater" (29:45). In the following verse, the relationship between invocation and enlightenment is expressed clearly: "O you who believe, invoke God with much invocation, and glorify Him early [in the morning] and late [at night]. He it is who blesses you, as do His angels, in order to bring you out of darkness into Light . . ." (33:41–43).

The deeper meaning of *islām,* as spiritual submission to the Real, is linked to the ease or expansion of the "breast" (*sadr*), and this in turn is associated with the heart, within the breast, which is receptive to the light and the remembrance of God, source of wisdom: "Is he whose breast God has opened up to submission—so that he follows a light from his Lord [like one whose breast remains closed to submission?]. So woe to those whose hearts have been hardened against the remembrance of God" (39:22). In the following verse, 39:23, the Qur'an speaks of hearts that "soften" (*talīnu*) to the remembrance. This softening can be understood in many ways, the most important perhaps being the serenity that comes to characterize the heart that, being expanded and illumined by the remembrance of God, is awakened to its own fundamental reality, and becomes attuned to the consciousness of God, which essentially defines that reality.

The importance of the quality of peace in relation to the heart and the wisdom that is rooted therein cannot be overemphasized. It is only in a state of peace that the heart reveals its true nature and the contents of its own consciousness. If the soul is dominated by its lower possibilities—anger, lust, jealousy, pride, etc.—then the heart is obscured by the "clouds" generated by these vices, and the wisdom of the heart will remain concealed. The soul at this stage of lowliness is referred to as the "soul which commands evil" (al-nafs al-ammāra bi'l-sū', 12:53). When its conscience is awakened, and it strives for virtue—that inner striving which the Prophet referred to as the "greatest struggle" (al-jihād al-akbar)—then it is qualified as "the self-accusing soul" (al-nafs al-lawwāma, 75:2). And when the soul is serene in the certainty of God, it is referred to as "the soul at peace" (al-nafs al-mutma'inna, 89:27). This peace or serenity, which allows the heart to yield to God and thereby reveal its deepest nature as primordial wisdom, can only come from God. It is not the kind of peace that comes from anything in the world or the ego: "He it is who has sent down the spirit of peace into the hearts of the believers, that they might add faith to their faith" (48:4).[48] This inward journey through deeper degrees of faith—going from simple conviction to heartfelt faith, from faith to certainty, and from certainty to gnosis—is proportioned to the revelation of the depths of the consciousness contained within the heart. This inward journey can also be understood as the path leading from human forms of wisdom expressed outwardly in thought and act, to the supra-formal essence of wisdom, mysteriously present in the heart.

Put differently, the immanent presence of God within the heart is revealed in the measure that the heart is at peace in the certainty of God. Knowledge *of* the heart transforms itself into knowledge *by* the heart, and it is this properly "heartfelt" knowledge that constitutes wisdom. So the acquisition of peace of heart (itmi'nān) is a condition for authentic wisdom, and this peace of heart, as mentioned above, can only come from God. We, however, have access to the key to this peace: the remembrance of God, which, like a magnet, attracts the divine grace of transcendent peace. Or rather, God attracts to Himself those who turn to him in remembrance: "God leaves whomever He will to stray, and guides to Himself those who turn to Him: those who believe and whose hearts are at peace in the remembrance of God. Is it not in the remembrance of God that hearts are at peace?" (13:27–28).

After the "Verse of Light," cited earlier, comes the following, which reinforces the relationship between invocation and enlightenment. It shows that the *dhikr*, the remembrance/invocation of God, is the key means by which the soul is rendered capable of receiving and reflecting the one and only light, that of God: "In houses God has allowed to be raised, and wherein His Name is remembered, therein He is glorified, morning and the evening, by men whom neither trading, nor sale distracts from the remembrance of God and the observance of prayer and payment of the alms" (24:36–37).

Imam 'Alī makes explicit the relationship between *dhikr Allāh* and enlightenment in his commentary on this verse:

> Truly, God has made the remembrance [*al-dhikr*] a polish for the hearts, by which they hear after being deaf, and see after being blind and yield after being resistant. . . . There have always been servants of God . . . with whom He held intimate discourse through their thoughts, and spoke with them through the essence of their intellects. They diffused illumination through the awakened light in their hearing and their seeing and their hearts, calling unto the remembrance of the days of God. . . . Indeed, there is a special group [*ahl*] who belong to the *dhikr*; they have adopted it in place of the world, such that "neither trade nor merchandise" distracts them from it. They spend the days of their life in it. . . . It is as though they had left this world for the Hereafter, and they are there, witnessing what is beyond this world.[49]

The reality of the divine presence bestowed by the remembrance comes to suffuse the whole of one's consciousness, so that nothing in the outer world distracts one from the remembrance. It is this perpetual, uninterrupted consciousness of God, in the very midst of one's daily activities, that defines the spiritual rank of the people Imam 'Alī is describing here. As seen above, he speaks about those whose hearts are already in Paradise, their bodies, only, being at work in this world. They have adopted the *dhikr* in place of the world, which means that they are permanently oriented to the remembrance of God, and this remembrance is a properly paradisal state of consciousness, here and now. For this reason, "it is as though they had left this world." In fact, they have not left it, outwardly or materially, for they engage in trade and do business like others. But unlike others, their inmost identity is fashioned by their remembrance, so worldly activity is no longer a distraction from God.

In the Sufi tradition, this condition is known as "seclusion in society" (*khalwat dar anjumān*), or being in the world but not of it. On account of their permanent remembrance, divine light radiates through them, helping others to attain enlightenment: "They diffused illumination through the awakened light in their hearing and their seeing and their hearts." Wisdom attained through remembrance shines through the souls of the wise. The wise, furthermore, are those most fully attuned to the qualities of God that define His intrinsic nature. They are the ones who know that the divine nature is essentially mercy, compassion, and love; and the comportment of the wise reflects these divine qualities. Again, according to Imam 'Alī: "The one who truly understands (*al-faqīh*), is he who never makes people despair of the mercy of God."[50]

The remembrance of God is described by Imam 'Alī as a "polish" (*jilā'*)[51] for the hearts by which they come to see and hear. This evokes the beatitude expressed by Jesus in his sermon on the Mount: "Blessed are the pure in heart, for they shall see God" (Matthew 5:8). The heart that has been purified comes to see the divine reality, and it is this vision of the divine that the "eye of the heart" refers to in so many traditions of the world.[52]

Returning to the chapter entitled "Luqmān," let us note that after the sage is told by God what the essence of wisdom is—to be grateful to God—Luqmān in turn teaches his son some of the forms that wisdom takes. These range from avoiding polytheism, being constantly aware of the divine omnipotence and omniscience, establishing regular prayer, to enjoining the right, forbidding the wrong, and being patient. The exhortation ends, significantly, with a warning against pride: "Do not turn your nose up [lit. "your cheek"] at people, nor walk about arrogantly, for God loves not the swaggering braggart. Rather, be modest in your bearing, and lower your voice" (31:18–19). This important passage concerning wisdom thus begins with gratitude and ends with humility. If gratitude is the key note accompanying and determining remembrance—which in turn enlightens the heart—then humility can be seen both as the cause and the consequence of remembrance. Indeed, at its deepest degree, humility is the key to the consummation of this remembrance, being the chief means by which the veil of the ego is removed—or at least thinned—thus allowing the wisdom of the heart to manifest. One aims to become '*Abd al-Hakīm*, "Servant of the Wise," which becomes a possibility in the measure that the ego is effaced, a self-effacement that can only be attained in the bosom of divine remembrance.

This relationship between remembrance and effacement is expressed in the following saying of Imam 'Alī:

Do not remember God absent-mindedly, nor forget Him in distraction; rather, remember Him with perfect remembrance [*dhikran kāmilan*], a remembrance in which your heart and tongue are in harmony, and what you hide conforms with what you disclose. But you will not remember Him according to the true reality of the remembrance [*haqīqat al-dhikr*] until you forget your own soul in your remembrance.[53]

It is important to note here that one cannot force oneself to forget oneself; one cannot consciously aim to be unself-conscious; the soul cannot wipe out the soul, any more than words can express the wordless. This is why the Imam does not simply say that one must forget oneself. He says: forget yourself *in your remembrance*. In other words, it is only by means of the totality of your concentration on God as the supreme "Other" that you can be granted the grace of self-naughting. To be unconscious of oneself does not necessarily imply being conscious of God; but, by contrast, the plenary consciousness of God cannot but entail the eclipse of self-consciousness, the sunrise at once negating and absorbing the light of the stars. This is what the Sufis refer to as *al-fanā'*, "extinction" or "effacement." As a result of the effacement of the ego which is wrought by the alchemy of remembrance, that which is realized in the sage is a knowledge that is not so much "of God" but "through God": the sage is called *al-'ārif bi' Llāh,* "the one who knows *through* God." The sage thus comes to participate in God's knowledge of Himself, this being the ultimate degree of *tawhīd,* "realizing oneness" through pure, unitive consciousness. This realization of oneness generates the awareness that everything that is manifested in the created realm is known to be divine in principle, and created only in appearance. Everything that is apparently possessed by the creature is revealed to be nothing but the effects of the divine qualities shining through the creature. This vision of the reality—at once exclusive and inclusive—of the divine qualities, is granted to the servant who is effaced in worship. This principle is alluded to in one of the cornerstones of Sufi doctrine and praxis, the *hadīth al-nawāfil,* the saying pertaining to supererogatory devotions:

My slave never ceases to draw near to Me through supererogatory devotions [*nawāfil*] until I love him. And when I love him, I am his hearing by which he hears, his sight by which he sees, his hand by which he grasps, and his foot by which he walks.[54]

While the obligatory prayers initiate man's movement toward God, those prayers offered to God not simply out of religious obligation but total spiritual dedication lead to the ultimate degree of *tawhīd*, the *deificatio* or *theosis* referred to in the Christian tradition. But this mystical realization of *tawhīd* cannot be attained without first accomplishing that prefiguration of effacement which *Islām*, "submission," brings about: obedient performance of the obligations of the revealed Law. It is this which is stressed in the first part of the *hadīth*: God says that nothing is more lovable to Him "than that which I have made obligatory." Conformity to the outward religious obligations is thus not so much a formal constraint that prevents one from realizing the essence, but the very ground upon which one ascends toward the essence.

This subordination of the will of the soul to the will of God is thus an inherent part of the process by which humility, prerequisite for wisdom, is attained. But humility, as mentioned above, is both condition and consequence of wisdom. The humility that flows as a consequence of realized wisdom is what one might call "ontological," in that it is now the fruit of an authentic knowledge of what is real: knowledge of That which alone is, and, as a consequence, knowledge of the nothingness of the self in the Light of divine Reality. We return to the saying of the Prophet, but from a different angle: "He who knows himself, knows his Lord." For he who knows that his Lord is alone real, knows that he himself is unreal. As Ibn al-'Arabī writes, in what can be read as a comment on this saying: "The final end and ultimate return of the sages . . . is that the Real is identical with them, while they do not exist."[55]

Ibn al-'Arabī distinguishes between two forms of spiritual wisdom or *maʿrifa*, the term preferred by the Sufis,[56] in relation to this saying of the Prophet. This distinction takes us back to our discussion of the "Wisdom of Divinity in the Word of Adam" in Ibn al-'Arabī's *Fusūs*. The first form of wisdom revealed by knowledge of oneself is "knowing Him as knowing yourself"—knowledge of oneself as a servant contains the logical corollary: knowledge of God as one's Lord. The second form of wisdom is "knowing Him through you as Him, not as you."[57] The possibility of this latter form of wisdom is predicated on the presence of divinity already "in" the soul. For the Sufis, God is present in the soul in the way sunlight is "in" a mirror reflecting it. The Light of God radiates from the sun of absolute Being, and can be reflected and refracted without the sun itself changing either its "location" or its essence in any respect. The reflected light "in" the mirror is not other than sunlight: the relative consciousness "in" the heart is not other than consciousness as such, the supreme Self or, in Qur'anic terms, the divine Witness, *al-Shahīd*. According to Ibn al-'Arabī, spiritual realization can be described as light returning to the root from which it was manifested:

The object of vision, which is the Real, is light, while that through which the perceiver perceives Him is light. Hence light becomes included within light. It is as if it returns to the root from which it became manifest. So nothing sees Him but He.[58]

Refracted light comes to realize its true nature as light: when the light within the heart as it were "merges" with the Light whence it was projected, the result is not two lights, one that can be called reflected or relative, the other original and absolute. Rather, it is a question of the relativity qualifying the reflected light within the soul being lifted, shed or effaced; and what was previously the lesser light—the ray of relative light reflected in the mirror of the heart—is now indistinguishable from Light as such. This is one way of understanding the meaning of the "subsistence" (baqā') of the individual after "extinction" (fanā'). That which subsists is Light as such, which penetrates and radiates through the individual soul, the veil of whose ego is now utterly transparent.

By means of this analogy with light it becomes easier to intuit what might be regarded as a contradiction in Sufi metaphysics: on the one hand, "none knows God but God," and on the other, the sage comes to know God by knowing himself, as the Prophet said. In terms of the analogy with light, one sees this apparent contradiction as a fruitful paradox: God Himself is the sole Light, which is the source both of consciousness and of being; there are signs of this Light for the relative soul both within itself, in terms of subjective consciousness, and on the horizons, in terms of objective being: "We shall show them Our signs on the horizons [around them] and in their own souls, such that it be clear to them that He is the Real" (41:53). But the very next sentence in this verse alludes to the mystical truth which is only fully accessible by virtue of the extinction of the self, the truth that God alone is that which is seen and that which sees: "Does it not suffice that your Lord is witness to everything?"[59]

Here, then, lies the deepest wisdom accessible to us: the wisdom that reveals to us the divine reality underlying, penetrating, and suffusing all that exists: "Wherever you turn, there is the Face of God" (2:115). But attainment of this wisdom is predicated upon the kind of vision granted by the heart that has been polished and purified by the remembrance of God. The heart then comes to see by the light of this remembrance, and with the eye of the Lord, not with its own eye.[60] The heart knows that "your Lord is witness to everything," and it knows it precisely because it sees through, *and not by means of,* the subjective veil of individual consciousness. The "vision of God" means, therefore, not that we see God; for the "vision *of* God" is nothing but *God's vision*: "Vision comprehends Him not, but He comprehends all vision; and He is the Subtle, the Aware" (6:103). His infinitely subtle awareness penetrates and thus "comprehends," encompasses, and transpierces all possible awareness: "There is nothing like Him; and He is the Hearer, the Seer" (42:11). To say that the ultimate wisdom consists in the realization that God alone can be qualified by true consciousness, that God alone knows God, and that He is therefore both the Witness and what is Witnessed, is to paraphrase in universal, metaphysical terms the first testimony of Islam: "There is no divinity but God," *lā ilāha illa'Llāh*. And to say that this ultimate wisdom is realized only by the purified heart of the effaced slave of the Wise (*'Abd al-Hakīm*) is to express in individual, mystical terms the second testimony: "Muhammad is the Messenger of God" (*Muhammad rasūlu'Llāh*).

Endnotes

1. Cited by Ibn Mājah. See the collection of sayings under the heading of "La Sagesse" (*al-hikma*), in the excellent compilation by Tayeb Chouiref, *Les Enseignements Spirituels du Prophète* (Wattrelos: Éditions Tasnim, 2008), vol. 1, pp. 179–191.

2. The word *humility* derives from the Latin *humus*, meaning "earth."

3. The Arabic word *dhikr* means remembrance, mention, and also invocation. The context in which it occurs determines which meaning, or combination of meanings, is intended.

4. Sufism refers to the range of mystical traditions in Islam. See Eric Geoffroy, *Introduction to Sufism—The Inner Path of Islam,* trans. Roger Gaetani (Bloomington: World Wisdom, 2010) for a useful overview; and Frithjof Schuon, *Understanding Islam* (Bloomington: World Wisdom, 1994), which is an exposition of the essential elements of the Islamic faith from the point of view of quintessential Sufism, grasped by the author as the expression, in Islamic mode, of the "perennial philosophy."

5. Martin Lings, *What is Sufism?* (Cambridge: Islamic Texts Society, 1993), p. 85.

6. The very notion of philosophy is inextricable from divine revelation, being seen in the Islamic philosophical tradition as having issued forth not from human invention but from the "niche of prophecy" (*mishkāt al-nubuwwa*). Seyyed Hossein Nasr, *Islamic Philosophy from Its Origin to the Present* (Albany: State University of New York Press, 2006), p. 3.

7. In referring to God as "Him," we are abiding by Islamic convention, the name *Allāh* being masculine in gender. Needless to say, the divine reality as such transcends gender specificity. However, when one mentions in Arabic the Essence of Allāh, *al-Dhāt,* one refers to "Her," the word *dhāt* being feminine in gender. It

is for this reason, among others, that so many Sufis poetically address the essence of God as "Laylā," a woman's name signifying "night," a symbol that evokes the saying of the Shulamite in the Song of Solomon, "I am black but beautiful." See, for an example of Sufi poetry of this genre, the Shaykh al-'Alawī's poem "Laylā," translated beautifully by Martin Lings in his biography, *A Sufi Saint of the Twentieth Century—Shaikh Ahmad al-'Alawī* (London: George Allen & Unwin, 1971), p. 225.

    8. All translations from the Qur'an are mine, but substantially based on the translations by M. M. Pickthall, Ali Quli Qara'i, and M. A. S. Abdel Haleem.

    9. Cousin and son-in-law of the Prophet, fourth caliph of Islam, first Imam of the Shi'is, was famously described by the Prophet as the gate to prophetic knowledge: "I am the city of knowledge," he said, "and 'Alī is its gate." Frithjof Schuon refers to 'Alī as "the representative par excellence of Islamic esoterism." *The Transcendent Unity of Religions,* Peter Townsend (trans.) (London: Faber & Faber, 1953), p. 59. For discussion of 'Alī's seminal role in the articulation of the Islamic spiritual tradition, see R. Shah-Kazemi, *Justice and Remembrance—Introducing the Spirituality of Imam 'Alī* (London: IB Tauris, 2006).

    10. The phrase "the clear book" is an allusion to the Qur'an's description of itself, *al-kitāb al-mubīn,* which can also be translated as "the clarifying book"; see 12:1, 26:2, et passim.

    11. 'Alī b. Abī Tālib, *Dīwān* ('Abd al-Rahmān al-Mustāwī, ed.) (Beirut & London: Dar al-Ma'rifa, 2005), p. 72. The poem begins with the following line: "Your remedy is within you, but you do not grasp it; and your sickness is from you, but you do not perceive it." The esoteric idea of man as microcosm, and the elaborate doctrine of "the Perfect Man" (*al-Insān al-kāmil*), associated with Ibn al-'Arabī (d.1240), is found here in seed form.

    12. *The Mantle Adorned—Imam Būsīrī's Burda* (Abdal Hakim Murad, trans.) (London: Quilliam Press, 2009), p. 122. This is arguably the most influential of all the poems in praise of the Prophet in the whole Islamic tradition.

    13. The word in Arabic is *sūra,* which literally means "form," but can also have a more abstract connotation, so that, for example, one of the derivatives of the root of the word is *tasawwur,* "mental conception." This harmonizes with the Platonic sense of *eidos,* which we translate as either form or idea, and refers to the essence or archetype of a thing.

    14. This saying is not found in the canonical compilations of Prophetic sayings but is nonetheless accepted by most Muslim scholars as regards its basic meaning, and is often quoted by Sufis. The great Sufi commentator 'Abd al-Razzāq al-Kāshānī (d.1329) identifies the Name of God with the Prophet, doing so in his commentary on the verse in which God addresses the Prophet: "So remember the Name of thy Lord" (73:8). Kāshānī interprets this Name to mean "your own self." *Tafsīr Ibn 'Arabī* (Beirut, 2001), vol. 2, p. 382. Another prophetic saying of great importance to the Sufis is this: "I am Ahmad [the celestial name of Muhammad] without the letter *mīm* [m]; I am an Arab without the letter *'ayn.* Who hath seen me the same hath seen the Truth." The name *Ahmad* without *mīm* becomes *Ahad,* "One"; the word

Arab without the *'ayn* becomes *Rabb,* "Lord." See Abū Bakr Sirāj ad-Dīn, *The Book of Certainty—The Sufi Doctrine of Faith, Vision, and Gnosis* (Cambridge: Islamic Texts Society, 1996), p. 3.

15. Farid ud-Din 'Attar, *The Conference of the Birds* (A. Darbandi, D. Davies, trans.) (Harmondsworth: Penguin, 1984), p. 219.

16. Cited in *Justice and Remembrance,* op.cit, p. 28.

17. S. H. Nasr, *Knowledge and the Sacred* (Albany: State University of New York Press, 1989), p. 311. One of the richest schools of wisdom in the Islamic tradition is that centered on the metaphysical principle of Light, the *Hikmat al-ishrāq* ('wisdom of illumination'), of which Shihāb al-Dīn Yahyā al-Suhrawardī (d. 1191) is the founder. See Seyyed Hossein Nasr, *Three Muslim Sages—Avicenna, Suhrawardī, Ibn 'Arabī* (Cambridge: Harvard University Press, 1964), chapter 2, "Suhrawardī and the Illuminationists," pp. 52–82, for an insightful and concise overview.

18. Q 2:25. This verse is given as the words uttered by the souls in Paradise upon being given fruits of the heavenly garden.

19. We have slightly modified Arberry's translation of this passage from Rūmī's *Discourses,* (London: John Murray, 1961), pp. 44–45.

20. Exoterically, these words are interpreted to mean: the Prophet is among you, one of you. But the word used in Arabic is *fī,* "in" or "within." This is why the Sufis have understood the verse to mean that the supra-personal "Muhammadan Reality" (*al-Haqīqa al-Muhammadiyya*) is within each person's heart. The Prophet testified to this dimension of his nature when he said: "I was a Prophet when Adam was still between [being fashioned by] water and clay." See Eric Geoffroy, *Introduction to Sufism,* op.cit., section entitled "The Model of Muhammad," pp. 43–55, for discussion of this saying in the context of a succinct presentation of the role played by the Prophet in Islamic spirituality.

21. It is on the basis of this innate inspiration fashioning the essence of the intellect that one can speak of the reciprocity between intellection and revelation.

22. See 17:61 et passim.

23. This is a *hadīth qudsī,* a saying in which God speaks in the first person through the Prophet. Though this saying is not found in the standard *hadīth* collections, this does not diminish its fundamental importance in the Sufi tradition, nor does it prevent the exoteric authorities from accepting its meaning. For the meaning harmonizes with the interpretation given by the companion of the Prophet, and one of the founders of the exegetical tradition, Ibn 'Abbās (d. 68/688) on 51:56, a verse in which God says that He *only* created mankind in order that they might "worship Me." According to Ibn 'Abbās, the word *worship* here means "know." At the end of his commentary on 51:56, the Ash'arite theologian and exegete, Fakhr al-Dīn al-Rāzī (d. 1209) cites the *hadīth* of the "hidden treasure," as well as the interpretation of Ibn 'Abbās. *Tafsīr al-kabīr* (Beirut: Dār Ihyā' al-Turāth al-'Arabī, 2001), vol. 10, p. 194.

24. Ibn al-'Arabī, *The Ringstones of Wisdom* (Caner Dagli, trans.) (Chicago: Kazi Publications, 2004), p. 3.

25. This saying is also ascribed to Imam 'Alī in the Sufi tradition. A good example of the way in which this saying was interpreted in this tradition is given

by the following commentary by a master of Shi'ite gnosis, Rajab Bursī (d. 1411): "The knowledge of the self is that a man knows his beginning and his end, from where he came, and to where he is going, and this is based on true knowledge of delimited existence. And this is knowledge of the first effulgence [al- fayḍ al-awwal] which overflowed from the Lord of Might. Then Being flowed from it, and was made Existence by the command of the Necessary Existent. . . . And this is the single point which is the beginning of the engendered things, and the end of all existent things. . . . The Essence of God is unknowable for man. So knowledge of Him is through His qualities. And the single point is a quality of God, and the quality [ṣifa] indicates the Qualified [mawṣūf], because by its appearance God is known." Todd Lawson, "'The Dawning Places of the Lights of Certainty in the Divine Secrets connected with the Commander of the Faithful' by Rajab Bursī (d. 1411)," in L. Lewisohn (ed.), The Heritage of Sufism—The Legacy of Medieval Persian Sufism (1150–1500), vol. 2 (Oxford: Oneworld, 1999), p. 271.

26. This word means both remembrance and invocation. The first relates to the principle of the awareness of divine reality; the second concerns the various means by which this consciousness of God is to be attained: prayer, supplication, glorification, praise, meditation, recitation of scripture, but most especially the continuous invocation of the Name or Names of God. Dhikr in the sense of remembrance denotes spiritual consciousness, and dhikr in the sense of invocation refers to the central methodic practice that generates this consciousness, which can also simply be called "wisdom." The importance of both senses of dhikr in relation to wisdom will be addressed shortly.

27. See note 1 above.

28. For discussion of this oft-quoted saying in the Sufi tradition see the excellent chapter by Martin Lings entitled "The Heart" in his What is Sufism?, op.cit., pp. 45–62.

29. For the complexity of types of linguistic implication (tadmīn) used in the Qur'an, see Adrian Gully, "Tadmīn: 'Implication of Meaning' in Medieval Arabic," Journal of the American Oriental Society, 117, no.3 (July–September 1997), especially pp. 471–476, where several Qur'anic illustrations of these different types of implication are given.

30. As J. Berque, a French scholar and translator of the Qur'an says: "It is not necessary to be a Muslim to be sensitive to the remarkable beauty of this text, to its fullness and universal value." Cited in Claude Gilliot and Pierre Larcher, "Language and Style of the Qur'an," in Encyclopaedia of the Qur'ān (Jane D. McAuliffe, ed.) (Leiden/Boston: Brill, 2002), vol. 3, p. 110.

31. For the saying of the Prophet and this citation from Rūzbihān, see Kristin Sands, Sufi Commentaries on the Qur'an in Classical Islam (Oxford: Routledge, 2006), pp. 8–11.

32. Cited in Justice and Remembrance, op.cit., p. 42.

33. When, in Arabic, superlatives are used, they are not to be understood only in an exclusive sense: phrases such as "the greatest" (akbar), and "the 'best" (khayr), as applied to the Prophet can also be understood inclusively in the sense of "unsurpass-

able," which implies "but not unequalable." While popular piety will ascribe to the Prophet a greatness that in fact cannot be equaled, the Prophet himself appeared to favor the idea that he was unsurpassable but not unequalable: "Do not say that I am better than Moses," he told his followers; and in another saying: "Do not say that I am better than Jonah." See Qāḍī 'Iyāḍ's *al-Shifā'* (Aisha A. Bewley, trans.) *Muhammad— Messenger of Allah* (Inverness: Madinah Press, 1991), p. 120. Likewise the Qur'an tells us that the believers do not differentiate between the Messengers (2:285 et passim).

34. Cited in *Book 20 of al-Ghazali's* Ihyā 'Ulūm al-Dīn (L. Zolondek, trans.) (Leiden: E. J. Brill), 1963, p. 21. The source of the saying is given there as the *Musnad* of Ahmad b. Hanbal, 2:381. See the discussion of this and similar sayings by Joseph Lumbard in his presentation of Sufism as the tradition of *ihsān,* spiritual virtue, excellence, or simply "making beautiful": "The Decline of Knowledge and the Rise of Ideology in the Modern Islamic World," in *Islam, Fundamentalism, and the Betrayal of Tradition* (Joseph E. B. Lumbard, ed.) (Bloomington: World Wisdom, 2009), p. 54.

35. The reason why the word *kafara* can be translated either in terms of ingratitude or disbelief will be discussed shortly.

36. Cited by Sayyid Haydar Āmulī in his commentary on the Qur'an, *al-Muhīt al-a'zam,* vol. 1, p. 266. The commentator cites this saying and then quotes certain verses of the Qur'an describing the drink that is given to the believers of different ranks in Paradise: 76:5–6; 76: 21; 83: 25–28 et passim.

37. *Meister Eckhart—Sermons and Treatises* (M. O'C. Walshe, trans. and ed.) (Longmead: Element Books, 1987,1989), vol. I, p. 50. See also our essay, "Eckhart's Image of the Eye and the Wood: An analogy which explains 'all that I have ever preached about,'" in *The Eckhart Review, 12* (Spring 2003), which discusses the principle of inward transformation through meditative prayer.

38. The relationship between integration of soul and wisdom is brought out clearly by Frithjof Schuon: "[T]he individual being cannot be reintegrated into the Absolute without all his faculties participating in due measure in the process. Spiritual Knowledge . . . brings into play all that we are, hence all the constituent elements, psychic and even physical, of our being, for nothing positive can be excluded from the process of transmutation; nothing can be destroyed, and therefore the psychic faculties or energies that form part of our reality and whose existence must have a meaning for us, have to be determined and canalized by the same governing Idea that determines and transforms thought." From the essay "Prayer and the Integration of the Psychic Elements," in his *The Eye of the Heart* (Bloomington: World Wisdom, 1997), p. 161.

39. Cited in *Justice and Remembrance,* op. cit., p. 111.

40. Ibid, p. 55.

41. The word *kawthar* also means "abundance." It is also interpreted as a reference to the Prophet's daughter, Fāṭima. These three meanings—celestial grace, abundance, and Fāṭima—are, needless to say, mutually inclusive.

42. Cited in Qāḍī 'Iyāḍ, *al-Shifā',* op. cit., p. 74.

43. Muhammad al-Ghazālī, *Ihyā' 'ulūm al-dīn* (Shaykh al-'Aydarūs, ed.) (Beirut: Dār al-Jīl, 1992), vol. 4, p. 334.

44. A well-known saying, cited in the biography of the Prophet by Ibn Isḥāq, *The Life of Muhammad—A Translation of Ibn Isḥāq's* Sīrat Rasul Allāh (A. Guillaume, trans. and ed.) (London: Oxford University Press, 1955), p. 183. See also Annemarie Schimmel, *And Muhammad Is His Messenger—The Veneration of the Prophet in Islamic Piety* (Chapel Hill/London: University of North Carolina Press, 1985), p. 50.

45. See Abū Bakr Sirāj ad-Dīn, *The Book of Certainty,* op. cit., pp. 1–11.

46. See Frithjof Schuon, *Stations of Wisdom* (Bloomington: World Wisdom, 2003) for a truly wise application of this fundamental discernment on those planes most directly concerned with the spiritual life.

47. Cited in *Al-Ghazālī—Invocations and Supplications* (Book IX of The Revival of the Religious Sciences) (K. Nakamura, trans.) (Cambridge: Islamic Texts Society, 1990), p. 8 (we have slightly modified the translation of the last sentence of the saying).

48. One thinks here of the saying of St Paul: "And the peace of God, which passeth all understanding, shall keep your hearts and minds through Christ Jesus" (Philippians 4:7).

49. Cited in *Justice and Remembrance,* op. cit., p. 142.

50. Ibid, p. 47.

51. Echoing the prophetic saying: "For everything there is a polish [*siqāla*, synonymous with *jilā'*] and the polish of the hearts is the remembrance of God." Cited in the collection of al-Bayhaqī. See Martin Lings, *Muhammad—His Life Based on the Earliest Sources* (London: George Allen & Unwin, and Islamic Texts Society, 1983), p. 328.

52. In his book entitled *Eye of the Heart,* Frithjof Schuon provides many examples of this doctrine in different spiritual traditions, and cites this particularly striking description by a sage of the Ogallala Sioux: "I am blind and I do not see the things of this world; but when the Light comes from On High, it illuminates my heart and I can see, because the Eye of the heart (*Chante Ishta*) sees all things. The heart is the sanctuary at the center of which is a small space where the Great Spirit (*Wakan Tanka*) lives, and this is the Eye of the Great Spirit by which He sees everything, and with which we see Him. When the heart is impure, the Great Spirit cannot be seen, and if you should die in this ignorance, your soul will not be able to return at once to the Great Spirit, but will have to be purified by wanderings across the universe. To know the Center of the Heart where the Great Spirit dwells, you must be pure and good and live according to the way that the Great Spirit has taught us. The man who is pure in this way, contains the Universe in the Pocket of his Heart (*Chante Ognaka*)." Frithjof Schuon, *Eye of the Heart* (Bloomington: World Wisdom, 1997), p. 9.

53. Ibid, p. 162.

54. *Saḥīḥ al-Bukhārī,* (Summarized) (M. M. Khan, trans.) (Madina: Maktaba Dar-us-Salam, 1994), no.2117, p. 992.

55. Cited by W. C. Chittick, *The Sufi Path of Knowledge—Ibn al-'Arabī and the Metaphysics of Imagination* (Albany: State University of New York Press, 1985), p. 375. We have modified Chittick's translation here, preferring "sages" to "gnostics" in the translation of the Arabic *'ārifūn.*

56. The root of *ma'rifa* is *'arafa*, "he knew," and it is this word that is used in the saying, "He who knows [*man 'arafa*] his Lord knows himself," and also in the divine utterance, "I was a hidden treasure, and I loved to be *known* [*u'raf*]. The connotation here is the kind of knowledge implied by recognition, or "re-cognition," as discussed earlier. The root of the word *hikma* is *hakama*, the principal meaning of which is to adjudicate, as in a dispute, whence *hākim*, "judge." The *hakīm*, however, is not just the "philosopher," he is also the physician: one whose medical knowledge goes beyond medicine conventionally understood, and is a true "healer" of both body and soul.

57. Ibn al-'Arabī, *Bezels of Wisdom* (R. W. J. Austin, trans.) (New York: Paulist press, 1980), p. 108.

58. Cited in *Sufi Path,* op. cit., p. 215.

59. For discussion of this theme see Kāshānī, *Tafsīr,* op. cit., vol. 2, p. 384.

60. "I saw my Lord with the eye of my heart," wrote Mansūr al-Hallāj (d. 922) in one of his poems, "I asked Him, who art thou? He said: Thou." Cited by Seyyed Hossein Nasr, "The Heart of the Faithful Is the Throne of the All-Merciful," in (*Paths to the Heart—Sufism and the Christian East* (J. S. Cutsinger, ed.) (Bloomington: World Wisdom, 2002), p. 45.

References

Al-Rāzī, F. (2001). *Tafsīr al-kabīr.* Beirut: Dār Ihyā' al-Turāth al-'Arabī, Vol. 10.

'Alī b. Abī Tālib. (2005). *Dīwān* (Ed.). 'Abd al-Rahmān al-Mustāwī. Beirut & London: Dar al-Ma'rifa.

Abū Bakr Sirāj ad-Dīn. (1996). *The book of certainty—The Sufi doctrine of faith, vision and gnosis.* Cambridge: Islamic Texts Society.

Arberry, A. J. (Trans.). (1961). *Discourses.* London: John Murray.

Attar, F. (1984). *The conference of the birds.* (A. Darabandi & D. Davies, Trans.). Penguin Classics.

Būsīrī, Muhammad. (2009) *Burda: The mantle adorned.* (Abdal Hakim Murad, Trans.). London: Quilliam Press.

Chittick, W. C. (1985). *The Sufi path of knowledge—Ibn al-'Arabī and the metaphysics of imagination.* Albany: State University of New York Press.

Chouiref, T. (Ed.). (2008). *Les enseignements spirituels du prophète.* Wattrelos: Éditions Tasnim, Vol. 1.

Geoffroy, E. (2010). *Introduction to Sufism—The inner path of Islam.* (R. Gaetani, Trans.). Bloomington: World Wisdom.

Al-Ghazālī, M. (1992). *Ihyā' 'ulūm al-dīn,* vol. 4. (S. al-'Aydarūs Ed.). Beirut: Dār al-Jīl.

Gilliot, C., & Larcher, P. (2002). Language and style of the Qur'an. In J. McAuliffe, (Ed.). *Encyclopaedia of the Qur'ān,* Vol. 3. Leiden/Boston: Brill, p. 110.

Gully, A. (1997). '*Tadmīn*: "Implication of meaning" in Medieval Arabic. *Journal of the American Oriental Society*, 117(3), pp. 471–476.

Ibn al-'Arabī, Muhyī al-Dīn. (2004). *The ringstones of wisdom.* (Caner Dagli, Trans.). Chicago: Kazi Publications.

Ibn Isḥāq, M. (1955). *The life of Muhammad—A translation of Ibn Isḥāq's Sīrat (Rasul Allāh)* (A. Guillaume, Trans. & Ed.). London: Oxford University Press.

'Iyād, Qāḍī. (1991). *Muhammad—Messenger of Allah.* (Aisha A. Bewley, Trans.). Inverness: Madinah Press.

Kāshānī, A. R. (2001). *Tafsīr Ibn 'Arabī.* Beirut:

Khan, M. (Trans.). (1994). *Sahīh al-Bukhārī,* (Summarized). Madina: Maktaba Dar-us‑Salam.

Lawson, T. (1999). The dawning places of the lights of certainty . . . In L. Lewisohn, (Ed.). *The heritage of Sufism—The legacy of medieval Persian Sufism, Vol. 2* (1150–1500). Oxford: Oneworld, p. 271.

Lings, M. (1971). *A Sufi saint of the twentieth century—Shaikh Ahmad al-'Alawī.* London: George Allen & Unwin.

Lings, M. (1983). *Muhammad—His life based on the earliest sources.* London: George Allen & Unwin, and Islamic Texts Society.

Lings, M. (1993). *What is Sufism?* Cambridge: Islamic Texts Society.

Lumbard, J. (2009). The decline of knowledge and the rise of ideology in the modern Islamic world. In J. Lumbard, (Ed.). *Islam, fundamentalism and the betrayal of tradition.* Bloomington: World Wisdom.

Nakamura, K. (Trans.). (1990). *Al-Ghazālī—Invocations and supplications. The Revival of the religious sciences,* (Book IX). Cambridge: Islamic Texts Society.

Nasr, S. H. (1964). Suhrawardī and the Illuminationists. In *Three Muslim sages—Avicenna, Suhrawardī, Ibn 'Arabī.* Cambridge: Harvard University Press, pp. 52–82.

Nasr, S. H. (1989). *Knowledge and the sacred* Albany: State University of New York Press.

Nasr, S. H. (2002). The heart of the faithful is the throne of the all-merciful. In J. Cutsinger, (Ed.). *Paths to the Heart—Sufism and the Christian East.* Bloomington: World Wisdom.

Nasr, S. H. (2006). *Islamic philosophy: From its origin to the present.* Albany: State University of New York Press.

Sands, K. (2006). *Sufi commentaries on the Qur'an in classical Islam.* Oxford: Routledge.

Schimmel, A. (1958). *And Muhammad is His Messenger—The veneration of the prophet in Islamic piety.* Chapel Hill/London: University of North Carolina Press.

Schuon, F. (1953). *The transcendent unity of religions.* (P. Townsend, Trans.). London: Faber & Faber.

Schuon, F. (1997). *The eye of the heart.* Bloomington: World Wisdom.

Schuon, F. (1999). *Understanding Islam.* Bloomington: World Wisdom.

Schuon, F. (2003). *Stations of wisdom.* Bloomington: World Wisdom.

Shah-Kazemi, R. (2003). Eckhart's Image of the eye and the wood. *The Eckhart Review, 12.*

Shah-Kazemi, R. (2006). *Justice and remembrance—Introducing the spirituality of Imam 'Alī.* London: IB Tauris.

Walshe, M. (Trans. & Ed.). (1987/1989). *Meister Eckhart—Sermons and treatises,* Vol. I. Longmead: Element Books.

Zolondek, L. (Trans.). (1963). *Book 20 of al-Ghazali's* Ihyā 'Ulūm al-Dīn. Leiden: E. J. Brill.

5

Wisdom

The Hindu Experience and Perspective

GEORG FEUERSTEIN

A Preamble about Hinduism

To begin with, Hinduism is *not* just a religion. It is best described as a culture within the Indian civilization, similar to Buddhism and Jainism. It has its own literatures (in Sanskrit and vernaculars), art forms, social customs, subcultures, religions, values, myths and symbols, distinct philosophical traditions, "sacred" languages (primarily Sanskrit and Tamil), and not least its own unique historical trajectory. Here I will extend the term *Hindu* back to the Vedic era, several thousand years ago, although this label is generally reserved for Indian cultural expressions that belong to the "orthodox" (*āstikya*) culture that is subsequent to, but affirmative of, the *Vedas*. The *Vedas* are a corpus of four hymnodies composed in archaic Sanskrit and comprising more than one thousand hymns. They are the oldest known Indo-European works, which were for several millennia transmitted orally by the priestly estate (mainly from father to son) before they were committed to writing late in the common era.

The *Vedas* are the religio-philosophical fountainhead of Hinduism. In recent years, the question of what is meant by "Hinduism" has been debated in certain scholarly (hermeneutical) circles. Not every Indologist would extend Yoga to the Vedic era, but I agree with Mircea Eliade (1973), among others, that Yoga is assuredly present everywhere in the civilization of India from the earliest times on. It is a theory-practice continuum and has indeed a chameleonlike quality: It can modify its philosophical ideas as readily as its practical elements.

East–West Encounter: The Larger Context

When, in the early nineteenth century, the first translations of India's vast Sanskrit literature appeared in Europe, the German Romantics enthusiastically and somewhat uncritically lapped up the ideas expressed in these works. Friedrich Schlegel, who looked for the "pinnacle of the romantic" in India, studied Sanskrit and in 1808 published his widely influential book *Über die Sprache und Weisheit der Indier* (*On the Language and Wisdom of the [East] Indians*). He did not put "wisdom" in quotation marks, but unhesitatingly presented the Indians as the wisest people on Earth and passionately argued for a cross-fertilization between East and West.

German Romanticism continued on mostly in nonacademic circles, especially among the American Transcendentalists, notably Ralph Waldo Emerson and Henry D. Thoreau. This popular movement spawned the dubious syncretism of Theosophy, which was, however, responsible for making many Yoga texts available in English early on. During the latter part of the nineteenth century, mainstream Western culture started to react against the earlier idealization and elevation of the East, causing a considerable polarization between the yeas and the nays. In a nutshell, this was the beginning of the split between "Eastern Wisdom" and "Western Thought." As time went by and Europe again remembered its own classical heritage of rationality, this contrast seemed forced and exaggerated, with "Western thought" and Western culture looking increasingly salutary. It was, so the theory went, after all more rational and less embroiled in religious and ethical concerns than the East—a notion that survived into the twentieth century and that here and there can still be encountered today.

With objectivism, empiricism, and intellectualism gaining momentum in the late nineteenth and culminating in the mid-twentieth century, the wisdom over which the Romantics waxed so eloquent increasingly seemed obsolete or became the target of vulgarization at the hands of peddlers of mystical and occult wares.

In his essay "Difficulties Encountered by a European in Trying to Understand the East," written in 1962, Carl Gustav Jung observed astutely:

> [W]e are fond of putting "Oriental wisdom" in quotation marks
> and banishing it to the dim region of faith and superstition. But

that is wholly to misunderstand the realism of the East. (Jung, 1962, p. 9)

Even though Jung had serious misgivings about Westerners naïvely "imitating" Eastern ways, he went on to say that "we have not the slightest justification for undervaluing" the East. He understood that the West was in the process of re-balancing itself by beginning to pay greater attention again to feeling and intuition (and thus also to wisdom) beyond mere intellectualism.

His critical attitude toward "pitiable imitators" notwithstanding, we cannot find fault with Jung's perspicacious observation made as early as 1933 in *Modern Man in Search of a Soul* that "while we are overpowering the Orient from without, it may be fastening its hold upon us from within" (pp. 215–216). This dialectical process has, in fact, greatly accelerated since he made that comment. Unfortunately, much of the contemporary popularization of Eastern thought and practices—including much of today's commercialized Yoga—offers superficial substitutes instead of bona fide wisdom that can heal our psyche.

Books such as the present anthology are, therefore, timely and vitally important. The encounter between East and West, which, as far as India is concerned, started well over two thousand years ago with its decisive influence on the Mediterranean. Yet, this encounter can only fulfill itself if we do not filter wisdom through our one-sided intellectualism. Instead, we must engage in an authentic dialogue, which implies that we must transcend our Western civilization's postmodern cynicism and shallow cosmopolitanism. We can do this only if we keep spiritual values firmly in the forefront of our deliberations and not shy away from *living* them either.

What is Wisdom?

The statements in the first section should have made it clear that whatever wisdom is, it is *not* a matter of abstract intellectual ideas. The difference is that wisdom has a living quality, intellectual ideas do not. Wisdom grows, transforms, and deepens a person; intellectual ideas at best broaden his or her intellectual horizon. Intellectual ideas are tied into other intellectual ideas to make a web of models or systems. Wisdom organically relates to other living values, which uplift and make whole. Intellectual ideas increase information and knowledge. Wisdom enhances the quality of life and is healing. As the German philosopher Nicolai Hartmann wrote in his book

Ethik (Ethics), published in 1926, wisdom "is ethical spirituality, namely the attitude of ethos, which governs all of life as a fundamental spiritual factor of humanity." We must, however, not simply equate wisdom with ethics; the emphasis is on spirituality.

What, then, is wisdom from the vantage point of a civilization—India— that from the earliest times has had a penchant for delving into the psyche and intelligently distilling from this exploration the best possible understand- ing that can serve both day-to-day life and also the highest spiritual aspira- tions pursued by only a small minority?

There is no easy answer to this question, because the Indian civilization spans roughly five thousand years and extends over numerous philosophical approaches. I will have to limit myself here to snapshots of the major develop- mental phases and orientations within so-called Hinduism, as well as to the Sanskrit language, which is the foremost medium for most of the Hindu wisdom literature. Within Hindu India, the traditions of Yoga, *Sāṃkhya,* and *Vedānta* stand out as primary soteriologies, that is, liberation teachings. I will therefore focus on them, and within them will have to limit myself to just a few select texts and authorities.

Sanskrit has six principal words connoting "wisdom," namely, *jñāna, prajñā, vidyā, veda, dhī,* and *manīṣā.* The first two terms come from the same verbal root, viz., *jña,* "to know." *Vidyā* and *veda* are both derived from the root *vid,* which also has the meaning of "to know." *Dhī* is related to the root *dhyai* "to contemplate," and the last-mentioned word is derived from the root *man* "to think."

All these terms can be found in conventional contexts, but in their spiritual application they have two principal meanings. The first is *liberat- ing gnosis* in the sense of transcendental realization. The second is what I call the *wisdom of the path* that springs from that gnosis. This resultant path knowledge can be communicated to other to guide them to that gnosis. In other words, wisdom is understood to be either an immediate experience, or realization, of the transcendental Reality, or it is helpful knowledge or insight based on that realization: knowledge that can be used as a guide by others, whether to live meaningfully and holistically or to gain for themselves the same immediate realization. In the latter sense, wisdom is insight-based knowing, which

1. is informed by a noncognitive, transcendental realization (i.e., illumination, *bodhi*) consisting in a Pure Consciousness Event (Forman, 1990). This is a rare "mystical" realization, which is typically described as "immediate," "unfiltered," or "without identifiable qualities";

2. exceeds the discursive, logical mind with its stepwise knowing, which tends to fixate on the material level of existence; that is, it is transconceptual and transrational;

3. is also not exhausted by the aesthetic (or feeling/valuing) sense; and

4. has practical value for wholesome (morally sound) living; and for

5. spiritual development, that is, development inclined toward transcendental realization;

6. is transmittable selectively and by extraordinary means to others; selectively, because it is received by those who are duly qualified for it, and by uncommon or paranormal means, because it is transplanted from consciousness to consciousness, or because it is given by psychoenergetic transmission (*sañcāra*).

Another way of tackling the earlier question is to say that wisdom is either a *direct* distillate of a personal transcendental realization or an *indirect* derivative of directly distilled wisdom, which is handed down through a chain of sagacious teachers.

Hindu Philosophy, Psychology, and Spirituality

From a Western perspective, Hindu wisdom falls under the three categories captured in the above subtitle, which represent three overlapping emphases rather than distinct subject matters. "Hindu Philosophy"—if *philosophía* is understood in the original sense of the word as "love of wisdom"—is, I propose, a fitting label for the Hindu teachings. This characterization applies particularly to the six "systems" (*darśana*), or views, that are thought to make up the classical sextad of Indian (Hindu) thought: Yoga and *Sāṃkhya, Vedānta* and *Mīmāṃsā, Nyāya* and *Vaiśeṣika*. Each of these systems has codified its main ideas and created aphoristic compositions on them called *Sūtras*. I will address only the first three traditions, because wisdom is arguably not a *major* focal point of the others.

As a philosophical system, Yoga largely coincides with the teaching found in Patañjali's *Yoga-Sūtra*, which is celebrated as the handbook of Classical Yoga. It consists of 195 Sanskrit aphorisms (*sūtra*), which purport to capture yogic philosophy and psychology up to the time of Patanjali (200–300

CE). His approach favors a problematic dualistic metaphysics—contrasting the multilevel Cosmos against the perennial transcendental Self (which exists as numerous "monads"). This metaphysical framework is in the service of the yogic path to Self-realization.[1] The stated goal is, similar to Gnosticism, "aloneness" (*kaivalya*)—the realization of the transcendental Self separate from the Cosmos. To get away from the logical impasse of ontological dualism, some modern scholars have sought to reinterpret this system.[2]

Sāṃkhya is a system of ontology that is closely allied with Yoga but does not incorporate a complex psychotechnology (of ecstatic states). At the practical level, it shares with Yoga the discipline of discernment (*viveka*) between the Real and the unreal, or between the Self and the non-Self (i.e., the ego-personality but also the Cosmos at large). It also places great emphasis on the practice of dispassion (*vairāgya*), or the act of mentally letting go of whatever has been recognized as unreal, or the non-Self. These two means are thought to bring the practitioner closer and closer to Self-realization. In its classical form, *Sāṃkhya* subscribes to the same strict dualism as Classical Yoga. But the preclassical and the postclassical variations of this system espouse nondualism. In other words, they affirm that there is an ultimate Singularity, which encompasses the transcendental Self (or Selves) and the Cosmos.

Vedānta, which grew out of the wisdom teachings of the ancient *Upaniṣads,* can be looked upon as a nondualistic counterpart to Yoga, and in fact the post-Patañjali schools of Yoga all adopted *Vedānta* rather than the strict dualism of the *Yoga-Sūtra*. The essence of *Vedānta* is the practice of *Jñāna-Yoga,* the path of liberating knowledge, or wisdom. This Yoga is first expounded under that name in the *Bhagavad-Gītā* (3.3) where the God-man Krishna distinguishes between *Jñāna-Yoga* for the *Sāṃkhya* followers and *Karma-Yoga* for the *yogins*. The former path proceeds by discernment and meditation firmly anchored in dispassion (*vairāgya*). The latter approach involves appropriate action without desire/craving for any reward accruing from one's deeds.

The classic representative of *Jñāna-Yoga* is the possibly seventh-century Śaṅkara, the great promulgator of the school of radical nondualism (*Advaita Vedānta*). He makes the point that we are *always* the Self. Our assumption that we are a particular body and mind is simply wrong and should therefore be abandoned. This understanding is not merely theoretical knowledge but rather is wisdom born of actual realization. Ignorance is erroneously seeing the ego, personality, body, or mind as the Self.

The spiritual path consists in the continuous remembering that one is in fact the Self, the transcendental Witness, rather than any witnessed object (including the body and the mind). Hence, liberation requires that we purify (i.e., polish the mirror of) the mind. In the *Upadeśa-Sāhasrī* (17.22), Śaṅkara states that this purification happens by means of the moral observations, self-restraint, sacrificial rituals, or austerities. The best discipline, according to him, is one-pointedness (*ekāgrya*)—or focusing—of the senses and the mind. Śaṅkara had a healthy respect for reasoning (*yukti*), but he did not place it above gnosis.

The Hindu heritage is a great deal vaster and more complex than the standard grouping of the above-mentioned six classical philosophical viewpoints suggests. The six systems were, for instance, preceded by the presystematic nondualist schools of the *Upaniṣads* and the epic schools. These traditions were succeeded by the ramifying, highly experiential schools of Tantra (emerging c. 500 CE), the Tantra-related body-oriented *Haṭha-Yoga* (probably separating out of Tantra c. 1000 CE), and the profoundly philosophical contemporaneous tradition of medieval Kashmiri Śaivism, and many others.

The term "Hindu Psychology," which is also sometimes applied to these traditions, is perhaps overloaded with too many Western concepts about psychology to prove useful. The important point is that while the Hindus have many intriguing insights into the human mind, especially the nature of consciousness, these have not been empirically tested (or are even testable), statistically quantified (or are quantifiable), or rendered sterile by being ripped out of the context of life and turned into totally abstract bits of information. Fortunately, the boundaries between psychology and philosophy have remained permeable in Hinduism. This is in distinct opposition to the Occidental approach, which strictly partitions them, just as it separates fact from value.

A demarcation is appropriate when it comes to delineating "Hindu Spirituality" from religion, so that the former term is relieved of typical preconceptions. If by "religion" we mean the kind of conventional religious ideas and practices with which we are familiar from the Judeo-Christian tradition of the West, then the Hindu teachings treated here cannot be characterized by this term, at least not without proper qualifications. But if we understand "spirituality" as an orientation that, firstly, goes beyond the level of conventional, largely imitative, moralistic, and theistic religiosity and, secondly, that is more akin to what we call "mysticism," we have indeed a plausible label for the Hindu teachings that concern us here.

The common ground between Hindu spirituality and mysticism, as I see it, is their concern with inner freedom, or liberation—hence their occasional characterization as "soteriologies" (from Greek *sotería*, "salvation"), or liberation teachings. By their own admission, liberation (*mokṣa, mukti, kaivalya,* etc.) is indeed their vital focus. It is this ideal that Hindu ethics proposes as the apex of its four-tier value pyramid: material welfare, pleasure, morality, and liberation. As the Polish-American philosopher Henryk Skolimowski, who champions a participatory way of thinking, acknowledges, "[p]hilosophy is a quest of liberation. . . . [It] seeks to elevate man, release him from bondage" (1994, p. 379). He believes that the West has installed reason as an autonomous agency, which "alienated itself from the overall quest of the liberation of man" (ibid.). Because of this, we can also no longer understand, appreciate, or even, I would argue, tolerate the close proximity between philosophy, spirituality, and morality that is natural to the Hindu sages. Yet, wisdom is not a merely rational quantity, and if we were to seek it through purely intellectual channels, it would always escape us, like sand running through our fingers.

Owing to the fact that wisdom is looking at life holistically, it can appreciate linkages—such as the linkage between fact and value—that simply escape the rational mind. Inevitably, this makes for an understanding of the world that is completely different from the West's intellectual comprehension. To the eye of wisdom, it is self-evident that mental transformation goes hand in hand with morality. There is no type of Yoga that exists without ethical guidelines. These must be implemented not by rote but by applying wisdom. Thus, wisdom lies at the heart of Hindu spirituality.

The Transcendental Witness— The Most Important Discovery of the Indian Sages

The Hindu philosophical-spiritual heritage is not primarily interested in the accumulation of abstract knowledge ("information"). Rather, it places a premium on the kind of insight that helps human beings not only to live a more meaningful, "meta-motivated" (A. H. Maslow) life but also, importantly, to fulfill their innate potential, which necessarily includes their *spiritual* possibilities. This type of knowledge is called "wisdom." This wisdom transcends the run-of-the-mill preoccupations of the majority of fellow humans—preoccupations that are summarized in the Hindu values of *artha* (material welfare) and *kāma* (pleasure). It also transcends the service usually associated with religion as a social enterprise and which, in India, is known as *dharma*. In other words, wisdom transcends the ordinary state of consciousness, or what Charles Tart styled the "consensus trance" of the average individual (1983). On this point, C. G. Jung noted: "One thing we ought never to forget:

almost the half of our lives is passed in a more or less unconscious state" (Foreman, 1990, p. 11). But we regularly and predictably forget. Our civilization does not have an equivalent to the four-values model of Hindu society—material welfare (*artha*), pleasure (*kāma*), morality (*dharma*), and liberation (*mokṣa*)—to remind us that human life is not exhausted by our habitual preoccupations.

At the apex of the value pyramid of Hinduism is *mokṣa, the grand ideal of liberation*, which is *in principle* available to everyone. This is *in actuality* pursued only by those few who are willing and able to let go of the allure of conventional life and feel irresistibly drawn to spiritual transcendence. With the demise of the Middle Eastern Gnostic movement and the Mediterranean mystery cults, Western civilization lost sight of this ideal. Yet, the possibility of spiritual liberation clearly remains an integral part of our human potential, as is recognized by the contemporary fields of Transpersonal and Integral Psychology.

The ideal of liberation, according to Hinduism, is closely allied with the concept of transcendental Consciousness, or Awareness (*caitanya, cit, citi*). This Awareness is not an accidental characteristic of the mind but the essential nature of the ultimate Self-Identity (*ātman, puruṣa*), which is why I use an initial capital for it. Whereas Jung made the Self the fulcrum of his concept of the Unconscious with its gallery of archetypes, the Hindus have since the earliest times regarded the Self as identical with sheer, unadulterated, immutable, and perennial Awareness. They argue that this Awareness is utterly different from the mind, from the brain-dependent consciousness. In Kantian terms, Awareness is the Thing in itself, apart from any conceptual overlay.

Western philosophers and psychologists have produced an entire library about the nature of consciousness. By and large, they have rejected any suggestion that there could be such a "thing" as pure Awareness. Introspection reveals to them only a cluttered mind, a tangled consciousness. Rightly so, because the average mind is the antipode to peacefulness and clarity, and it is filled with all sorts of contents.

This, however, has not been the experience of the Hindu sages. Their analyses of highly *disciplined* introspective states revealed to them an entirely different picture. They came to see a resting mind that manifests a reality in which knowledge is, as the *Yoga-Sūtra* (1.48) states, "truth bearing" (*ṛtambhara*). That is, they saw things as they are in themselves, not filtered through the discursive mind, not modified by emotions or motivations—pure Awareness. This is gnosis. I admit, this is a huge claim, which can only be verified or falsified in the context of yogic discipline. That is to say, it is not a matter of mere faith. Rather, the claim is perfectly testable by anyone willing to undertake a course of yogic discipline.

In his edited anthology *The Problem of Pure Consciousness: Mysticism and Philosophy,* Robert K. C. Forman, a professor of religion, rightly rejects the perennialist notion that all mystical experience inevitably means contact with an absolute reality. By contrast, he and the twelve contributors to the anthology favor a constructivist view, which assumes that *some* mystical experiences are "significantly shaped and formed by the subjects beliefs, concepts, and expectation" (1990). However, Forman argues that one specific type of mystical experience which he labels a "Pure Consciousness Event" (PCE) exists and is *not* constructed by the usual epistemological processes. Wisdom, as gnosis, is strongly related to, or identified with, the contentless PCE, as it occurs at the most advanced level of spiritual maturation. This is an important point, which removes gnosis from the realm of subjectivity and opinion.

The Mind as Object

Our mind has the extraordinary capacity to cognize the objective world *and* simultaneously to know that it is cognizing. This is the duo of *awareness* and *self-awareness* respectively. *Vedānta, Sāṃkhya,* and Yoga are agreed that the ultimate Self-Identity (*ātman, puruṣa*) is pure, transcendental Awareness. Consequently, the mind (*citta*) cannot be endowed with the same feature. In fact, these three traditions maintain that the mind, as a property of the insentient Cosmos (*prakṛti*), has no consciousness in itself but borrows it from the Self. Representing in a way all the above-mentioned traditions, the *Sāṃ khya-Kārikā* (verse 11) speaks of the Cosmos as nonconscious (*acetana*) and nondiscerning (*avivekin*)—always in comparison with the Self. Rather, the above-mentioned three traditions regard ordinary consciousness as a product of the intersection between transcendental Self-Awareness (*caitanya, cit, citi*) and the structures of the insentient mind. The mental phenomenon of consciousness, then, is not an epiphenomenon of the brain but a product of the Self and the mind together.

The three traditions insist that this relationship is not an actual connection as between two material things. Given that the Self is *transcendental* and the mind is an *empirical* structure, this could never be. *Vedānta* postulates simply that the world is false (*mithyā*), which does not mean it is nonexistent but merely that it is not in truth the way it appears to the unenlightened mind. The *Upadeśa-Sāhasrī* (12.1), which is correctly attributed to the great *Advaita Vedānta* preceptor Śaṅkara, states:

Just as [a person wrongly] looks upon the body bathed in sunlight
as luminous, so he thinks that the mind illuminated by the Seer
is the Seer [itself].[3]

Only some radical forms of Vedāntic nondualism, as we find it in the
thirty thousand verse *Yoga-Vāsiṣṭha* for instance, affirm that the world is
absolutely illusory. Whether false or illusory, the world *appears* as real due to
spiritual ignorance (*avidyā*), the exact opposite of wisdom. This ignorance,
which is not merely the absence of knowledge, or wisdom, but decidedly
wrong knowledge, is eliminated by gnosis; then the world stands revealed as
the ultimate Reality (*ātman* or *brahman*).

Sāṃkhya and Yoga speak of an "association" or "correlation" (*saṃyoga*)
between Self and mind. They compare the mind to a clear crystal, which is
"colored" by objects as they present themselves to the mind. They are made
visible by the innate "luminosity" of the Self, which is the perennial Witness
that is said to apperceive the mind's cognitions. Witnessing is made possible
by the eternal Self's immutability (*apariṇāmitva*). If the Self would undergo
change, it could never apperceive the ever-changing mind. The correlation
is lifted when spiritual ignorance (*avidyā*) is eliminated by the dawning of
gnosis in the highest state of ecstasy, which is known as *dharma-megha-samādhi*
("cloud of *dharma* ecstasy") leading directly to liberation (*kaivalya*).

Upon liberation, or Self-realization, the mind is wholly "destroyed" or
"dissolved." In ordinary language, "destruction" or "dissolution" of the mind
is equivalent to insanity. This is not the meaning either phrase has in Yoga.
In the dualistic systems of Classical Yoga and also Classical *Sāṃkhya*, liberation must logically be equivalent with psychophysical death. The reason for
this is that the Self is transcendental, that is, *beyond* the Cosmos (including
the body and mind), so that Self-Realization is necessarily a transcendental
event (and not a mere cognitive event). Strangely, however, Classical *Sāṃ
khya* subscribes to the notion that some form of Self-realization during the
embodied condition is possible despite its radical ontological dualism, and
the same claim has been made by Western scholars for Classical Yoga.[6]

The nondualist systems of thought understand Self-realization unequivo-
cally as *transcendence* of the mind and the emergence of wisdom (resulting
from Self-realization) rather than involving psychophysical demise: the mind
is left very much intact and fully functional; yet, the enlightened being no
longer identifies with it or the body but rather with the transcendental
Witness-Self. This allows for the paradoxical condition of "living liberation"
(*jīvan-mukti*), that is, liberation while the body and mind of the realized
adept are still intact.

Voluntary Discipline

Yoga, which has been shaped over literally hundreds of generations, is tried and tested. A teacher recommends to students only what has worked for him or her. Generations of *yogins* learned from the errors of their predecessors, and, we may assume, progressively passed on better instructions. Almost every teacher is a link in a preceptorial lineage (*paramparā*), which gives him or her a certain legitimacy and authority. In addition, a realized teacher gives the disciple a direct glimpse—a personal taste—of the truth of which he or she speaks. This is done in various ways, which all involve so-called parapsychological abilities. This directly transmitted gnosis is even more important than the orally related wisdom teachings.

In order to attain liberating gnosis, the collective wisdom of the path must guide our every step and lead us to gnosis. Just as scientists stand on the shoulders of their predecessors, so the sages of Yoga depend on the wisdom of their teachers and grand teachers in a line of spiritual transmission (*sañcāra*). We find the preclassical teachings of *Sāṃkhya* and Yoga articulated particularly in the post-Buddhist *Kaṭha-Upaniṣad* and the *Bhagavad-Gītā*. The former scripture (1.2.2) has this relevant stanza:

> Both the good (*śreyas*) and the pleasant (*preyas*) affect a man. The wise discerns [carefully between them]. The wise chooses the good over the pleasant. The dimwit, out of [a desire for] gaining or keeping (*yoga-kṣema*) [worldly things], chooses the pleasant.

So, one of the functions of wisdom is to point us in the right direction. A closely related function is to show us the steps of the path to liberation. As the *Kaṭha-Upaniṣad* (1.2.4ff.) notes, ignorance and wisdom lie far apart and thus require a modicum of wisdom to be distinguished. The person who is motivated by worldly matters and goods—that is, by greed—is not likely to know the difference or choose correctly. In other words, to gain wisdom we must be somewhat wise already, which the Indians would explain as having a good karmic quality. Those who lack rudimentary wisdom are incapable of even hearing the wisdom teachings. In the absence of wisdom, even the most astute intellectual will find the yogic teachings a sealed book. As the *Kaṭha-Upaniṣad* (1.2.7) states, there are many who hear but do not understand. The *Bhagavad-Gītā* (2.67) puts it thus:

> When the mind is governed by the roaming senses, then it carries away wisdom like the wind [carries away] a ship at sea.

Even if we happen to be born with little native wisdom, we are not condemned to the gloom of ignorance forever—a hopeful message. Our mind contains an inborn capacity for wisdom. This is expressed in the teaching about the so-called *buddhi,* or "wisdom-faculty," often called "higher mind." Thus, the *Bhagavad-Gītā* (2.49) advises: "Seek refuge in the wisdom-faculty!" That is to say, find your innate wisdom. Diligent study of the wisdom literature no doubt serves—and is meant to serve—this process of discovery.

What I have called the wisdom of the path is solidified in the moral disciplines and practices of self-restraint, which in Classical Yoga are known respectively as *yama* and *niyama,* as well as in the practical instructions passed on from teacher to disciple by word of mouth. The wisdom of the path is also in part thematized in the philosophical teachings.

Thus, for instance, in explaining the spiritual process, Patañjali emphasizes the role of discernment (*viveka*). This quality is also fundamental to *Sāṃkhya* and *Vedānta*. At the beginning level, this practice is applied to separating the Yoga practitioner's personal belongings from his or her sense of self (e.g. "I am not my car") and subsequently, the sense of self (or identification with the body and mind or social roles)—e.g. "I am not a parent, such-and-such professional, or party member"—from true Self-Identity (*ātman, puruṣa*).

All eight constituents (*aṅga*) of the yogic path are designed to jointly lead to liberation. The well-known eight limbs are moral discipline (*yama*), self-restraint (*niyama*), posture (*āsana*), breath-control (*prāṇāyāma*), sensory inhibition (*pratyāhāra*), concentration (*dhāraṇā*), meditation (*dhyāna*), and ecstasy (*samādhi*). Each constituent practice is intended to progressively promote the yogic process of "inward-mindedness" (*pratyak-cetana*). The first limb creates the right social conditions for this work of self-transformation, while the second limb purifies the *yogin*'s inner environment. Posture, which in the *Yoga-Sūtra* means meditation posture, stabilizes the body and directly initiates desensitization to the external world; breath-control opens up the subtle inner world; the three remaining limbs—collectively called "inner limbs" (*antar-aṅga*)—tackle the mind directly, bringing it under increasingly refined voluntary control.

In Vedānta, discernment takes the form of the well-known *neti neti* ("not this, not that") procedure, as epitomized in the *Nirvāṇa-Ṣaṭka*. Verse 1 in part reads: "I am not reason, intuition, egoity, or memory. Neither am I hearing, tasting, smelling, or sight; neither ether/space nor earth; fire or air." Everything inside and outside must be carefully distinguished from the transcendental Self. In Yoga, discernment is pursued especially through the multilevel process of ecstasy (*samādhi*) where the mental environment is exceedingly simplified. The main focus of attention here is the distinction between the purest part of the mind, which is called *buddhi* (in the sense of "awakened intelligence") and the transcendental Self. At the higher levels of ecstatic elevation, the *buddhi* becomes so luminous (i.e., transparent) as to seem almost identical with the Self. Only a properly trained mind can differentiate them.

The philosophy of *Vedānta,* which grew out of the unsystematized nondualist teachings of the early *Upaniṣads,* has its own spiritual path composed, in the first instance, of the following three practices: "hearing" of the traditional wisdom (*śravaṇa*), reflection (*manana*) on the received wisdom, and contemplation (*nididhyāsana*) on it. The *Vedānta-Sāra,* a late-fifteenth-century manual, lists the following "four means" (*catur-sādhana*) in addition to the preceding three practices:

1. discernment (*viveka*) between the eternal and the temporal realities, the singular eternal Reality being the Absolute (*brahman*);

2. dispassion (*virāga*) in regard to the benefit in worldly and otherworldly terms;

3. calm (*śama*) consisting in self-restraint (*dama*), chastity (*uparati*), endurance (*titikṣā*), contemplation (*samādhāna*), and faith (*śraddhā*);

4. desire for liberation (*mumukṣutva*).

The above four levels are the analog of the multistage path of Classical Yoga. They comprise what is known as *Jñāna-Yoga,* the Vedāntic path of wisdom.

Karma-Yoga, the path of self-transcending action, was formulated in the *Bhagavad-Gītā* in the context of *Vedānta* (as well as *Sāṃkhya* philosophical ideas). *Karma-Yoga* revolves around the ethical concept of *svadharma,* which is one's personal (*sva*) moral law or norm. It corresponds at least in part to the Kantian categorical imperative. Now, we cannot know the *svadharma* arising from our "own being" (*svabhāva*) unless we are attuned to wisdom. The *Gītā* (2.51–2.53), therefore, recommends the practice of *buddhi-yoga,* the discipline of having the "wisdom-faculty" (*buddhi; Greek: nous*) guide our actions:

The wise [who are] *buddhi*-yoked, who have renounced action-born fruit, who are liberated from the bondage of birth [and death]— they go to the region [that is] free from ill.

When your wisdom-faculty has traversed the thicket of delusion, then you will acquire disinterest in what will be heard and what has been heard [i.e., mundane knowledge].

To ask again: What is wisdom? The *Bhagavad-Gītā* (18.20–22) answers this question in keeping with a tripartite model:

[The wisdom] by which the one immutable state-of-existence is seen in all beings, undivided in the divided—that wisdom know as *essential*.

But [that] wisdom which recognizes through separateness various distinct states-of-being in all beings—that wisdom know as *dynamic*.

Again, [that wisdom] which clings to a single effect as if [it were] the whole, without [due] cause, without concern for reality and [which is] slight—that is described as *turbid*.

Thus, wisdom can be said to range from moderate insight to the ultimate realization of gnosis. In other words, wisdom is progressive, depending on the purity or lucidity of the mind.

The progressive nature of wisdom and hence of spiritual development is made evident in the *Yoga-Vāsiṣṭha,* a massive text of 32,000 verses on radical Vedāntic nondualism. This text distinguishes seven stages of wisdom:

1. *śubha-icchā* ("desire for the good")—this is the first step on the spiritual path when the seeker realizes there is more to life than eating and drinking, making money, sexing and pleasurizing, and when he or she wants more and begins a quest; in other words, wisdom is dawning, and the name of this initial stage indicates that from the outset, the path of wisdom has a moral component;

2. *vicāraṇā* ("consideration")—through the study of the wisdom literature and by frequenting the company of wise and saintly people, the seeker begins to ponder his or her options more deeply and thereby awakens the impulse to liberation;

3. *tanu-mānasā* ("refinement of thought")—the seeker develops a degree of indifference to worldly things, which frees up attention for the spiritual process; at this stage, wisdom is gathering momentum;

4. *sattva-āpatti* ("attainment of being")—the seeker becomes capable of entering into ecstatic states (*samādhi*) and of delving into pure Awareness; this is the level when wisdom becomes gnosis;

5. *asaṃsakti* ("nonattachment")—by being in touch with Reality, the world is recognized as a mere mental construct of the mind;

6. *padārtha-abhāvanā* ("nonexistence of reality")—the advanced seeker, now an accomplished adept, recognizes the world to be as unreal as a dream;

7. *turyagā* ("immersion into the Fourth")—here the adept transcends everything by fully "entering" into the ultimate Reality; this nondual Reality is known as the "Fourth," because it goes beyond the three mundane states of consciousness of waking, dreaming, and sleeping; this final level is no ordinary ecstatic state but liberation itself.

Several centuries after Patañjali, the tradition of Tantra elaborated its own distinct "psychotechnology," often incorporating the eight limbs of the *Yoga-Sūtra*. One of the elements of the comprehensive Tantric path is physical purification (*śodhana*), which acquired prominence in *Haṭha-Yoga*—an offshoot of the pan-Indian movement of Tantra. *Haṭha-Yoga* is undoubtedly the most somatic type of Yoga, and it is shot through with a host of magical ideas and practices. Some Western critics have therefore dismissed it as a degenerate form of Yoga, though this branch of the yogic tree has gained great popularity in the modern West. In North America alone, upward of fifteen million people are practicing *Haṭha-Yoga* in its various "styles" (a modern concept).

A significant aspect of Tantra and *Haṭha-Yoga* is the awakening of the psychospiritual energy known as *kuṇḍalinī-śakti*. This energetic aspect of Consciousness is traditionally understood as the *magna mater* of wisdom. When galvanized into action, it unleashes all sorts of spiritual knowledge, or wisdom. The "serpent power," or "goddess power," as this energy has been dubbed, must be guided from the base of the spinal axis (where it lies dormant) to the crown of the head, which is the connecting point to pure Awareness, called Śiva. This practice is fundamental to the bipolar nondualism—Śiva and Śakti, Awareness and Power—of the Tantric tradition. When the serpent power rises to the crown, the resulting state of transconceptual ecstasy (*nirvikalpa-samādhi*), which is a form of supraconscious ecstasy, is considered to be equivalent to the reunion of Śiva (pure Awareness) and Śakti (the power aspect of Awareness).

The emergence of Tantra was paralleled by a florescence of the emotive-devotional elements of Indian culture, especially the folk traditions. This led to the crystallization of *Bhakti-Yoga*, the spiritual path of devotion, as codified in the two *Bhakti-Sūtras* (one by the sage Nārada and the other by the sage Śāṇḍilya). *Bhakti-Yoga* is undoubtedly the most religious branch of Yoga, which is also the most Indian. It naturally also involves doctrine, rituals of worship, sacrificial offerings, chanting, prostration, shrines, pilgrimages, and so on. This type of Yoga has become well known in the West through the proselytizing International Society of Krishna Consciousness, which is a branch of the school founded by the fifteenth-century teacher Caitanya.

All these means are understood as embodied wisdom. The final goal is liberation in the infinite company of the Ultimate Personal (*puruṣottama*), which is a state of superlative devotion. Some teachers of this tradition understand devotion (*bhakti*) as a form of incommensurable wisdom.

The Ladder of Ecstasy Leading to Gnosis

The forté of Yoga are the various ecstatic states, which precede liberation. The *yogin* progressively moves through the various levels of ecstatic realization until the dawning of *nirvicāra-vaiśaradya*, or "the autumnal-lucidity of [the ecstatic state] beyond understanding." It is in this advanced form of *conscious* ecstasy that "truth-bearing insight" (*ṛtambharā prajñā*) arises. This is an extraordinary, spontaneous knowing, which has nothing to do with ordinary discursive thinking but everything to do with wisdom. The "subtle" (or nonmaterial) object held in the mind during this type of conscious ecstasy (*samprajñāta-samādhi*) is directly and fully understood as it is in itself. This state creates nonafflicted (*akliṣṭa*) unconscious activators (*saṃskāra*) that eventually clear out other activators in the depths of the mind.

The ultimate phase of *conscious* ecstasy—the lower category of ecstasy—is the "vision of discernment" (*viveka-khyāti*). Here the mind has become so pure that it catches glimpses, as it were, of the transcendental Self. Discernment between the purified mind (called *buddhi*) and the transcendental Self qualifies as a type of wisdom. At its peak, this elevated realization yields sevenfold wisdom (*prajñā*), according to the *Yoga-Sūtra* (2.27):

1. that which ought to be prevented (viz. future suffering) has been prevented;

2. the causes of suffering have been eliminated once and for all;

3. complete cessation of mental activity has been accomplished;

4. the vision of discernment, which effects the cessation of conceptual mental activity, has been applied;

5. sovereignty of the higher mind (*buddhi*) has been established;

6. the ultimate constituents (*guṇa*) of body, mind and Cosmos, have become reabsorbed into their transcendental matrix out of which they emerged;

7. the transcendental Self abides in its essential nature; that is, it is not mixed up with the mind (and Cosmos at large).

To move still farther up the ecstatic ladder into the *supraconscious* ecstasy—the higher category of ecstatic realization unaccompanied by cognition—the *yogin* must inwardly renounce any vestigial clinging to the elevated state of *conscious* or *cognitive* ecstasy. When he does so, he comes to enjoy the imponderable condition of *dharma-megha-samādhi*, or "the cloud of *dharma* ecstasy." It is not clear what the term *dharma* stands for here, though it reminds us that Patanjali borrowed considerably from the Buddhist tradition. The Vedāntic *yogin* Vijñāna Bhikṣu equates the condition of *dharma-megha* ecstasy with living liberation (*jīvan-mukti*), which precedes the supreme realization of postmortem liberation. If true, we could argue that in this connection *dharma* stands for the virtues that spontaneously manifest in the *yogin* at this advanced level.

The state of supraconscious ecstasy (*asaṃprajñāta-samādhi*) has no conscious contents (that is, no awareness of a mental object) and has only a remnant of unconscious activators left. When these "seeds" (*bīja*) in the unconscious mind are completely dissolved, this is known as *nirbīja-samādhi*, which is a supraconscious transitional state leading to liberation that involves the death of the physical body.

Wisdom of the Path

Wisdom of the path, which gradually leads to gnosis, includes insight into such key ideas as suffering (*duḥkha*), karma, and unconscious activators (*saṃskāra*), etc. As I said above, wisdom of the path is distilled experience. All these ideas have an experiential basis and are meant to be translated into practice. The basic recognition that, in the words of the *Yoga-Sūtra* (2.15), "everything is suffering" is the starting point of spiritual life. This insight clearly requires a basic level of wisdom. Therefore, Patañjali adds the qualifying word *vivekinah* to the quoted phrase, which means "for the discerner," that is, for the sagacious person who has insight into life. In his *Yoga-Bhāṣya* on this aphorism, Vyāsa remarks that the discerning *yogin* is as sensitive as an eyeball.

A foolish individual, who does not see clearly, thinks that life is "just grand" and that there is absolutely nothing wrong with it. He or she does not notice the full extent of suffering entailed in birth, growing up, adult life, and old age; or the suffering involved in illness or loss, or in envy, jealousy, anger, and lust. The ignorant individual also knows nothing about the unconscious activators (*saṃskāra*), which are produced by every thought and action and which, in countless numbers, form the "karmic deposit" (*karma-āśaya*) that conditions the psyche, perpetuates suffering, and leads from lifetime to lifetime in an endless cycle.

There are, then, numerous obstacles to wisdom. It could be said that the psychological constitution of the ordinary worldling (*saṃsārin*) is not conducive to the emergence of wisdom. Such a person prefers consoling delusions over actual reality, comfort over discipline, pleasure over love, quick answers over responsible solutions, ego-driven motivations over the pursuit of what Abraham H. Maslow labeled "meta-values," and so on.

And yet, there also is within us a wellspring of knowing. This permanent transpersonal core acts as an attractor to itself. Patañjali wrests from his metaphysical dualism the following explanation (see *Yoga-Sūtra* 3.35): The "seen" (i.e., the mind and experienced Cosmos) has the twofold purpose of either facilitating the witnessing Self's apperception of the world or its liberation from it. It is all a matter of how we perceive things. That is to say, it is all a matter of wisdom.

Implications for Individuals and Society

Hinduism has an uncommonly wide spectrum of wisdom teachings. Since wisdom, unlike knowledge, has a timeless quality, these teachings should be as relevant today as they were in bygone ages. This raises the legitimate question of why, if wisdom is perennial, it should come in so many varieties. Here we must differentiate between wisdom and philosophical opinion. Briefly stated, wisdom has a quality that, regardless of the philosophy in which it is embedded, supports psychological integration and empowers the individual to progress along a spiritual trajectory. If we were to look deeply enough, we would find that certain core values and practices of wisdom—such as discernment and mental renunciation (i.e., nonattachment)—can be found across diverse traditions. Their wellspring is gnosis, or the direct realization of transcendental Reality. How this realization is subsequently interpreted—whether as Self, the nondual Absolute, or *nirvāna*—depends on historical and personal factors. Some sages have therefore chosen to remain silent, though others have opted to endorse the philosophical-spiritual tradition with which they were aligned.

Without question, our era is in dire need of wisdom. We have become super-clever but, as many critics of modern civilization are wont to point out, our lack of self-knowledge and emotional maturity are matchless and calamitous. Our insistence on separating values from facts has driven us into an ethical quagmire. We are unable to cope with the enormous complexity of our postmodern civilization. Most importantly, we are destroying our planet's natural environment at such a precipitous pace that critics can be excused for thinking that our species is on a mad suicide mission.

Sadly, the Westernization of India is fast undermining that country's spiritual traditions. The baneful effects of this process can be seen in Yoga, which has been "internationalized" to suit essentially Western tastes and purposes. The imitation feared by C. G. Jung is rampant, and it is doubtful that Hinduism still has the vitality and clarity to resist the allure of the West and continue to influence us in benign ways.

I believe that the burden is almost exclusively on our side: We, as Westerners, must learn to approach Hinduism—and other cultures—humbly as open-minded dialogue partners, so that we can benefit from its wisdom teachings without simply discarding our own Western experience. European Romanticism had the right energy for this task but not the appropriate circumspection. Perhaps now, well over a century later, we can muster a more balanced attitude. As far as I can tell, nothing can be lost, but everything can be gained from this.

Summary and Conclusions

Wisdom and actual gnosis are central to Yoga, which not only has liberation for its ultimate "goal" but involves an intricate psychotechnology comprising many ecstatic states. Most Western students of Yoga will probably never experience these *samādhis,* which presuppose an exceptional cultivation of the yogic path, notably meditation. But the cartography developed by Yoga adepts over the centuries reveals to us the astonishing spectrum of our common human potential. Moreover, the wisdom distilled in the course of Yoga's exploration of the possibilities and limits of the human mind can serve anyone who desires to live more holistically and sanely even without attempting to attain special mental states, the Pure Consciousness Event, or Yoga's grand ideal of spiritual liberation.

Endnotes

1. The phrase "Self-realization" was made popular in the West by the school of Paramahansa Yogananda. The Sanskrit sources use *ātma-* or *purusha-jñāna* ("Self-knowledge").

2. See, e.g., Ian Whicher, *The Integrity of the Yoga Darśana: A Reconsideration of Classical Yoga* (Albany: State University of New York Press, 1998). See also Christopher Key Chapple, *Sāṃkhya-Yoga: Proceedings of the IASWR Conference, 1981* (Stony Brook: The Institute for Advanced Studies of World Religions, 1983), pp. 103–119; and Lloyd W. Pflueger, "Dueling with Dualism: Revisioning the Paradox of *Puruṣa* and *Prakṛti,*" in Ian Whicher and David Carpenter (eds.), *Yoga: The Indian Tradition* (London and New York: Routledge Curzon, 2003), pp. 70–82.

3. This and all other renderings from the Sanskrit found in the present essay are the author's.

References

Eliade, M. (1973). *Yoga: Immortality and freedom.* Princeton: Princeton University Press.

Feuerstein, G. (2008). *The yoga tradition: Its history, literature, philosophy and practice.* (3rd ed). Prescott, Ariz.: Hohm Press.

Forman, R. (Ed.) (1990). *The problem of pure consciousness: mysticism and philosophy.* Oxford: Oxford University Press.

Halbfass, W. (1988). *India and Europe: An essay in understanding,* Albany: State University of New York Press.

Hartmann, N. (1926). *Ethik.* Berlin: Walter de Gruyter.

Jung, C. (1962). "Difficulties encountered by a European in trying to understand the East." Reprint (1978) In: *Psychology and the East* (p. 9.). Princeton: Princeton University Press.

———. (n.d.). *Modern man in search of a soul.* New York: Harvest Books (first publ. 1933).

Maslow, A. H. (1964). *The farther reaches of human nature.* New York: Viking Press.

Sarbacker, S. R. (2005). *Samādhi: The numinous and cessative in Indo-Tibetan Yoga.* Albany: State University of New York Press.

Skolimowski, H. (1994). *The participatory mind: A new theory of knowledge and of the universe*. London: Arkana/Penguin.
Tart, C. (1983). *States of consciousness*. El Cerrito, Cal.: Psychological Processes Inc.

Internet Resources

www.traditionalyogastudies.com

6

The Innate Awareness of
Buddhist Wisdom

ARI GOLDFIELD

The inner movements of consciousness:
When their true nature is not realized, are ignorance itself.
This is the root of all karma and disturbing emotions.
When their true nature is realized, consciousness is self-aware wisdom,
The source of all positive qualities.

—Milarepa, the great eleventh-century Tibetan Buddhist yogi

To perfectly realize wisdom—to gain enlightenment—is Buddhism's highest goal. The Buddha gave volumes and volumes of teachings on wisdom. Over the centuries, in the Asian countries where Buddhism has flourished scholars and meditation masters have expanded on the Buddha's teachings by composing innumerable philosophical texts, meditation guides, poems, parables, and songs that describe how to realize wisdom: through the inner activities of study, reflection, meditation, and through the outer activity of conduct in the world. Countless practitioners have devoted themselves to this pursuit; many by spending good portions of their lives in meditation retreat.

Over the last few decades, Asian masters have begun transmitting Buddhism's notions of wisdom to Western disciples. And a growing number of Westerners are taking in these teachings; interacting with them through the traditional inner and outer activities, but also exploring them from a variety of new perspectives: scientific, academic, artistic, and psychological. Westerners are now teaching Buddhism, translating it, writing about it, and contributing to a dialogue (which, admittedly, in some circumstances more resembles a debate or even fierce argument) about what Buddhism is, what it actually means, and what relevance it has for us.

My own Buddhist teacher, the Tibetan master Khenpo Tsültrim Gyamt-so Rinpoche, gives a simple name to this rich process occurring on multiple levels of individual, relationship, and society—he calls it "research." Khenpo Tsültrim believes research a vital activity (while not losing, as best we can manage, empathy and a spacious perspective), and encourages his students to engage in active, continuing investigation, in order to discover wisdom—and experience it—in an immediate, individual, and unique way. The Buddha himself urged his followers to make their discovery of wisdom their own personal journey, teaching:

> Just as a merchant buying gold
> Would examine the gold by melting, cutting, and rubbing it,
> So monks, nuns, and the wise
> Should not accept my teachings out of faith,
> But only after analyzing my words thoroughly. (Gyamtso, 1997)

The implications here are that what others accept as wisdom, we need not accept ourselves unless we have independently confirmed it to be so; and what we may believe to be wisdom will not be so for others. It may even be that what will appear as wisdom to us now may not do so a year after our present epiphany. Buddhism teaches that when examining its doctrinal explanations of wisdom, remembering these points is essential to the examination and to the development of wisdom itself.

Thus, as we begin our exploration of Buddhism's perspectives on wisdom, it is worthwhile to engender a spirit of inquiry, discovery, and experience. We will probably be frustrated if we aim to pin down Buddhist wisdom as being "this" or "that"—as any one particular description, teaching, meditation practice, or way of acting in the world. Although in this chapter we will consider the aspects of what might comprise a tentative definition of Buddhist wisdom, Buddhism itself teaches that wisdom cannot truly be defined. Yet, by keeping our minds as open as possible to what wisdom might be, and how we might find it, we give ourselves the best chance of doing so. The modern Zen Buddhist master Shunryu Suzuki advised:

> Our "original mind" includes everything within itself. It is always rich and sufficient within itself. You should not lose your self-sufficient state of mind. This does not mean a closed mind, but actually an empty mind and a ready mind. If your mind is empty, it is always ready for anything; it is open to everything. In

the beginner's mind there are many possibilities; in the expert's mind there are few.

[T]he most difficult thing is always to keep your beginner's mind. . . . This is also the real secret of the arts: always be a beginner. Be very, very careful about this point. If you start to practice zazen, you will begin to appreciate your beginner's mind. It is the secret of Zen practice. (Suzuki, 1973)

A Tentative Definition of Buddhist Wisdom

From this perspective of "beginner's mind," let us consider the following as a tentative definition of Buddhism's notion of wisdom:

> Wisdom is an innate awareness of our own true nature and the true nature of the outer world; is experientially spacious, blissful, and clear; imbued with love; and is inseparable from altruistic ethical conduct. It is cultivated on a gradual path of meditation, with the guidance of qualified teachers.

One reason why this definition is tentative is that it is my own "best effort." In this chapter I will present evidence for it, but others could certainly take different perspectives based on their own knowledge of Buddhism's vast and varied scholarly and meditative traditions.

Yet another reason for it being tentative was alluded to above: Buddhism teaches that *any* definition of *any* phenomenon—"from form through omniscience" (as the texts like to describe the range of phenomena from the most common to the most sublime)—must be tentative because when closely analyzed, internal contradictions, questions, and paradoxes reveal themselves. If anything is certain, it is that gaining awareness of these uncertainties is an essential part of the process of growing in wisdom. Therefore, identifying these problematic areas will be a part of this chapter as well.

Let us now explore the individual components of this definition.

Wisdom Is Innate

> I have found the Buddha in my own mind,
> And the treasure of everything I need is overflowing from inside.
> E ma, what a wonderful miracle!
> E ma, how amazing!
>
> —Jamgön Kongtrül Lodrö Tayé, nineteenth-century Tibetan Master

The primary canonical source for the teachings on wisdom's innateness is Maitreya's[1] *Treatise on Buddha Nature*. This text explains that the core of every conscious experience we have from birth to death is the Buddha Nature—pristine awareness that is the essence of enlightenment. As pure water is fully present in a muddy river; as pure gold is fully present in gold ore, so the Buddha Nature is fully present within all states of mind. Maitreya described this innate wisdom in the following way:

> Mind's abiding nature is luminous clarity,
> Like space, it does not change.
> Attachment and other disturbing emotions, arising from mistaken
>   thoughts,
> Are fleeting and do not afflict it at all.

This text calls innate wisdom the "element," because wisdom is the fundamental constituent or *element* of consciousness, whether it is a moment of consciousness of an enlightened buddha or of a confused sentient being. All consciousness is essentially made of the same luminous awareness, and that awareness is the wisdom mind of the Buddha. Luminous awareness is an inalienable part of who we are. In the context of Maitreya's text, the oft-appearing Buddhist term *emptiness* refers to how this luminous awareness is "empty" of flaw, but is not empty of its own unsurpassable qualities, such as clarity, wisdom, love, bliss, and courage—the qualities of enlightenment.

We may ask, "If the nature of our consciousness is wisdom, why do we not experience it? Why are we not the enlightened Buddha already?" The text addresses this paradox by stating that the only difference between the Buddha and ordinary beings is that the Buddha has seen through the fleeting obscurations of disturbing emotions, and has realized the luminous nature of mind, while ordinary beings have not yet done so. Thus, innate wisdom is like the sun shining behind clouds—although there are clouds in the sky that prevent one from seeing the sun, the sun is still there, always shining. No matter what difficult circumstances we may be facing, the wisdom inherent in the core of our awareness can never be taken away from us or lost—it is always safe.

In fact, the text states that our experience of suffering actually proves that the true nature of our experience is wisdom beyond suffering. For if disturbing emotions and painful experience really were the nature of mind itself, we would not experience them as unpleasant—we would not seek to be free from them. What keeps us constantly in motion, constantly in pursuit of happiness and in avoidance of pain, is the freedom from pain and suffering that is our inherent nature. The basic quality of intelligence is the desire to be rid of the bonds of pain and to be happy and free, because happiness and freedom are vitally part of our basic identity.

Since each sentient being shares this longing for happiness, it is also the bond of commonality that is the source of universal love, compassion, and empathy. As the Dalai Lama observes,

> Human beings by nature want happiness and do not want suffering. With that feeling everyone tries to achieve happiness and tries to get rid of suffering, and everyone has the basic right to do this. In this way, all here are the same, whether rich or poor, educated or uneducated, Easterner or Westerner, believer or non-believer, and within believers whether Buddhist, Christian, Jewish, Muslim, and so on. Basically, from the viewpoint of real human value we are all the same. (1984)

Thus, innate wisdom manifests as the energizing force for the lives of all conscious beings, and is also what makes each of our lives valuable and deserving of respect—both from others and from ourselves. The Buddha taught:

> All wandering beings are completely pervaded by the enlight-
>   ened essence,
> All wandering beings, without exception, are precisely buddha,
> Therefore, all sentient beings are worthy. (*Samadhi-raja-sutra*)

The modern Tibetan master Chögyam Trungpa emphasized this connection between innate wisdom and intrinsic value. He coined a new term for the wisdom that is classically known as the Buddha Nature, calling it "basic goodness," which he described as "the ground or root of wakefulness and sanity that exists as a potential within every human being" (1984). Having this nature of basic goodness endows us with the capacity to live a wise and free life:

> As human beings, we are basically awake and we *can* understand reality. We are not enslaved by our lives; we are free. Being free, in this case, means simply that we have a body and a mind, and we can uplift ourselves in order to work with reality in a dignified and humorous way. . . . Life is a humorous situation, but it is not mocking us. We find that, after all, we can handle our world; we can handle our universe properly and fully in an uplifted fashion. (ibid.)

One benefit of the teachings on innate wisdom is that they help us relax from what can be a desperate search for happiness outside of ourselves. Trungpa wrote of "the basic problem" of how "you never feel satisfied even if you get what you want, because you still *want* it so badly" (1973/2008). Gaining confidence in one's basic goodness, one realizes that there is no need to feel that one is missing something or is somehow incomplete. As Jamgön Kongtrül sang,[2] the treasure we can so desperately seek is actually to be found in the intrinsic awareness that is right within our own mind. Milarepa echoed this:

> When there's nothing to look for, that's the greatest thing to
>   find—
> It's the precious treasure of innate mind. (He-ru-ka, 1488)

There are also problems in Buddhism's teachings on wisdom being innate. Students often begin to believe that there is something wrong with them if they have not succeeded in experiencing their wonderful innate qualities. They view themselves as flawed and inferior because they are still hampered by their emotions, and develop a concept of "enlightenment" that becomes so distant from their own actual experience that they set themselves a goal that no one could ever achieve. They do often imagine, however, that someone else has actually achieved it—has achieved success where they have so far failed—and in so doing elevate teachers to a status of perfection that ignores the teachers' humanity. This can lead to a blind, unquestioning worship of teachers, who can never be wrong because the student is by definition obscured, while the guru is by definition enlightened. The result is a Buddhist community that resembles less a forum for wisdom to develop, and more a cult where intelligence and independent reasoning are stifled. Therefore, it is vital to keep one's intelligence sharp; as it is to recall that Maitreya's stated purpose for teaching that wisdom is innate was to help people be free of discouragement and self-judgment.

Let us now explore the next element of Buddhist wisdom's definition.

Wisdom Is Experiential Awareness

> Kye ho! This self-aware original wisdom
> Leaves speech's path, eludes concepts' grasp.
> I, Tilli, have nothing to teach to you,
> This wisdom knows itself—that's how to know!
>
> —the Indian master Tilopa (tenth/eleventh c. CE)

Although the great Buddhist masters have given countless teachings and writ-ten innumerable treatises on wisdom, those same masters hold that wisdom can actually be neither transmitted by a teacher nor learned by a student. A classic parable warns that just as if when someone points out the moon, one were to focus one's gaze on the pointing finger rather than on the moon itself, so it is that if one gets caught up in the teachings' words, one misses the teachings' essential point.

The reason for this is that actual wisdom cannot be expressed in words or conceived of in thoughts. It is not mere intellectual knowledge. Rather, it is an experiential awareness—direct; unmediated by thoughts; unobscured by words; felt and known deeply in body and heart as well as in mind. It is pure knowing, unlimited by concepts of there being something to know and someone who knows it. When Tilopa sang of wisdom as being "self-aware," he was alluding to this nondual quality of awareness—how it knows in a way that transcends a separation between knower and known. As the Buddha taught in the *Kalachakra Tantra*, "In this enlightened dimension, knower and known are one" (Lodrö Tayé). And the Indian master Nagarjuna (seventh c. CE) wrote,

> All conceptual focus dissolves,
> All fabrications are at peace.
> The Buddha did not at any time
> Teach the Dharma to anyone. (*Dbu ma rtsa ba shes rab*)

The meaning of Nagarjuna's latter two lines is that the actual meaning of the Dharma—the teachings—cannot be described, even by the Bud-dha. At the same time, the actual meaning of the teachings can be *known* by wisdom-awareness that transcends what can be analyzed or taught. As Milarepa sang:

> This wisdom, mere self-awareness,
> Is inexpressible in speech,
> And unknown to logicians. (He-ru-ka, 1488)

This is the difference between what is called the "Dharma of transmission"—the words of the teachings—and the "Dharma of realization"—the wisdom of knowing the teachings' meaning in experiential awareness. And in this experiential awareness, Milarepa explains, is freedom—the freedom from the limitations of subject-object duality; from the habitual tendency to view some objects as desirable and productive of pleasure and others as unpleasant and productive of suffering; and from the internal struggles that this creates. For Milarepa, to refrain from all those confused tendencies is wise, as he sang:

> When I realize wisdom beyond thought,
> I forget everything included in perceiver and perceived—
> It is fine to forget these causes of happiness and pain. (ibid.)

It may seem that a wisdom beyond duality might be dull, static, or lifeless, but it is actually explained to be an awareness endowed with great energy and strength. According to the classic texts, progress in realizing wisdom brings extraordinary benefits, including mental clarity, peace, and happiness. Many of these benefits have been confirmed by contemporary research.[3] And these benefits arise primarily from realizing one's own true nature. Milarepa sang:

> There's a whole lot of power in my view
> Free from extremes, beyond concepts.
> There's a whole lot of power right here in the heart
> Of what's been pure from the very start. (ibid.)

The energetic power of wisdom is emphasized especially in the tantras, which the Indo-Tibetan tradition calls its esoteric system of teaching and practice. The *Hevajra Tantra* extols "nondual wisdom" as "glorious." It describes how singing and dancing are highly beneficial methods for meditating on the nondual wisdom that is the innate essence of emotional experience:

> For yogis and yoginis whose anger is completely pure,
> Their singing songs is completely pure mantra
> And their dancing is meditation,
> So yogis and yoginis—always singing and dancing! (*Hevajra Tantra*)

And yet, a danger of the teachings on the nonconceptual, nondual qualities of wisdom is that practitioners often believe that in order to gain realization they must somehow stop thinking; must conquer their emotions and rise up and out of them. When people attempt that, they are prone to reject their emotions, falling into the trap of what John Welwood calls "*spiritual bypassing* . . . a common tendency . . . among Western spiritual seekers to use spiritual ideas and practices to avoid dealing with their emotional unfinished business" (2002). Stephen Batchelor observes how this separation of spiritual and emotional life actually has its roots in the way Buddhism is practiced in the East: "In India, China, Southeast Asia, or Tibet, it was always the serene, world-renouncing contemplative monk who represented the ideal of a Buddhist life" (2010). Although the ancient Eastern masters did teach that in the search for wisdom, thoughts and emotions should not be abandoned, Batchelor notes how most of those masters were themselves "world-renouncing contemplatives" who had abandoned living in society. All of this messaging from the East has led to a Western paradigm of

> the good Buddhist . . . as an unflappable beacon of smiling calm, ready to respond at any moment with a kind gesture or some choice words of wisdom. As a way of coping with the hectic pace and stress of modern life, the housewife or business executive alike is encouraged to become a monk in lay clothing. (ibid.)

But people can suffer from striving to achieve that goal. When meditation is used to escape from the psyche rather than illuminate it, no matter how brilliant that meditation may seem, it does not produce wisdom. The question, then, is can one find a relationship between thoughts, emotions, and nonconceptual awareness? That is the topic of the next section.

Wisdom Knows Our Own True Nature

> Look for wisdom within your disturbing emotions.[4]
>
> —Tibetan Buddhist Proverb

> When you do not see your disturbing emotions and your wisdom as different,
> You have mastered realization.
>
> —Milarepa

> Desire, perfectly pure, and transcendent wisdom, perfectly pure, are not dual, cannot be made dual, are not separate, and are not different. Anger, perfectly pure, and transcendent wisdom, perfectly pure, are not dual, cannot be made dual, are not separate, and are not different.
>
> —The Buddha, in the Great Sutra of Transcendent Wisdom in 100,000 Verses

Upon initially encountering the descriptions of wisdom as nonconceptual and nondual self-awareness, one's reaction may be that these teachings are incredibly profound, or else incomprehensible. The common quality of both these reactions is that what is described seems very far from our ordinary experience. For this reason, the Indian Buddhist masters Dignaga (sixth c. CE) and Dharmakirti (seventh c. CE) went to great lengths to explain how to find this nondual self-awareness right within our ordinary experiences of consciousness.

Dignaga defined this self-awareness as "a nonconceptual, unmistaken awareness that experiences itself," and explained that "desire and all the rest" of our thoughts, emotions, and feelings "are self-awareness, concept-free" (Gyamtso, 1997). To explain how this is, the experience of eating sugar candy is used as an example. Imagine eating a delicious piece of chocolate, and then attempting to describe your experience to people who have never eaten chocolate before. When they ask you: "What is it like to eat choco-late?" you could reply: "it tastes rich, creamy, sweet, and delicious." If they then ask: "What are 'rich,' 'creamy,' 'sweet,' and 'delicious,' like?" you are left saying something such as: "They are like mmm-mmm." Buddhism calls such an expression a "term of experience"—it is not a word; yet it is not com-pletely outside the sphere of language. But if the person then asks, "What is 'mmm-mmm' like?" then you cannot answer. The conversation has hit up against the core of conscious experience, in which there is active knowing, but which cannot be described or even conceived of. This is self-awareness.

Of self-awareness at the core of emotional experience, Dharmakirti wrote:

> Happiness does not depend on others;
> Words have no power to describe it.
> Therefore, self-awareness of joy
> Is free of the bonds of expression. (Gyamtso, 1997)

That "happiness does not depend on others" means that one knows one's own emotional state without having to ask anyone else what it is—it is exclusively the private sphere of experience of the individual person. And if that person states that they are happy or sad, no matter how many thou-sands of others may claim otherwise, who can truly know what the person's emotional experience is, except that person's mind as it knows itself? This self-awareness of emotions, much like the self-awareness of the experience of eating chocolate, is inexpressible. Joy, anger, jealousy, love, and sadness can be named in phrase, poetry, and song, but when one asks: "What is that emotional experience actually like?" it is taught that even the Buddha's tongue remains mute.

Thus, an emotion at its core is an experience of pure knowing; of freedom from the limitations of expressions of "good" or "bad," "pleasant" or "unpleasant"; and freedom from the beliefs that those expressions carry with them. Thus, emotions, even negative ones, can yield an experience of freedom and purity, inseparable from the purity of self-aware wisdom itself, as the Buddha described in the *Great Sutra of Transcendent Wisdom* (*Prajna-paramita*). From such an experience, one realizes that wisdom is actually not to be found somewhere different from even afflictive emotions themselves. As Milarepa sang, this is an extraordinarily beneficial thing to realize (He-ru-ka, 1488).

In this way, our innate wisdom is fully present in and aware of the variety of our thoughts, feelings, and emotions, but at the same time is devoid of our normal habits of favoring some experiences and shunning others. Our innate wisdom is aware of our experiences so deeply and intimately that it knows what these experiences actually are—the energetic play of nondual, luminous awareness itself. Thus, our wisdom knows who we are and what we are about, down to the very core of our being.

The Progressive Stages of Developing Wisdom

Given the profundity of what they set out to explain, Buddhist teachings also make use of a series of progressive stages to explain wisdom's realization of our true nature.[5] This true nature is often referred to as "emptiness," and the first stage in this progressive explanation describes how the fundamental aspect of emptiness is selflessness. Selflessness means that in genuine reality, nothing resembling a truly existent personal self can be found—there is no "I" or "me" in the nondual expanse of genuine reality.

The reason why selflessness is the first, fundamental stage, is that all suffering arises from a mistaken belief that a self truly exists. When a person thinks: "I am angry," "I am anxious," or "I am in pain," the common denominator is a belief that there is truly an "I" to have this difficult experience. There is also the tendency of identifying oneself with the positive and negative status of one's body, wealth, fame, success, and relationships. People define themselves by whether or not they look good, feel good, succeed, have pleasing connections with others, or do not. Since all of these criteria are subject to change beyond anyone's control, identifying oneself with them is a certain source of anxiety and pain. This is why Buddhism considers it essential to realize that "I am not defined by my success or failure," because no such self can be identified.

For what is it that constitutes this "I," this self? Is the self our body, our mind, or is it some combination of both? One is encouraged to logically

[8] Blessed are the pure in heart, for they will see God.

analyze body and mind to see if a self can be found there, and many techniques are taught for how to do this. Nagarjuna, the Indian master who is probably Buddhism's most famous exponent of logical analysis, taught one such method in his text *The Fundamental Wisdom of the Middle Way*:

> If the self were the aggregates,
> It would be something that arises and ceases.
> If the self were something other than the aggregates,
> It would not have the aggregates' characteristics. (Gyamtso, 2003)

The aggregates refer to the components of body and mind. Nagarjuna points out how everything in body and mind is continuously arising and ceasing. The cells in the body constantly dissolve and are replaced by new ones; thoughts and feelings form in the mind and then disappear. The self, therefore, cannot be identical to body and/or mind, because if it were, then I would die each time my cells, thoughts, or feelings ceased. Nor, however, could I be different from body and/or mind, because if I existed as a different substance from body and mind, what would I be? I would not have body and mind's characteristics—I would not be able to move, think, or feel. Therefore, the self is not the same as body and mind, nor is it different from them, and there is no third possibility for its existence.

Thus, it is taught that the true nature of the self is selflessness, and the self that appears to exist when we think "I" and "me" is only illusory and dreamlike—appearing, while at the same time empty of truly existing. This is the meaning of the famous line from the Buddha's *Heart of Wisdom Sutra*: "Form is empty; emptiness is form." As Khenpo Tsültrim (1997–2008) sings:

> Since when I analyze I cannot find the self,
> I am certain that the self that appears is an illusion.

One might imagine that the realization of selflessness would be tantamount to experiencing extinction. In fact, those who claim to have realized this aspect of wisdom describe it as great liberation, because being free from thinking one's identity is confined to a small body and ego feels wonderful, they say. In the modern Tibetan master Kalu Rinpoche's (ca.1980) words:

> If you wake up to . . . reality,
> You will know that you are nothing,
> And being nothing, you are everything.

Following the teachings on selflessness come those on the emptiness of all phenomena. In what are considered the most profound of these explanations, the true nature of reality is explained to be emptiness because reality is ultimately *empty* of any concept of what it might be. If something can be conceived of or described, it is only *relatively* existent—it exists only in relation to something else, like the notions of big and small, poor and rich, good and bad, happiness and unhappiness, and woman and man. Genuine reality, however, transcends all of these relatively existent concepts. Relative and ultimate are what Buddhism calls the *two truths*. The Indian master Shantideva (eighth c. CE) explained:

> Relative and ultimate—
> These are the two truths.
> Concepts are described as relative;
> The ultimate is not the object of conceptual mind. (*Byang chub
>   sems pa'i spyod pa la 'jug pa*)

If we apply this to ourselves, we can see how wisdom can realize that relative truth and ultimate truth exist inseparably in all phenomena. For example, when I refer to my body, I think of it as "me" or "self," but everyone else thinks of it as "you" or "other." My father thinks of me as "son," my sister as "brother," my wife as "husband." A tiger or mosquito would see me as "food," while for the parasites living in my stomach, I am a "home." So what am "I," really? The true nature of self—and of other, son, husband, and all other labels—transcends all concepts of what it might be.

Realizing this transcendent quality of phenomena's true nature, simplicity beyond concept, is described as a yogic experience of wonder and amazement. The adept Nyima Bepa sang:

> Look at your body—it was never born
> Look at mind—simplicity
> Reality, non-duality
> Leaving thinking mind far behind
> So I don't know anything! (Wangchuk Dorje)

Thus in the end, wisdom cannot be described as knowing any concrete, conceivable "thing." And yet, the pure energy of its awareness can be experienced in a way that transcends concepts. Each of the five main disturbing emotions is taught to embody this pure energy of awareness—this wisdom—in its own unique way. When the true nature of anger is realized, it is "mirror-like wisdom," because the angry mind is also bright and clear, like a shining mirror. Desire's true nature is "discriminating wisdom," because desire is inquisitive of even the tiniest details of the objects of its passion. Jealousy is ultimately "all-accomplishing wisdom," pride is "the wisdom of equality," and stupidity is the "wisdom of the expanse."

When one is open to and embraces the emotions, free from rejecting some and clinging to others, one can experience their underlying nature, the pure and protean energy of self-aware wisdom. Chögyam Trungpa (1973/2008) explains:

> Tantra teaches not to suppress or destroy [the] energy [of thoughts and emotions] but to transmute it; in other words, go with the pattern of energy. . . . When one goes with the pattern of energy, then experience becomes very creative. . . . You realize that you no longer have to abandon anything. You begin to see the underlying qualities of wisdom in your life situation. . . . If you are highly involved in one emotion such as anger, then by having a sudden glimpse of openness . . . you begin to see that you do not have to suppress your energy . . . but you can transform your aggression into dynamic energy.
>
> If we actually feel the living quality, the texture of the emotions as they are in their naked state, then this experience also contains ultimate truth. . . . We discover that emotion actually does not exist as it appears, but it contains much wisdom.

Although these teachings on emotions' wisdom-essence are incredibly profound, a problem with the methods taught for how to implement them is that they can be too simplistic; too much a cure-all that ignores the depth and complexity of emotional patterns. For example, Milarepa gave the instruction:

> Throughout the day and night, look at your mind—
> When you look at your mind, you don't see anything.
> When you don't see anything, let go and relax. (He-ru-ka, 1488)

This style of teaching is beautiful in its simplicity and profundity. And in the medieval era of its formulation and use, perhaps teachings like this one were sufficient. For modern people (including Buddhist teachers themselves, from both East and West), however, reliance on such maxims to the exclusion of other methods of more deeply exploring and engaging the psyche can leave whole areas of emotional content suppressed under the surface of meditative experiences of peace and clarity that are superficial and fleeting. The result is that the practitioner experiences the repetition of painful emotional patterns without knowing where they come from or what to do about them, other than to continue to use meditation techniques that are actually ineffective. Fortunately, Buddhist psychologists such as Jack Kornfield, Rob Preece, and John Welwood have pioneered an effort to see how modern psychological techniques of deeper emotional inquiry can enhance Buddhism's classic wisdom teachings, and make them more efficacious and relevant in the modern world.

Wisdom Knows the True Nature of the Outer World

For Buddhism, wisdom about the true nature of the outer world lies in a deep understanding of the interdependent nature of things. The Buddha himself taught that to know interdependence is to know the essence of his teachings.

The basic principle of interdependence is that things exist only in dependence upon their causes and conditions. The Buddha gave the example of a rice seedling—it does not exist independently with any essence of its own, but rather is the product of many causal factors, such as a rice seed, nutritious soil, sunlight, water, and the efforts of a farmer. So it is with all phenomena in the universe—they arise when their causes and conditions coalesce, and they cease when those causes and conditions disperse.

Knowledge of this interdependent quality of things brings an understanding of impermanence—how it is that everything in the universe is subject to continuous change. From the tiniest particles of matter to the simple and complex life forms on this planet, to the planets and the stars themselves, all things arise, abide, and cease. In fact, everything is changing moment by moment, and nothing stays the same from one instant to the next. The Buddha called such a contemplation of impermanence "the king of all meditations," because as one gains more and more familiarity with how the nature of all phenomena is a continual flow of change, one's fixation on phenomena as being rigidly one way or another begins to lessen. When one has certainty in impermanence, one is less disturbed when things seem bad, and less carried away when things seem good. This is the foundation of equanimity. One begins to know that since whatever identity something seems to have is just a fleeting snapshot, bound to transform into something else, then nothing really "exists" with any fixed identity at all. This "emptiness" of static identity is an important aspect of the true nature of things. As Nagarjuna wrote,

> By understanding arising, you understand cessation.
> By understanding cessation, you understand impermanence.
> By understanding impermanence,
> You realize the truth of genuine Dharma. (*Rigs pa drug cu pa*)

Another vital understanding here is that of the interdependence of opposites. Superficially, the phenomena in a pair of opposites—such as right and wrong, poor and rich, good and bad—appear to exist separate and distinct from one another. However, to take the first pair as an example, what a person considers to be right depends on their notion of wrong, and vice versa. And being right would have no meaning unless there were others who were wrong. Thus, the more a person believes that being right is the source of their positive and distinct identity, the more they depend on their notion of what is wrong in order for their identity to survive. The more a person clings to one pole in a pair of opposites in hopes of avoiding the other, the more the other is actually present.

Knowing this about opposite phenomena helps us to avoid the stubbornness, fear, and rigidity that accompany clinging to opposites as being independently existent—a tendency that the Buddha called "clinging to extremes." We understand that we can never destroy what we find undesirable or threatening, for the more we seek to do so, the stronger it becomes. So we develop the spaciousness of view that allows opposites to coexist.

The masters describe how when this understanding deepens, it manifests as the realization of equality. Equality means that the true nature of reality transcends concepts of opposites, contradictions, differences, or conflicts. Equality is not a blank state or a vacuum, because opposites continue to appear to the mind that possesses this realization. However, they are known to be interdependent and actually unreal, the union of appearance and emptiness, like opposites appearing in a dream. The Indian master Shantarakshita (eighth c. CE) describes the realization of equality in this song:

> While nothing ever moves from equality's expanse
> Appearances magically shine.
> Many rivers flow into the great ocean where the water has the
>   same salty taste.
> Many they may be, but they taste the same,

In this, there is nothing different.
Everything there is, all of existence has the flavor of the native
state.
How wonderful, how happy—as happy as can be! (Wangchuk
Dorje)

Wisdom Is Experientially Spacious, Blissful, and Clear

From Shantarakshita's song, we glean that for Buddhism, wisdom is more
than just knowledge—it is a felt experience. And the three main qualities
the masters describe as accompanying their experience of wisdom are spaciousness, bliss, and clarity.

Wisdom's freedom from fixation allows it to feel good; the sun is a
useful metaphor to explain how this is so. The sun holds and emits tremen-
dous energy that sustains our lives and makes us feel warm and comfortable.
Yet if on a sunny day we hold a magnifying glass over our skin, we fix
the sun's energy into too small a space, and we experience pain. Similarly,
when mind's powerful innate awareness gets fixated on an internal feeling
or thought, or on an external event, individual, or object, it feels tight, tense,
and uncomfortable. Free from that fixation, the energy of awareness feels
unconstrained and naturally relaxed.

The spacious quality of the wisdom mind was described beautifully by
the Tibetan yogi Gotsangpa Gönpo Dorje (twelfth-thirteenth c. CE) in his
song *Swinging the Lance in Open Space.* The title's metaphor is used to describe
the quality of how wisdom is unimpeded by fixation. If one attempted to
swing a lance around indoors, one would knock things over, and be blocked
from having much experience of freedom. But outside, one can swing a
lance around freely, without impediment. This is Gotsangpa's experience of
wisdom:

Experiences flow naturally, without hindrance,
Free of fear, despair, and worry,
Conquering dualistic fixation, I am triumphant—
My activity is like swinging a lance in open space. (Darpo, 1994)

The great Tibetan yogini[6] Machik Labdrön (eleventh-twelfth c. CE)
instructed her disciples to meditate in a way that would connect them with
wisdom's spaciousness when she sang: "Let mind rest as space; Let it rest
without focal reference point" (Lodrö Tayé). And Milarepa used his own
metaphors to sing of spaciousness:

Like an eagle soaring into the stratosphere,
The yogi with confident insight is blissful.
Like a strong wind traveling throughout the sky,
The yogi neither impeded by nor stuck on anything is blissful.
    (He-ru-ka, 1488)

As Milarepa described, wisdom's spaciousness is accompanied by a feeling of bliss. This bliss is not found by shunning pain in favor of pleasure, however. Rather, it manifests when one is able to open to and experience the underlying energy of self-awareness that is the inexpressible nature of happiness and suffering alike. Free from the struggle of fighting negative feelings and clinging to positive ones, one feels relaxed, peaceful, and genuinely happy.

The danger in following these teachings is that, in an attempt to rest in space-like freedom from fixation, practitioners may dissociate from their feelings and rest in a superficial spaciousness that is actually a cold detachment. It is therefore vital for meditators to be honest with themselves and make sure that they are aware of their emotional experiences—we can only connect with self-aware wisdom through our feelings and not in spite of them. When Milarepa sang: "Suffering is blissful, so I am happy" (He-ru-ka, 1488), we see how he experienced his suffering and identified it as such, and at the same time he opened to suffering's essential nature, which is what felt blissful.

To ensure that her students did not avoid their feelings, Machik Lab-drön sent them to sleep alone overnight in charnel grounds and other desolate places that everyone was certain were haunted by demons. Machik instructed her disciples to let fear arise, and then look directly into its essential nature—to search for fearlessness within the fear itself. In this spirit, the modern master Jack Kornfield (1993) gives the following meditation advice:

> Notice what feelings and thoughts are present. In particular, be aware of any feelings or thoughts you are now struggling with, fighting, denying, or avoiding. Notice them with an interested and kind attention. Let your heart be soft. Open to whatever you experience without fighting. Breathe quietly and let it be. . . . Invite all parts of yourself to join you at the peace table in your heart.

This fearlessness and honesty are part of wisdom's experiential clarity. When wisdom-awareness does not deny the fear, loneliness, mistrust, hostility, and vulnerability that lurk in the shadows of the psyche, but rather, acknowledges them and willfully opens to their experience, mind and heart feel clear and bright. Milarepa sang:

> Even confused thoughts themselves are clear light that shines
>   so brilliantly.
> Experiences so bright like sun and moonlight,
> Without any direction, clarity shines timelessly.
> You cannot find it, so you cannot say what it is.
> So many kinds of certainty shine like the stars in the sky.
> Whatever arises is the greatest bliss. (He-ru-ka, 1488)

Wisdom Is Imbued with Love

Milarepa sang that wisdom is "an open sky of pure love," in which "the clouds of compassion gather perfectly, sending down a steady rain of enlightened activity" (He-ru-ka, 1488). This love and compassion flow both to oneself and to others. For oneself, rather than shunning, contracting from, or struggling against who and what one is, wisdom holds one's experiences in deep acceptance and loving embrace. It does the same when it beholds the beings, events, and phenomena of the outer world. It is even able to hold in loving awareness the anger, violence, injustice, and pain appearing internally and externally, without denying them in fearful or Pollyannaish myopia. Wisdom is known as the *Great Mother*, because to experience it is to feel held in love that is strong and unchanging, and to feel the ability to hold oneself and others in the same way.

In order to manifest wisdom that is imbued with love, Buddhism's view is that cultivating love and compassion is a vital part of spiritual practice. Without feeling love, a person can never fully manifest the wisdom that is its richest potential. Recognizing this, Chandrakirti (an Indian master of the sixth-seventh centuries CE) placed the following verse at the beginning of his seminal treatise on the development of wisdom, *Entering the Middle Way*:

> Since I assert that loving-kindness itself is the seed of the Vic-
>   tors' abundant harvest,
> Is the water that causes it to flourish,
> And is its ripening that allows it to be enjoyed for a long
>   time,
> At the very outset, I praise compassion. (*Dbu ma la 'jug pa*)

If there is any danger in Buddhism's teachings on love and compassion, it is in their emphasis on self-sacrifice. For example, in a text that is renowned in Tibet for its teaching on compassion, the following verse appears:

> All suffering comes from yearning for your own happiness;
> The perfect buddhas are born from the intention to benefit
> others.
> Therefore, fully exchange your own happiness for the suffering
> of others. (Thogme)

Buddhist psychologists have documented the detrimental effect that unskillfully cultivating this mindset of self-sacrifice can have. Rob Preece (2006) writes:

> I recall a young Western Tibetan Buddhist nun. . . . She tried hard to live the pure, selfless existence she saw exemplified in the teachings. She seldom if ever considered her own needs. She would sleep very little and constantly worked to take care of others. . . . Sadly, it was evident that beneath this utter dedication to serve . . . was a desperately sad and unhappy person. She would seldom acknowledge this because to do so would be to think of herself. Suppressing her own inner need or pain was crucial to her.

When something like this happens, the spiritual path leads not to wisdom but to self-loathing and self-oppression. The key to avoiding this, while still cultivating the love and compassion that are so essential to wisdom, is to recall that "the ideal of . . . total selflessness must be born out of a healthy sense of self-worth and self-love" (ibid.). This self-love is not selfishness; rather, it emerges as a natural result of deeper and subtler levels of awareness of what is happening within one's own being. The obstacle to love is when one experiences an emotion but contracts from it in fear. When that fear is present one cannot love oneself, and one feels discomfort rather than empathy when others show evidence of emotional experience. So Chögyam Trungpa (1984) advised:

> That mind of fearfulness
> Should be put in the cradle of loving-kindness.

The more one does this—the more one lovingly knows and accepts oneself—the more one will lovingly be able to know and accept others. True wisdom is deeply loving, and true love is profoundly wise.

Wisdom Is Inseparable from Altruistic Ethical Conduct

The Buddha has taught:
You cannot cultivate wisdom without performing altruistic activity.
You cannot perform altruistic activity without cultivating wisdom.
Be careful not to abandon either.

—The Indian Master Atisha Dipankara (tenth-eleventh c. CE)

Thus, Buddhism considers wisdom and altruistic conduct to be vital parts of one whole. If one attempts to cultivate wisdom without performing altruistic activity, that effort is explained to be actually just a self-serving method of gaining mental peace, but peace that is not genuine because it is antagonistic to others sharing its space. Similarly, without wisdom, altruistic activity runs into obstacles, both internal and external. For the mind not trained in wisdom has a strong ego-fixation, and believes that the external world is solid in its appearance and rigid in its ways. As a result, altruistic impulses are easily overwhelmed by frustration, impatience, stubbornness, and anger. Such a mind tends to have fixed ideas of right, wrong, good, and bad. It seeks to impose these ideas on the outside world, and believes that converting others to its own views, protecting what is right, and destroying what is wrong are part of altruistic action. With this kind of outlook, altruistic action can become a daily struggle that leaves one with feelings of bitterness, depression, and burnout.

For these reasons, the Buddha taught that genuine wisdom is like the eyes that give altruistic activity the power to see. Wisdom produces the energy, creativity, and adaptability of altruistic living in the world. Chögyam Trungpa (1991) taught that we possess the wisdom that altruistic activity needs when we

acknowledge that the world around us is workable. . . . [I]t is not a hard-core, incorrigible world. It can be worked with within the inspiration of the buddhadharma, following the example of Lord Buddha and the great bodhisattvas.[7] We can join their campaign to work with sentient beings properly, fully, and thoroughly—without grasping, without confusion, and without aggression. Such a campaign is a natural development of the practice of meditation because meditation brings a growing sense of egolessness.

Wise altruistic conduct is also taught to be flexible, and the texts give examples of occasions when great practitioners performed what appeared to be nonvirtuous actions that in fact were beneficial. However, the danger of

Buddhism's flexible code of conduct is that practitioners and teachers will act in ways that cause harm, claiming (or having others claim for them) that their conduct is beyond reproach because of their pure altruistic motivation, and their possession of wisdom greater than that of their critics. This danger, warned of by the ancient texts, plays out in modern Buddhist communities as well, sometimes with well-publicized, dramatically unfortunate results. Since all Buddhists—teachers and students alike—are human beings, it is impossible that this danger will ever vanish. However, when teachers, practitioners, and communities are open, honest, and encourage dialogue about conduct, the danger can be minimized. Wisdom and ethical conduct flourish in the light of inquiry, not in the darkness of secrecy or silence.

Wisdom Is Cultivated on a Gradual Path of Meditation with the Guidance of Qualified Teachers

Although wisdom is innate, if it is to manifest, it must be cultivated with the guidance of qualified teachers. Tilopa, who realized the nature of his mind by meditating while working at pounding sesame seeds, sang:

> An ignorant person may know that oil exists in a sesame seed,
> But does not know the methods for extracting its essence.
> Like that, original wisdom is innate within the hearts of all
>   beings,
> But if a guru does not demonstrate the methods for realizing
>   it, it remains hidden. (Lodrö Tayé et al.)

One cannot gain wisdom just from reading books or watching videos; rather, wisdom is born from the living relationship between student and teacher. Over time and by way of close, sustained interaction, student and teacher become familiar with each other in a deeper and more intimate way. Mutual trust and openness grow. The teacher becomes subtly able to assess what instructions and methods (both conventional and unconventional!) the student needs, and the student becomes more adept at putting those into practice. Through trial and error the student's own wisdom grows, and as this happens, in mind and heart the student feels more and more connected with the teacher's own wisdom.

The texts describe three steps in this process of cultivating wisdom: listening, reflecting, and meditating. *Listening* refers both to studying the teachings on how to cultivate wisdom, and listening to a living teacher. The students *reflect* on what they have heard, asking questions of their guides, and exploring together with them the terrain of their own personal wisdom journey. The purpose of this second step is to uncover doubts, questions, and uncertainties in order to come to one's own personal understanding. If this is not done, forcing oneself to meditate according to instructions one does not accept as personally true does not produce wisdom, but rather frustration, denial, and dissociation from one's authentic inner wisdom voice.

The third step is to gain *meditative* experience of what one has heard and reflected upon. There are two phases of meditation: "calm-abiding" (*sha-matha* in Sanskrit) and "superior insight" (*vipashyana*). At first these phases are practiced sequentially; then gradually one is able to combine them. The purpose of calm-abiding is to help calm whatever busyness, tension, and anxiety exist in the mind, so that mind can abide in meditative concentration without distraction. Of the many methods of calm-abiding meditation, the most widely practiced is placing one's attention on one's breath. In the stage of superior insight, one looks with one's "eye of wisdom" directly at the true nature of reality, and thereby actualizes self-aware wisdom itself, inexpressible and inconceivable. The Tibetan master Rangjung Dorje (thirteenth-fourteenth c. CE) describes this experience in the following way:

> Looking again and again at mind that cannot be looked at,
> Unseeable reality is seen vividly, just as it is. (Dorje)

One can practice meditation anywhere from ten minutes a day to spending weeks, months, and even years in formal meditation retreat. It is highly beneficial to periodically practice meditation in retreat, even if only for a few days at a time. The masters teach, however, that it is important to view one's whole life as an opportunity to meditate. As Milarepa sang:

> Going, wandering, sleeping, resting—I look at mind
> This is virtuous practice without sessions or breaks! (He-ru-ka,
>   1488)

Thus, an essential component of meditation is that one be able to integrate it into the rest of one's life; otherwise, it becomes just one more thing one *does* rather than part of the fabric of how one *lives*. In this regard, Tilopa is a good example for the modern practitioner—Tilopa meditated for twelve years in solitary retreat but did not gain final realization; it was only when he moved to a village, got an ordinary job, and began meditating while working that his spiritual practice yielded its ultimate fruit of his being able to recognize the nature of his mind.

Concerning one's teachers (and it is perfectly acceptable to have one or more than one), they should be *qualified*. Students are exhorted to examine teachers carefully to make sure they have the necessary ability and experience to be their guide. And students seek *guidance* from their teachers on this path, not commands. To blindly obey a teacher is dangerous and contradictory to the wisdom path. For it is logical that one only grows in wisdom by keeping one's critical faculties switched on, and by learning to question, investigate, and explore ever more subtly and precisely, even (and perhaps especially) with regard to those persons whom one trusts as one's guides along the way.

Buddhist Wisdom—An Evolutionary Process

From the inception of Buddhism itself, Buddhist wisdom has been an evolutionary phenomenon. The Buddha often taught by way of dialogue with his students, with the content of their questions shaping the style and substance of his answers. Later, in the centuries following the Buddha's death, many new volumes of his teachings on wisdom appeared. This sparked great debates in India about whether these teachings were actually the Buddha's words. To this day, some systems of Buddhist practice are founded on the belief that they were so, while others disagree. And when both the original and later teachings made their way from India to other countries, the way they were taught, studied, and practiced changed along with their location. Now, Western thought, psychology, and systems of politics, law, economics, sciences, religion, arts, and ethics are all interacting with and shaping a view and practice of Buddhism very different from the ones that existed in Buddhism's mother countries, which themselves had evolved over time!

This chapter has explored aspects of Buddhism's wisdom tradition, its profound strengths and also its potential pitfalls. Perhaps this tradition's greatest strength, however, lies in its ability to self-reflect, and as a result, to adapt, grow, and evolve. For travelers on the wisdom journey who are open to such self-reflection, even missteps lead to the desired destination. As Khenpo Tsültrim Gyamtso (1997–2008) sings:

> Making mistake after mistake, I walk on the authentic path,
> Forgetting and forgetting, I rely on unforgetting mindfulness,
> Experiencing confusion after confusion, I search for the
>   unconfused true nature.

Endnotes

All translations from Tibetan are my own.

1. Maitreya is traditionally known as the "Buddha's regent," and the texts name him as the buddha of the next eon.

2. Singing *doha* (Sanskrit for "songs of realization") is a traditional Buddhist teaching device and meditation practice. For further explanation, see Gyamtso, 2010, 71–76.

3. Many of these benefits have been verified by contemporary research. See Hoffman, S. G., Sawyer, A. T., Witt, A. A. & Oh, D., "The effect of mindfulness-based therapy on anxiety and depression: A meta-analytic review," *Journal of Consulting Clinical Psychology* 78, no. 2 (2010): 169–183. doi: 10.1037/a0018555; Shapiro, S. & Carlson, L., *The art and science of mindfulness* (Washington, DC: American Psychological Association Press, 2009); and Walsh, R. & Shapiro, S., "The meeting of meditative disciplines and Western psychology: A mutually enriching dialogue," *American Psychologist* 61 (2006): 227–239.

4. The five root "disturbing emotions" or "mental afflictions" (Sanskrit: *kleshas*) are: desire, anger, jealousy, pride, and stupidity.

5. For an in-depth presentation of the stages of meditating on emptiness, see Gyamtso, 2010, 21–67.

6. A yogini is a female yogi.

7. Literally translated, *bodhisattva* means "Courageous Ones of Enlightenment," and refers to Buddhist practitioners who have vowed to help all beings reach enlightenment. Bodhisattvas are taught to be courageous because they are willing to go to great lengths to help those in need.

References

Batchelor, S. (2010). *Confession of a Buddhist atheist*. New York: Spiegel & Grau.

Chandrakirti. *Dbu ma la 'jug pa* [Entering the middle way]. Retrieved from: http://www.aciparchive.org/ace/#lyt%28vol%29col%28tendg%29title%282791%29sq%28dbu%20ma%20la%20%27jug%20pa%29hit%28first%29pg%28401%29.

Dalai Lama, The Fourteenth (*Bstan-'dzin-rgya-mtsho*). (1984). *Kindness, clarity, and insight* (J. Hopkins, Trans.). Ithaca: Snow Lion Publications.

Darpo, Y. (1994). *Rgod tshang pa mgon po rdo rje'i rnam thar* [The life story of Gotsangpa]. Xining: Mtsho sngon mi rigs dpe skrun khang.

Dorje, R. *Nges don phyag rgya chen po'i smon lam* [Aspiration Prayer for Mahamudra, the Definitive Meaning]. Retrieved from: http://www.dharmadownload.net/pages/english/Texts/texts_0054.html.

Wangchuk Dorje. *Lhan cig skyes sbyor gyi zab khrid nges don rgya mtsho'i snying po phrin las 'od 'phro* [The profound instructions on connate union: The radiant activity at the heart of an ocean of definitive meaning]. Retrieved from: http://www.dharmadownload.net/pages/english/Texts/texts_0051.htm.

Gampopa. *Dam chos yid bzhin gyi nor bu thar pa rin po che'i rgyan* [A wish-fulfilling jewel of genuine dharma: The ornament of precious liberation]. Retrieved from: http://www.dharmadownload.net/pages/english/Texts/texts_0028.htm.

Gyamtso, Khenpo Tsültrim. (1997). *Blo rtags kyi rnam gzhag rigs gzhung rgya mtsho'i snying po* [Presentation of the classifications of mind and logic: The essence of the ocean of texts on logic]. New York: Nitartha International.

―――. (1997–2008). Unpublished poems. In possession of Ari Goldfield.

―――. (2003). The sun of wisdom: Teachings on the noble Nagarjuna's fundamental wisdom of the middle way. (Ari Goldfield, Trans.). Boston: Shambhala Publications.

Hevajra Tantra. Retrieved from: http://tbrc.org/link/?RID=O1PD92753|O1PD927 531PD92757$W20866#library_work_Object-O1PD92753|O1PD927531PD9 2757$W20866.

He-ru-ka, T. (1488). *Rnal 'byor gyi dbang phyug chen po mi la ras pa'i rnam mgur* [The life and songs of Milarepa, the great lord of yogis]. Retrieved from: http://www.tibet.dk/pktc/tibdtexts.php.

Kalu Rinpoche. (ca.1980). Unpublished poem. In possession of Susan Skolnick.

Karpo, P. *Rnal 'byor bzhi'i bshad pa don dam mdzub tshugs* [An explanation of the four yogas called: Pointing out genuine reality]. Retrieved from: http://dharmadownload.net/pages/english/Sungbum/004_Padma%20Karpo/004_Padma%20 Karpo%20Sungbum%20pages/padma%20karpo_21_zha.htm.

Kornfield, J. (1993). *A path with heart: A guide through the perils and promises of spiritual life.* New York: Bantam Books.

Lodrö Tayé, J. *Shes bya kun khyab mdzod* [The treasury of knowledge]. Retrieved from: http://www.tibet.dk/pktc/tibdtextsandrefs.htm#Shesbyadzod.

―――, et al. *Bka' rgyud mgur mtsho* [An Ocean of Songs of Realization of the Kagyu Lineage]. Retrieved from: http://www.dharmadownload.net/pages/english/Texts/texts_0056.htm.

Maitreya. *Theg pa chen po rgyud bla ma* [The treatise on the buddha nature]. Retrieved from: http://www.dharmadownload.net/pages/english/Texts/texts_0015.htm.

Nagarjuna. *Dbu ma rtsa ba shes rab* [The fundamental wisdom of the middle way]. Retrieved from: http://www.aciparchive.org/ace/#lyt%28vol%29col%28tendg %29title%282752%29sq%28dbu%20ma%29hit%28first%29.

―――. *Rigs pa drug cu pa* [Sixty stanzas of reasonings]. Retrieved from: http://www.aciparchive.org/ace/#lyt%28vol%29col%28tendg%29title%282753%29sq %28rigs%20pa%20drug%29hit%28first%29.

Prajna-paramita-sutra [The Buddha's sutra called: "Transcendent wisdom"]. Tibetan Volume VI.

Preece, R. (2006). *The wisdom of imperfection: The challenge of individuation in Buddhist life.* Ithaca: Snow Lion Publications.

Samadhi-raja-sutra [The Buddha's sutra called: "The king of meditative states"].

Shantideva. *Byang chub sems pa'i spyod pa la 'jug pa* [Entering the bodhisattva's way]. Retrieved from: http://asianclassics.org/release6/flat/TD3871M_T.TXT.

Suzuki, S. (1973). *Zen mind, beginner's mind* (pp. 17–18). New York: Weatherhill Press.

Thogme, N. *Rgyal sras lag len sum cu so bdun ma* [The thirty-seven practices of a bodhisattva]. Retrieved from: http://www.dharmadownload.net/pages/english/ Natsok/0012_Tibetan_German/Tibetan_German_0003.htm.

Trungpa, Chögyam. (1973/2008). *Cutting through spiritual materialism. Shambhala Library Edition.* Boston: Shambhala Publications.

———. (1984). *Shambhala: The sacred path of the warrior.* Boston: Shambhala Publications.

———. (1991). *The heart of the Buddha.* Boston: Shambhala Publications.

Welwood, J. (2002). *Toward a psychology of awakening: Buddhism, psychotherapy, and the path of personal and spiritual transformation.* Boston: Shambhala Publications.

Bibliography

Chödrön, Pema. (2001). *The places that scare you: A guide to fearlessness in difficult times.* Boston: Shambhala Publications. Powerful, practical explanations of how to transform difficult emotional patterns and develop self-confidence, love, and inner peace by one of Buddhism's great Western teachers.

Dalai Lama, The Fourteenth (*Bstan-'dzin-rgya-mtsho*). (2005). *The universe in a single atom: The convergence of science and spirituality.* New York: Morgan Road Books. The Dalai Lama sees scientific and Buddhist inquiry and analysis as complementary rather than competitive. In this insightful volume, he explores what science and spirituality can learn from each other, and how they can be brought together for the benefit of the world.

Rahula, W. (1974). *What the Buddha taught, revised and expanded edition.* New York: Grove Press. A classic introduction to the core teachings of Buddhism, as conveyed in the words of the Buddha's first teachings.

Sogyal Rinpoche. (1992). *The Tibetan book of living and dying.* San Francisco: Harper Collins. A wonderful guide to integrating meditation into life and its transitions, including the ultimate transition of the dying process.

Trungpa, Chögyam (1976). *The Myth of Freedom and the Way of Meditation.* Boston, Shambhala Publications. In one volume, this brilliant master presents the essential teachings on the stages of Tibetan Buddhist view and meditation in modern and accessible language and style.

7

Wisdom and the Dao

LIVIA KOHN

Wisdom arises from original nonbeing,
Brightly it illuminates the ten directions.
Combined in the void, formed in the mysterious empyrean—
It pours from the various heavens as flowing fragrance.
Its wonders are beyond belief,
Its empty impulse truly beyond the real.
It is right there, yet it is not—
It is not there, yet nothing is without it.

—Chant at Daoist ordination from *Guanshen dajie,* fifth c.

Introduction

The Daoist tradition evolved over two and a half millennia. It understands wisdom as the proper apperception of Dao and the recognition of how to realize it in everyday life. Its vision of wisdom is highly practical—how to perceive reality in the best possible way and how to apply this perception in the world to the benefit of all. It comes with a number of practices, the most elementary of which are physical and ethical in nature. First, one learns how to perceive one's body as a continuous energetic flow. Then one works with society, nature, and the cosmos in terms of energetic exchange. To do so most efficiently, one observes a series of precepts that prevent one from committing serious infractions on the cosmic order.

The underlying worldview is a mixture of rational, prerational, and transrational modes of cognition. It centers on Dao, which is best described as organic order in the sense that it is not willful, not a conscious, active creator

Def. of Tao

or personal entity but an organic process that just moves along. Beyond this, Dao is also order—clearly manifest in the rhythmic changes and patterned processes of the natural world. As such it is predictable in its developments and can be discerned and described (Schwartz, 1985, p. 179). Its patterns are what the Chinese call "self-so" or "nature" (*ziran*), the spontaneous and observable way things are naturally. Yet, while Dao is nature, it is also more than nature—its deepest essence, the inner quality that makes things what they are. It is governed by laws of nature, yet it is also these laws itself.

In other words, it is possible to explain the nature of Dao in terms of a twofold structure. The "Dao that can be told" and the "eternal Dao," already contrasted in the first chapter of the *Daode jing* (Book of Dao and Its Virtue), the oldest Daoist text ascribed to the philosopher Laozi and dating back to about 400 BCE. The eternal Dao, then, is the mysterious, ineffable Dao at the center of the cosmos—a force entirely beyond ordinary thought and human reasoning. The peripheral Dao, on the other hand, is the visible and tangible force that manifests in the natural cycles of the world, which are seen both rationally in terms of natural cycles such as night and day, winter and summer, but also prerationally in terms of numerous divine entities such as gods, ghosts, and ancestors as well as in terms of patterns of energetic impulse and response made accessible through the so-called pseudo-sciences of fortune-telling, astrology, physiognomy, and the like (Kohn, 2001; Schipper, 1985).

The text describes the eternal Dao as invisible, inaudible, and subtle. It is "infinite and boundless," "vague and obscure"; it cannot be named, precedes and transcends all existence (ch. 14), and is beyond ordinary perception. Neither senses nor intellect can reach it, and the only way to realize it is by letting ordinary human faculties go, by cultivating intuition and spiritual levels of wisdom, by becoming subtler and finer and more potent, more like Dao itself.

Dao at the periphery, on the other hand, is manifest and clearly visible. It is characterized as the give and take of yin and yang, apparent in multiple pairs of complementary opposites. It is the natural ebb and flow of things as they rise and fall, come and go, grow and decline, emerge and die. It is the nature of life to be in constant motion. Things always move in one direction or the other: up or down, toward lightness or heaviness, brightness or darkness. Nature is a continuous flow of becoming that can be perceived with the senses, analyzed and classified with the intellect, and adapted to in body, mind, and behavior. Wisdom here can still be intuitive, but it also means the exact knowledge, the proper understanding, the intentional adaptation of Dao as manifest nature.

There is no radical break between the two levels of Dao: both function in perfect harmony and are fundamentally good. Wisdom means to realize this inherent cosmic goodness in everything that is and activate it in personal practice. The goodness of Dao in essence goes beyond all human guidelines because it is cosmic and natural, and both cosmos and nature are cruel and unjust at times: they do not have a set of values that can be defined or to which they can be (Kohn, 2004; 2010).

At the same time, human beings can intuit the goodness of Dao as a sense of well-being and inner harmony which, using their limited sensory and intellectual faculties, appears in behavioral and conceptual guidelines on the peripheral level. Social structures and moral rules thus form part of the cosmic harmony that Daoists embody, and their being in the world increases the quality of life around them. Nevertheless, Daoists who have realized the wisdom of the eternal Dao are not per se moral or accountable to social standards. Rather, they are transmoral or supramoral, postconventional in that they go beyond the demands of human society in a spontaneous sense of cosmic oneness.

The main force connecting the two layers, moreover, is a vital energy known as *qi*. *Qi* is the concrete aspect of Dao, the material energy of the universe, the basic stuff of nature.

Originally associated with concrete phenomena such as mist, fog, and moving clouds, *qi* also denotes anything perceptible but intangible: atmosphere, smoke, aroma, vapor, a sense of intuition, foreboding, or even ghosts. There is only one *qi,* just as there is only one Dao. But it, too, appears on different levels of subtlety and in different modes. At the center, there is primordial *qi,* also called prenatal, true, or perfect *qi*; at the periphery, there is earthly *qi,* sometimes described as postnatal *qi*. Both are classified according to categories such as temperature, density, speed of flow, and impact on human life (Kohn, 2005; 2008a). *Qi* is the basic material of all that exists. It animates life and makes events unfold. Human life is the accumulation of *qi*; death is its dispersal. After receiving a core potential of primordial *qi* at birth, people throughout life need to sustain it. They do so by drawing postnatal *qi* into the body from air and food, as well as from other people through sexual, emotional, and social interaction. But they also lose *qi* through breathing bad air, overburdening their bodies with food and drink, and getting involved in negative emotions and excessive sexual or social interactions. Learning how to manage *qi,* then, is the main way of reconnecting to the inherent wisdom of Dao at the peripheral level; refining *qi* to pure spiritual potency is the essential way of realizing wisdom in conjunction with the eternal power of creation, of achieving a mystical union with Dao.

Historically, the Daoist tradition unfolded in three major stages: the teachings of the ancient philosophers Laozi and Zhuangzi from the fourth to second century BCE; the rise of various religious organizations with a new, complex cosmology of immortality and more concrete *qi* practices in the early middle ages (second–sixth c. CE); and the heyday of Daoist culture under the Tang dynasty (618–907), when the religion formalized the adoption and integration of large sections of Buddhist worldview and practice. Its modern form, which has evolved in multiple schools and numerous different trends since the tenth century, combines these three fundamental aspects of philosophy, immortality, and Buddhism in a variety of new ways, providing multiple roads of accessing wisdom and allowing individuals to realize Dao in their particular way (Kohn, 2008a).

The Philosophy of Wisdom

In their presentation of Daoist wisdom, the ancient philosophers emphasize the importance of overcoming limited human perception in favor of mystical oneness with Dao. Both the *Daode jing* and the *Zhuangzi* see human consciousness as a deviation from, or loss of, Dao and find that cultural attainments and dualistic thinking—dividing the world according to right and wrong, good and evil, big and small, etc.—cripple people's instinctive nature: not only their eyes and ears but also their spontaneous inner goodness.

At birth, people are at one with Dao: they naturally know how to be truly and wholly in the world. As these things are lost, formal moral codes and social rules, documented especially in the so-called Confucian virtues, rise to the fore. The conscious discrimination of dualistic categories such as right and wrong replaces the original wisdom of spontaneous intuition. As a result, human beings impose their conceptions and wills on nature instead of following it along. All official rules and personal guidelines to correct behavior can do little to patch up the deficiency. Instead of the organic order of Dao, disorder and confusion prevail in the world. As the *Daode jing* describes it, when the great Dao declined,

> There were benevolence and righteousness.
> Knowledge and wisdom appeared,
> There was great hypocrisy. (ch. 18) (Bynner, 1944, p. 46)

The *Zhuangzi* concurs with this and outlines four stages that saw the development of culture and the establishment of classificatory consciousness. It says:

People of old had perfect knowledge. How was it "perfect"? They thought in a way that matched the stage before things existed. Their knowledge was perfect and exhaustive; nothing could possibly be added to it. Next, they saw things as existing, yet they did not yet make any distinctions among them.

Then a stage came when people made distinctions among things, but they had as yet no sense of right and wrong. When right and wrong began to appear in people's minds, the Tao was destroyed. The destruction of the Tao, then, meant the beginning of personal preference and one-sided love. (ch. 2) (Watson, 1968, p. 41)

"Knowledge" (*zhī*) usually refers to intellectual and sensory apperception, the dualistic division of the world into various categories. Wisdom, in contrast, is its more intuitive, spiritual dimension, expressed in its cognate *zhi,* written with the same character plus the word for "sun" or "illumination." The two Chinese words have the same pronunciation but with different tones. Perfect knowledge, then, is wisdom. It means perfecting perception back to the spontaneous intuition we are born with, a way of relating to life and world in a nondual, nondiscriminating manner. To express this release of dualistic classifications and conscious discrimination, the texts use the negative: non-knowledge (*wuzhi*), also rendered "unknowing." It indicates a way of perceiving and relating to things immediately as they are, matching Dao in harmony and oneness.

Letting Go

To achieve such wisdom, the individual has to let go of conscious learning and give up all attempts at contrived knowing or "sageliness," instead recovering the lost state of spontaneous apperception and return to original simplicity. The *Daode jing,* accordingly, advises people to lead a simple life on the outside and develop a pure mind within. It is especially incumbent upon those in authority to recover the purity of Dao. Only the ruler's virtue can lead the country as a whole to a full recovery of cosmic harmony.

Give up learning and be free from fear,
Give up sageliness and discard knowledge—
The people will profit a hundredfold.
Give up benevolence and discard righteousness—
The people will recover filial piety and love.
Give up skill and discard profit—

There will be no more thieves or robbers.
These four are mere ornament and not enough.
Therefore make the people hold on to these principles:
Manifest plainness and embrace simplicity,
Reduce selfishness and have few desires. (ch. 19) (Addiss &
    Lombardo, 1993; Schwartz, 1985)

But how to go about attaining these inner states of immediacy and simplicity? For this, the most accessible aspects of Dao are used as bridges: the cosmic energy of *qi,* present in all that lives, and the One, the state of primordial unity within. Thus, the *Daode jing* advises to "concentrate energy" and "embrace the One," to become like an infant, develop pure insight, and attain a state of nonaction (*wuwei*) (ch. 10). Another instance, where the negative is used to express a release from ordinary consciousness and modes of living, "nonaction" essentially means to get out so Dao can flow freely through oneself into the world—i.e., developing an attitude not unlike the Christian "Let go and let God." By extension, as spelled out in the texts, nonaction means to sense the movements of cosmic *qi* intuitively, never imposing individual, personal preferences on the flow of nature. One may act in the world, but should not do so willfully or being driven by egotistic purpose. Instead, one should recognize the signs of the cosmos and act along with all in perfect harmony. This is the wisdom of Dao: it brings personal contentment, social stability, and cosmic peace.

The *Zhuangzi,* too, supports this quest for simplicity and immediacy of perception and offers two passages that provide a glimpse of spiritual practices and stages of attainment. First, it describes a practice call "mind fasting," placing instructions in the mouth of Confucius:

Unify your will and don't listen with your ears but listen with your mind. No, don't listen with your mind, but listen with your *qi.* Listening stops with the ears, the mind stops with matching [perception], but *qi* is empty and waits on all things. Dao gathers in emptiness alone. Emptiness is the fasting of the mind. (ch. 6) (Mair, 1994, p. 32)

To reach the inner emptiness of Dao, one thus begins with an act of will, turns one's attention inward, and withdraws the senses, using instead the mind, the flow of consciousness, to relate to things. Then one gives that up, too, and moves on to working with pure *qi,* practicing a contentless, nonconceptual meditation that allows both senses and conscious mind to dissolve in favor of intuitive awareness: the senses being understood as the root of the emotions or "passions and desires," while the conscious mind is seen as the agency that creates mental classifications such as "right and wrong." The state to be achieved is one of "emptiness," characterized by the absence of conscious evaluation and a freedom from strong emotions yet full of openness to Dao. The texts again use the negative to express this, speaking of "no-mind" (*wuxin*), indicating that one lets go of the classifications and directionalized thinking that make up ordinary waking consciousness.

Wisdom is thus achieved through the dissolution and letting go of knowledge: it is the expression of the purified mind of *qi*, which goes along with all. The *Zhuangzi* calls the mind that works in wisdom "Heaven's storehouse—one fills it, yet it is never full; one drains it, yet it is never empty" (ch. 2). Like the ocean, like Dao, like pure spirit, this mind is beyond time and space, it is called "one-with-Heaven" and the "seat of the spirit" (ch. 15).

Oblivion and No-Mind

The other passage in the *Zhuangzi* that describes the movement away from ordinary and toward perfect awareness speaks about "sitting in oblivion" (*zuowang*) (Kohn, 2010). The classical passage is part of a dialogue of Confucius and his disciple Yan Hui. Yan Hui reports that he is "getting better" at attaining Dao. When Confucius asks what he means, Yan Hui says he has "become oblivious of benevolence and righteousness," two essential Confucian virtues that represent a step away from Dao. Confucius tells him that this is good, but that he has not gone far enough. At their next meeting Yan Hui says he has left behind "rites and music," taking aim at the fundamental Confucian ways of formally relating to the world. When Confucius tells Yan Hui that he still has a ways to go, he leaves, then reports again:

"I am getting there!"

"How so?"

"I can sit in oblivion!"

Confucius was startled: "What do you mean, 'sit in oblivion'?"

"I let my limbs and physical structure fall away, do away with perception and intellect, separate myself from body-form and let go of all knowledge, thus joining Great Pervasion. This is what

I mean by 'sitting in oblivion.'" (Watson, 1968, p. 90; Graham, 1981, p. 92; Mair, 1994, p. 64)

This "oblivion," then is an advanced state of meditative absorption, achieved after more common features of worldly connection, social rules, and formal virtues are eliminated. Also explained with the phrase "making one's body like dried wood and one's mind like dead ashes" (chs. 2, 22), it means that one has let go of emotions and desires and cut off ordinary sense perception. Completely free from dualistic thinking or bodily self-consciousness, oblivion represents a state where there are no boundaries between things and where the person as person has lost himself (Santee, 2008, p. 116).

The two passages on "mind-fasting" and "oblivion" are the only passages in the *Zhuangzi* that indicate concrete practices. Nothing further is known about practitioners' discipline—ethical, social, physical—in early Daoism. However, the *Zhuangzi* offers a vivid parable about what wisdom means at the time. In the parable "Knowledge Wandered North" (ch. 22), a figure called "Knowledge" goes wandering in the far north, the direction where the sun is hidden before it rises in the east, in Chinese cosmology associated with water, winter, and deep darkness, and the place of true wisdom. In this barren void, Knowledge meets a figure called No-Action No-Speech whom he asks about the best way to understand Dao, the most efficient adjustments of lifestyle, and the optimal methods of attainment. "No-Action No-Speech made no answer. It was not that he made no answer, he did not know *how* to answer."

Not deterred by this failure, Knowledge continues his quest, moving slightly farther south, "where he climbed to the top of Lonely Pass. There he saw Crazy Crooked and asked him the same questions." Crazy Crooked assures him that he knows, but "just as he wanted to speak he had already forgotten what he wanted to say." From here Knowledge continues, again moving farther south and thus closer to civilization. He manages to get an audience with the Yellow Emperor who explains to him that he should "let go of all thinking and be free from conscious organization; to let go of all life-style concerns and be free from any sense of practice; and release all prerequisites and be free from any systematic path." He also makes it clear that only No-Action No-Speech is really close to Dao and that even Crazy Crooked who is far advanced in oblivion still has not quite attained it yet (Kohn, 2011, p. 105). All words, all concepts, all methods only indicate the direction, just as the saying notes: the finger pointing at the moon is not the moon.

What, then, happens when people reach oblivion, find a state of "no-action no-speech" no-mind? They attain a level of inner truth and authentic wholeness, which the classics describe in the concepts of essential nature (*xing*) and destiny (*ming*). The two terms indicate the particular inborn characteristics of beings—their genetic makeup—and the position they are born in—their social circumstances and opportunities. Everyone at birth receives a particular share or "allotment" of Dao that determines his or her station in life and developmental potential: this is original destiny, the command every one gets from the universe to come to life in this particular shape and situation. Birth occurs when the various cosmic potencies take physical shape, when they receive ordered structure or principle. This, then, determines the particular essential nature, the unique character and abilities of beings, the patterns they use to make their life in the world (Brokaw, 1991, pp. 25–30). The goal of mind-fasting and oblivion, the overcoming of knowledge in favor of no mind and nonaction, the ideal of wisdom, then, is to find this true pattern, one's perfect authenticity, what Western books call the "higher self." By realizing essential nature, people recover the connection to the inherent power or virtue (*de*) of Dao and reach back to original oneness. They thus attain a state of cosmic harmony within that allows them to fully realize destiny and merge with the great flow of Dao, that is, "join the Great Pervasion" of all.

Social Activation

The ideal person who reaches this state is called the sage in the *Daode jing*. A text addressed to the various local lords of a war-torn country, it gives advice to the ruler and defines the sage as one who stands at the apex of human society and mediates between Heaven and Earth, a sacred shaman-king. The sage has fully realized Dao: his mind is beyond time and space, free and open like Heaven and Earth. He is impartial and aloof, fully attuned to the flow of nature. Because of his eminent position in society, moreover, he is a channel of cosmic *qi*: his very being shares Dao. Thus, he inevitably imparts purity and harmony to others and wherever he goes, all around him partakes of cosmic oneness. As the *Daode jing* says:

> Heaven is eternal and Earth everlasting.
> Heaven and Earth can be eternal and everlasting,
> Because they do not exist for themselves.
> Thus they can exist forever.
> Therefore the sage places himself in the background,
> But finds himself in the foreground.
> He puts himself outside,
> And yet he always remains. (ch. 7) (Chan, 1963, pp. 142–143)

More than just an authentic person in and for himself, the sage is a catalyst of goodness in the society around him. He filters the benevolent and creative powers of Dao into the world and by his very being makes the world a better place, one where Dao is heard more fully and serves universal goodness. The sage intuits the subtle energetic patterns of the world and always channels the essence of Dao, which means peace and stability. Far from being a world-denying hermit, nor yet consciously striving to improve or "save" the world, he has a great deal of social responsibility, connecting to Dao not merely for himself but for everyone and giving maximum help and support to all beings, society, and the cosmos (Kohn, 2002).

The *Zhuangzi* sees the ideal human less in social terms and focuses more on the personal characteristics. Rather than sage (*shengren*), it speaks of "perfected" (*zhenren*), a term that consists of the two words "true" and "human" and has been variously rendered "true man," "authentic person," "genuine human being," and "real mensch." It says:

> The perfected of old did not resent being humble, did not take pride in success, and never plotted their affairs. From this basis, they could be without regret if things went wrong, remain free from self-congratulations when they went right.
>
> For this reason, they could climb high places without getting scared, dive into water without getting soaked, and pass through fire without getting hot. Their understanding was such that they could rise up and join Dao at all times.
>
> The perfected of old slept without dreaming and woke without concerns. Their food was plain and their breath deep: in fact, the perfected breathes all the way to the heels while the multitude breathe just to the throat. (ch. 6) (Graham, 1981, p. 84)

Content with whatever is, being fully present in the present moment, such people accept reality as it is: if things go wrong, they deal with it; if things go well, they deal with it. They do not engage in intense emotions, are in fact "without feelings"—calm, balanced, equanimous, at peace. In addition, they don't worry about problems: they pass through potentially dangerous situations unscathed and without getting upset. Their sleep is deep and undisturbed, their breathing full and relaxed. Connected to Dao at all times, they are free from stress, let themselves be as they were meant to be, and allow all others the same freedom.

The society that is created by such people is one of authenticity and simplicity where, as the *Daode jing* says, sophistication, culture, and luxury as well as ritual propriety and formal moral codes are a thing of the past. People once again live in small communities, take care of their simple needs, and stay within familiar boundaries (ch. 80). Each individual having fully found his or her ideal way of being in the world, there is no need for social climbing or competition: Dao provides all beings with just the skills and inherent urges needed to make a complete and fully integrated society.

The *Zhuangzi* expresses the same idea with the concept of "skills" or "knacks," telling stories of various people who naturally master certain things: swimming, carpentry, butchery, archery, and so on, in each case making a perfect contribution to society (ch. 19). The bottom line is that the more one is in tune with one's inner self, the more natural and more fluid are one's actions: "If you join an archery contest and shoot to win a nice brick, you will be skillful. If you shoot for a fancy buckle, you will be nervous. If you shoot for a gold bar, you will be a wreck." Social harmony, then, follows naturally from individual alignment with Dao, from fully living one's truth.

Embodied Wisdom

In the early middle ages, Daoism became an organized religion and developed a different approach to wisdom under the influence of Chinese medicine— treating the body with acupuncture through centers and conduits of *qi*—and the belief in immortals—spirit beings residing in lofty paradises among the stars. In this context, Daoists somatized wisdom, mapping a restructuring of consciousness and refined ways of living in the world along the lines of the systematic refinement of *qi.* They not only taught practitioners to see energy as a key factor in life and world, but also to sense it at a subtle level, to realize its pervasion of all that exists (and thus the ultimate oneness of all), and to manipulate their reality of being *qi*.

chi

Continuing to the present day, Daoist wisdom therefore means to give up seeing self and world in terms of solid, stable, concrete entities and instead perceive cosmic oneness in everything, manifest in different oscillations and frequencies of energetic flow. It means to refine one's senses and the mind to be able to feel and sense energy patterns in oneself, other people, animals, institutions, events, and all material objects and to respond to these energy patterns spontaneously and immediately from a position of pure *qi*. The purer one's own energetic flow, the more one radiates harmony in one's environment and all the way across the planet and into the galaxy. At the same time, the refined Daoist also receives energetic impacts from the cosmos—gods, immortals, stars, ancestors, and all beings on the planet. Wisdom is thus the perception of self and cosmos as flowing energy combined with the awareness of ultimate oneness and the complete interconnection of everything. It also means the refinement of one's own energies to a level of purity, so that the flow is unimpeded and Dao can freely manifest.

To get to this state, Daoists work with *qi* in various ways. Their basic understanding is that the human body consists of two aspects of *qi*: a basic primordial or prenatal *qi* that connects people to the cosmos and determines both their essential nature and destiny; and a secondary, earthly or postnatal *qi* that is replenished by breathing, food, and human interaction, and helps the body survive in everyday life. Both forms of *qi* are necessary and interact constantly with each other, so that primordial *qi* is lost as and when earthly *qi* is insufficient, and earthly *qi* becomes superfluous as and when primordial *qi* is complete—as is the case with the embryo in the womb. People, once born, start an interchange of the two dimensions of *qi* and soon begin to lose their primordial *qi* as they interact with the world through shallow breathing, improper nutrition, emotional outbursts, sensory overloads, and intellectual tensions.

Three Levels

Most people begin their practice at a point when they already have lost a certain amount of primordial *qi* and thus the authenticity of their original, true self. Many times the wake-up call is that they get sick and encounter difficulties in life, suffer an impairment of energetic flow that gradually leads to decline and death. Daoist practice, then, proceeds in three levels: healing, longevity, and immortality, which match what we would call beginning, intermediate, and advanced.

The first level is healing, the replenishing and rebalancing of *qi* with medical means such as acupuncture, massages, food cures, and herbs, combined with an increased awareness of *qi*-patterns and conscious lifestyle choices. This allows practitioners to awaken to the subtleties of *qi* in their bodies and come to see themselves and the world around them as flowing energies. It increases awareness of the interconnectedness of all and the impact one's attitude and actions have on other people and the world. It is wisdom as applied to one's own life and leads to a fundamental feeling of personal well-being.

Having attained good health, Daoists move on to a second level of practice by increasing their primordial *qi* to the amount they had at birth or even above it. To do so, they follow various longevity techniques—dietary control, herbal remedies, sexual hygiene, deep breathing, physical movements, and mental purification—to take charge of their *qi*-exchange with the environment and cultivate themselves (Kohn, 2005, pp. 5–6). Wisdom here is the attainment of a higher level of purity, a refined energetic state. More than just feeling good, one becomes a being of Dao and is subtly aware of the energetic patterns in the environment, adjusting perception, lifestyle, and interactions to the ever-changing flow of *qi*. The practice increases health and vigor, allows people to live to advanced old age, and opens the path toward the full realization of cosmic authenticity.

Beyond that, if Daoists desire to become immortal and attain the heavens of the gods, they continue on to the third level, transforming all their *qi* into primordial *qi* and further refining this *qi* to even greater subtlety. This subtle *qi* eventually turns into pure spirit, with which practitioners increasingly identify to become transcendent spirit-people. The path that leads there involves intensive meditation and trance training as well as more radical forms of diet and other longevity practices.

In contrast to the first two levels of healing and longevity, where the goal is to prolong life and attain perfect harmony with the flow of nature, immortality implies the overcoming of the natural tendencies of the body and its transformation into a different kind of *qi*-constellation. Wisdom in healing and longevity means attaining spontaneous intuition and a sense of flowing along with *qi* in the world through physical, energetic techniques. Wisdom in immortality, on the other hand, is a state beyond perception, a mystical oneness with Dao as creative source, a transcendent mind and cosmic perspective. Practitioners who reach this level bypass death, since they do not identify with the body or worldly self any longer. While still in this world they have supernatural powers, such as telepathy, teleportation, clairvoyance, and so on. When ready to leave, they pass to a different sphere, but this has no impact on their continuation as spirit-persons: it merely means taking up residence in an otherworldly paradise.

Practices

As regards specific practices, the very same techniques appear on all three levels, albeit in different ways and with caution. Certain practices that are useful in healing may be superfluous in the attainment of longevity, while some applicable for immortality may even be harmful when healing is the main focus. Take breathing as an example. When healing or extending life, natural deep breathing is emphasized, with the diaphragm expanding on inhalation. When moving on to immortality, however, reversed breathing is advised, which means that the diaphragm contracts on the in-breath. Undertaking this kind of reversed breathing too early or at the wrong stage can cause complications, from dizziness to disorientation or worse (Kohn, 2008b).

The same also holds true for dietary practices. While certain foods and herbs may be prescribed to heal and balance the body, the best way to stay healthy and extend life is by eating moderately and in natural balance by partaking of all the different food groups and matching foods to the seasons. Thus, one should eat warming foods in winter and cooling foods in summer; prepare foods in accordance with the celestial constellations; observe the various food taboos associated with one's astrological signs; use locally grown and organic ingredients as much as possible; and systematically and in accordance with one's personal constitution supplement regular foodstuffs with herbal and mineral substances.

However, as practitioners become more proficient at controlling their diets, they can gradually wean themselves from ordinary foodstuffs, replacing grains and heavy foods with raw vegetables, fruits, and nuts. They can then increase herbal supplements, liquid nourishment, focused breathing, and concentrated internal guiding of *qi* to the point where they do not need any food to sustain themselves but can live entirely on *qi*. This process of removing ordinary food in favor of breath is called "abstention from grain." An advanced form of fasting, undertaken for weeks or sometimes months, it lightens the body's structure in favor of subtler energies and a finer cosmic awareness, but if done without proper preparation or stopped too abruptly may cause major damage to the physical system (Kohn, 2010). The most potent application of these Daoist methods to practical wisdom is on the level of longevity techniques: they raise the individual's awareness of *qi* in self and world and provide numerous concrete ways of modifying, balancing, and enhancing it. In other words, a Daoist living in wisdom would conceive of his own person, all people, living beings, and even inanimate objects as different aspects of *qi*, being subtly aware of the energetic vacillations and modulations as they occur in the ongoing rhythm of yin and yang, rise and fall, on and off.

Continuously refining her subtle energetic perception and intuition of *qi*, she would find a dwelling that matches the principles of Feng Shui, the art of siting and placement, and arrange all rooms and furniture to provide a maximum smoothness in *qi*-flow: no *shaqi* or "killing" currents (such as open hallways or drain pipes) that make energy rush through and take all good fortune away; nor any *siqi* or "dead energy" (such as clutter or massive furniture), which causes heaviness, darkness, and blockages (Rossbach, 1983). She would live a life of simplicity, letting herself be guided by the currents and patterns of life around her as well as by her own inner truth.

By the same token, a Daoist would match his diet to the seasons and eat a variety of foods but never to satiation, then engage in various energy exercises—slow movements in coordination with mental focus and deep breathing not unlike Indian yoga, traditionally called *daoyin* (lit., "guiding and stretching") and today best known under the name *qigong* (lit., "energy work") (Kohn, 2008b).[1] He would also be part of a Daoist community: worship the deities and honor the scriptures, study more advanced meditation techniques, and engage in social and communal activities, helping the poor and aiding the less fortunate.

There are no solid rules required of all: some Daoists are vegetarians, some eat meat, others live mainly on *qi*; some Daoists are married, some are single, others are celibate; some Daoists are hermits, some live in monasteries, others have families and work in the world; some are artists who live for their own gratification, some are workers in the employ of companies, others are businessmen who run major organizations, charities, and even entire school systems (such as in Hong Kong). The core of Daoist wisdom, in its embodied form as much as in the ancient philosophy, is authenticity and being true to one's Heaven-given nature and destiny. It is made more accessible through the subtle awareness and active modification of *qi,* but the essence of the vision is still the same—and so is the personal and social ideal on the mundane plane, on which the transcendent goal of immortality is superimposed.

The Buddhist Impact

Buddhism entered China in the first century CE and was soon identified vaguely as a strange version of Daoism. It began to exert a strong influence on Chinese religious culture in the fifth century, when a major translation project created a standardized form of Buddhist terminology (Tsukamoto, & Hurvitz, 1985). Ever since, Chinese popular religion and Daoism have been pervaded by Buddhist concepts and practices, most importantly the complex of karma and ethics. This significantly changed the nature of Daoist wisdom, raising it beyond the philosophical and practical to a cosmic and universal level and leading to the way it is still realized today.

The doctrine of karma and rebirth says that people's personality characteristics and life events are the result of earlier deeds in body, speech, and mind and that the chain of cause and effect continues over many lifetimes. The teaching places human beings in a concrete network of social and universal interaction, creating responsibility beyond one's own body and immediate kin and encouraging virtues such as compassion and visions of universal salvation. These are cultivated through years of intense meditation practice. Eventually, karmic patterns dissolve and a new perspective of life and self emerges, a new dimension of wisdom or "insight"—Sanskrit *prajñā,* Chinese *hui.* In China, the doctrine leads both to increased demands for an ethical life and to more systematic forms of meditation practice.

Precepts

In the fifth century, Daoists began to absorb Buddhist doctrine and practice. Following the Buddhist model, they established various sets of precepts, geared to curb sensory impulses and enhance social responsibility. Thus, for example, the sixth-century work *Zhihui dingzhi jing* (Scripture on Setting the Will on Wisdom), a work of the Numinous Treasure school, the first and most active in integrating Buddhist teachings (Zürcher, 1980), lists ten basic precepts. These consist of the five basic Buddhist precepts to abstain from killing, stealing, lying, sexual misconduct, and intoxication, plus five self-admonitions to act in harmony and with compassion. The latter are:

6. I will maintain harmony with my ancestors and family and never disregard my kin.

7. When I see someone do good, I will support him with joy and delight.

8. When I see someone unfortunate, I will support him with dignity to recover good fortune.

9. When someone comes to do me harm, I will not harbor thoughts of revenge.

10. As long as all beings have not attained the Dao, I will not expect to do so myself. (Kohn, 2004, p. 64)

Followers who take these precepts dedicate themselves to supporting living beings in various situations of life and swear the Daoist equivalent of a bodhisattva vow not to attain personal salvation unless and until all living beings do so also. To bring the message of social interconnection home, the precepts are supplemented with a set of fourteen principles of self-control, personal resolutions that guide practitioners to behave graciously and with kindness in various social situations. For example: "When I speak with another's lord, I shall feel gracious toward his country"; "When I speak with another's father, I shall feel kind toward his son"; "When I speak with a stranger, I shall feel protective about his country's borders." The rules teach practitioners to be sympathetic and identify with the plights and loyalties of others in different situations. They create a conscious awareness of the feelings and views of others, encouraging harmonious communities and an altruistic mindset. As practitioners deeply engage in the mental repetition of these resolutions, they increasingly realize the interconnectedness of all life and begin to evolve in wisdom.

Lay practitioners could take these ten precepts in an ordination ceremony, which also involved chanting the "Ode to Wisdom" cited in the beginning, which describes the cosmic origins of this Buddhist dimension of wisdom and its power in the world. The ceremony would bestow the rank of Disciple of Pure Faith upon them, an advanced status that came with a formal transmission of the *Daode jing* and certain related texts. The title is adopted from Buddhism and denotes a fully initiated yet still beginning Daoist who has spent some time as an Officer of Dao but has not yet entered the higher levels of ordination. To take this level of ordination was very common under the Tang, as numerous Dunhuang manuscripts document (Schwartz, 1985; Benn, 2000). Wisdom as the personalized, intuitive understanding of cosmic interconnectedness in this organized religious context is thus systematically nurtured and formally venerated as a goal.

Sensory Control

More advanced practices involved a stronger control over the senses. For example, the *Shangpin dajie* (Great Precepts of the Highest Ranks), another text of the Numinous Treasure school, presents a set of "Six Precepts of Wisdom" as essential blocks against passions induced by the five senses and the mind. For example,

1. Let not your eyes gaze widely or be confused by flowery colors lest you lose their clarity and diminish your pupils, their radiance no longer bright and penetrating.

2. Let not your ears be confused in their hearing or obscured by the five sounds lest you harm spirit and destroy uprightness, hearing bad sounds everywhere.

These precepts caution against overindulgence in the senses, which cause turbidity in the mind and loss of *qi* in the body. They merge Buddhist-inspired practice with the *Daode jing* warning against overloading the senses and the somatic understanding of Daoist practice as the refinement of qi flow. As the practitioner purifies himself internally, he or she becomes independent of impulses and reactions due to sensory stimulation. Then she begins to see self and world from the perspective of Dao and thus awakens to wisdom as a cosmic form of transpersonal cognition. This eventually leads to extreme subtlety of perception, when intuition and energetic awareness are so strong that they supersede sensory knowledge. Advanced Daoists (and modern qigong masters) commonly communicate telepathically, heal at a distance, move to far places in spirit, see into past and future, and so on—demonstrating various extraordinary powers often (erroneously) described as "supernatural."

Classical texts call these powers the "six pervasions," matching the six superior powers of a buddha: universal vision and hearing, knowledge of other minds, seeing former lives, multilocation, and superconsciousness. Daoists describe them as

> pervasive sight, pervasive hearing, pervasion of the void [air, smells], pervasion of emptiness [sound], pervasion of clarity [objects], and pervasion of the subtle [thoughts]. These six pervasions mean that nothing is left unpervaded. Through them the six passions are laid to rest and the inner spirits naturally return. Inner oneness naturally arises, and your vital essence is naturally strong. You reach long life and eventually go beyond death. (Kohn, 2004, p. 35)

In other words, as each sensory organ is transformed and reorganized in the move from passion to compassion and from separation to oneness, ordinary sensory faculties are refined to sublime subtlety and the paths of transrational cognition are opened. The practitioner fully merges with the core flow of Dao at the center of the universe, attaining, for example, the "eyes of Heaven," seeing everything as if from the perspective of Dao itself:

> With the eyes of Heaven one's understanding is lofty and wisdom pervades all without limits. Above and below, in the four corners and eight directions, nothing is not illumined, nothing is not radiantly bright.

The ordinary eyes of the practitioner, by avoiding the intricacies of worldly vision and being shaded against the enticing patterns of outside life, are made susceptible to the subtler and more brilliant vibrations of the light of Heaven. When the inner eye joins with cosmic radiance, their merged vibrations obliterate blockages and expose all to a pervading, penetrating light. "As long as people pattern themselves on Heaven, the bright pupils in the eyes can freely follow the radiance of the five colors." Similarly, all the other senses are transformed from a mundane to a cosmic level, so that the Daoist—as already postulated in the *Zhuangzi*—learns to see, hear, and feel through Dao rather than through the limited agents of the body-mind.

Conclusion

Wisdom in the Daoist tradition means two things. The first is the intuitive connection to an innate authenticity of being. This entails a sense of destiny and immersion in Dao as it animates the world through its material aspect, the universal life force known as *qi*. The second is mystical union with Dao as the creative core power of the universe. This means overcoming the boundaries of the body-mind and refining one's self through meditative absorption and sensory restructuring.

Daoist concepts of wisdom evolved over three historical phases. Ancient philosophers saw wisdom in contrast to knowledge and described it in terms of unknowing, no-mind, and nonaction, a letting go of dualistic classifications and emotional reactions in favor of a flowing along with Dao. Early medieval Daoists saw wisdom as a function of *qi,* achieved through the embodied perception of self, others, and world as energetic flow which allowed the subtle appreciation of deeper patterns of reality and opened the path to higher stages. Under the impact of the Buddhist karma doctrine, moreover, Daoists connected wisdom to ethical rules, interpreting it as a sense of social connectedness and the intricate awareness of how one's own mental states contribute to both one's own fate and the situation of the world. On higher levels, wisdom, moreover, meant the shining forth of universal radiance through the individual body-mind, the transformation of identity and senses toward oneness with Dao, and the attainment of subtle levels of perception. In all cases, the key is the intimate, intuitive, and embodied connection to Dao, the sense of flow and openness to all.

Endnote

1. Created intentionally and by political design as a cheap form of health care for the masses by the Chinese Communist Party in 1947, qigong is a system of slow body movements in coordination with deep breathing and mental guiding of

body energies that releases tension, effects healing, and contributes greatly to overall well-being. Adapting techniques from traditional Daoist and medical practices such as *daoyin,* the CCP yet set out to transform them, cleansing the methods of all ancient cosmology and "superstitions" and making them compatible with modern science. Over the five decades of its existence, Qigong has mutated wildly, serving the changing needs of the world's most populous country.

In the 1950s it was undertaken only in specialized clinics reserved for party cadres; in the 1960s, under the Cultural Revolution, it was outlawed as traditional superstition; in the 1970s, the time of "qigong fever," it became the people's prime choice of leisure and health activity, and numerous new methods, forms, and sequences were created; in the 1980s, it reached its heyday and many people experienced so-called extraordinary powers; in the 1990s, charlatans gave it a bad name and the political aggression of Falun gong caused it to be outlawed; in the 2000s, it has remained illegal and today is not practiced in China except in closely supervised medical clinics, where "meditation" is a dirty word.

Its first inroads in the West occurred in the early 1980s, and Western qigong to the present day continues the healing techniques of the 1970s, often taking recourse to traditional cosmology and meditation. For a thorough outline of the nature and history of qigong, see Wisdom and the Tao (Palmer, 2007).

References

Addiss, S. & Lombardo S. (1993). *Tao Te Ching.* Indianapolis: Hackett Publishing Company.

Benn, C. (2000). "Daoist ordination and *Zhai* rituals." In L. Kohn, (Ed.). *Daoism Handbook.* (309–338). Leiden: E. Brill.

Brokaw, C. (1991). *The ledgers of merit and demerit: Social change and moral order in late imperial China.* Princeton: Princeton University Press.

Bynner, W. (1944). *The way of life according to Lao Tsu.* New York: Perigree.

Chan, W. (1963). *A source book in Chinese philosophy.* Princeton: Princeton University Press.

Graham, A. C. (1981). *Chuang-tzu: The seven inner chapters and other writings from the book of Chuang-tzu.* London: Allan & Unwin.

Kohn, L. (2001). *Daoism and Chinese culture.* Cambridge, Mass.: Three Pines Press.

———. (2002). "The sage in the world, the perfected without feelings: Mysticism and moral reponsibility in Chinese religion." In G.W. Barnard & J. Kripal (Eds.), *Crossing boundaries: Essays on the ethical status of mysticism.* (288–206). New York: Seven Bridges Press.

———. (2004). *Cosmos and community: The ethical dimension of Daoism.* (p. 35). Cambridge, Mass.: Three Pines Press.

———. (2005). *Health and long life: The Chinese way.* Cambridge, Mass.: Three Pines Press.

———. (2008a). *Introducing Daoism.* London: Routledge.

———. (2008b). *Chinese healing exercises: The tradition of Daoyin.* Honolulu: University of Hawai'i Press.

———. (2010). *Sitting in oblivion: The heart of Daoist meditation.* Dunedin, Fla.: Three Pines Press.

———. (2011). *Chuang-tzu: The Tao of perfect happiness.* (Selections Annotated and Explained.) Woodstock, Vt.: Skylight Paths Press.

Mair, V. (1994). *Wandering on the way: Early Taoist tales and parables of Chuang Tzu.* New York: Bantam.

Palmer, D. (2007). *Qigong fever: Body, science and utopia in China.* New York: Columbia University Press.

Rossbach, S. (1983). *Feng Shui: The Chinese art of placement.* New York: Dutton.

Santee, R. (2008). "Stress management and the *Zhuangzi.*" *Journal of Daoist Studies,* 1: 93–123.

Schwartz, B. (1985). *The world of thought in ancient China.* Cambridge, Mass: Harvard University Press.

Schipper, K. (1985). "Taoist ordination ranks in the Tunhuang Manuscripts." In G. Naundorf, K. H. Pohl, & H. H. Schmidt. (Eds.). *Religion und Philosophie in Ostasien: Festschrift für Hans Steininger.* (pp. 127–148). Würzburg: Königshausen and Neumann.

Tsukamoto, Z. & Hurvitz, L. (1985). *A history of early Chinese Buddhism.* (2 vols.) Tokyo: Kodansha.

Watson, B. (1968). *The complete works of Chuang-tzu.* New York: Columbia University Press.

Zürcher, E. (1980). "Buddhist influence on early Taoism." *T'oung Pao, 66*: 84–147.

Bibliography

Dyer, Wayne W. (2007). *Change Your Thoughts—Change Your Life: Living the Wisdom of the Tao.* Carlsbad, Cal.: Hay House. A modern translation and new interpretation of the ancient classic on the basis of year-long personal practice, with subtle insights and guided meditations.

Kohn, Livia, and Michael LaFargue, eds. (1998). *Lao-tzu and the Tao-te-ching.* Albany: State University of New York Press. An edited volume of twelve essays that provide access to the history, legend, exegesis, and modern relevance of the ancient Daoist classic.

Kohn, Livia. (2005). *Health and Long Life: The Chinese Way.* Cambridge, Mass.: Three Pines Press. A comprehensive overview of the theory and methods of Chinese medicine and longevity in relation to Daoist practice and modern physics.

———. (2010). *Sitting in Oblivion: The Heart of Daoist Meditation.* Dunedin, Fla.: Three Pines Press. A comprehensive discussion of oblivion practice through the ages, including translations of major Tang works on Daoist meditation under Buddhist influence.

————. (2011). *Chuang-tzu: The Tao of Perfect Happiness. Selections Annotated and Explained.* Woodstock, Vt.: Skylight Paths Press. A new rendition of selections from the second major Daoist text, arranged by topic and interpreted for contemporary relevance and applicability.

————, ed. (2011). *Living Authentically: Daoist Contributions to Modern Psychology.* Dunedin, Fla.: Three Pines Press. A collection of twelve essays by psychologists and Daoist practitioners on the profound implications of Daoist thought and practice in modern psychology.

Internet Resources

www.daoiststudies.org. Resources on the study and appreciation of Daoism.
www.legacyofdao.org. Making Daoist wisdom available in the contemporary world.
www.jadedragon.com. Connecting ancient thought, holistic health, and martial arts.

8

The Confucian Pursuit of Wisdom

Michael C. Kalton

Introduction

The three religious traditions of East Asia, Confucianism, Daoism, and later Buddhism (imported from India), were referred to in Chinese not as "religions," but as "teachings" or "instructions" (*jiao*). This fits well the topic of this volume, for it indicates that the very nature of the religious enterprise was understood in China as a matter above all of guidance in how to live. Wisdom, in this framework, stands at the very center of religious practice, with the supernatural more or less present depending upon the cultural milieu of the times. As Confucius (551–479 BCE) himself put it in answer a question about how the spirits of the dead and the gods should be served, "You are not able to serve man. How can you serve the spirits?" "May I ask about death?" "You do not understand even life. How can you understand death?"[1]

The this-worldly orientation of Confucian wisdom is often referred to in Western literature as a form of "humanism." This terminology obscures more than it clarifies the nature of Confucian wisdom, for Confucians find a sort of guidance and sacrality in "this" world that our Western religious traditions locate in a transcendent "other" world. If we take wisdom broadly defined as the understanding and practice of the full profundity of what it means to be human, it is important to see from the beginning that Confucians located the profound in the life-giving conduct of government, social, and family relationships as carried on in everyday life.

So much is this the case that the classical Chinese character *lün* commonly translated as "ethics" means literally "relationship," and the character *ren,* which expresses the highest excellence of human spiritual attainment (often translated as "humanity," "benevolence," or simply "the good") is in fact a compound made up of the character for "person" and the character for "two." That is, the epitome of human wisdom and spiritual attainment can be expressed as two people conducting themselves in appropriate relationship to one another.

Mencius (372–289 BCE), the second great Confucian thinker, makes clear this centrality of relationships in a passage that became a major reference for the entire subsequent Confucian tradition:

> Comfortably housed but not properly taught, they become almost like animals. The sage [Shun] worried about this and appointed Xie to be Minister of Instruction, to teach the relations appropriate to human beings: between father and son, there should be affection; between ruler and minister, righteousness; between husband and wife, attention to separate functions; between old and young, proper order; between friends, trustworthiness.[2]

These Five Relationships, as they are called, seem very mundane, deceptively simple and perhaps in some respects time and culture bound in their expression. But for more than two thousand years they have expressed for Confucians the depth and perfection of human conduct. As the essence of what needs to be learned and understood by humans, these Five Relationships have traditionally been inscribed prominently on the walls of the most prestigious centers of learning in East Asia.

Over many centuries, Confucians have elaborated this learning, first with a complex cosmology and later with a metaphysical framework that could support sophisticated inner cultivation techniques. But even fleshed out fully with a vision of the cosmos and a profound analysis of the dynamics of the human psyche, we shall find that Confucian wisdom never leaves this home ground. How to conduct lives of life-giving relationship with our fellow humans, and, I would now add, with the entire community of life, remains the most complex, the most profound challenge of the human mind-and-heart. We shall see that the understanding and personal formation that enables us to meet this challenge is the constant and final measure of Confucian wisdom.

The Nature of Confucian Wisdom

Sagehood

However described, wisdom is on the side of the profound rather than the superficial; it has to do with an understanding and a way of conducting one's life that reaches into the depths. What depths? Superficiality and profundity are not objects or facts one can observe. These terms refer rather to a widely shared understanding that the experience of life is itself dimensional, such that a deeper penetration discloses more than is evident at the surface. In some traditions, this "deeper" may be a perception of a divine or ultimately real within, in comparison with which phenomenal reality seems but a shadowy illusion. In other traditions, one may discover the workings of an awe-inspiring Will and Presence in the unfolding process of life. Confucian profundity assumes a rather different, seemingly more mundane reality. In order to appreciate its depths, we will have to consider the emergence of the Confucian understanding of what it means to be human and of the nature of the encompassing reality within which we find ourselves.

Mencius described wisdom as the fully developed form of our innate sense of right and wrong. This seemingly simple proposition, however, needs considerable unpacking. What do we mean by right and wrong? What kind of faculty is an innate sense of right and wrong? Why does the guidance provided by this sense so often seem to miss the mark, and what can we do to refine it? The answers to these questions will take us into analyzing what it means in the East Asian context to be a sage, for the sage is the embodiment of wisdom.

Both the Daoist and the Confucian traditions share assumptions about the nature of the world to the extent that they describe a sage in a similar fashion: the sage is a person in such discerning contact with every unfolding situation that he or she can respond with spontaneous appropriateness. This general description gives us two closely intertwined facets of wisdom to be investigated. First, there is the question of spontaneity, just doing it right without having to fret and think about it. What kind of metric of sagacity or profundity can that be? And then there is that wonderfully vague but pregnant term, *appropriate*. What is the measure of what fits and what does not fit in a given situation? What might distinguish a profound from a superficial response?

Spontaneity or Self-so and the Mind-and-Heart

The Western world has generally followed an ancient Greek description of our inner life as comprised of three faculties: intellect, feelings, and will. This is congruent with our notions of reason as the ideal guide in the exercise of an autonomous free will as we make critical decisions between good and evil. East Asian thought, in contrast, has followed a paradigm less centered on human agency and more concerned with the fit of our activity with the situation within which it arises. Human beings are viewed as always situated, always engaged in a relational matrix. Hence, our activities are not simply self-originated, but emerge as responses to their situation, and the question of good and evil morphs into a matter of whether and how the response fits the situation. Like an archer aiming at a target, one's response hits the mark or misses, is closer or farther from enhancing the flow of life.

The term *spontaneity* in our description of the sage is a common translation of the Chinese, *zi-ran*, literally "self-so." Confucians shared with the Daoists a sense of a world of all-encompassing, normative, and guiding pattern, namely, *dao*. Sharing in this pattern, living creatures are "self-so" set up to respond appropriately to their situations, much as our hearts and lungs are set up to work together. The spontaneity or self-so appropriateness of sage activity, therefore, belongs to a much broader pattern of the dynamic natural (*zi-ran*) behavior of the world. But why then are we not all sages, spontaneously appropriate in our responses?

We shall find layers in the way the unfolding tradition answered that question. But from the beginning, by framing the question in terms of situated, responsive beings, attention was directed to the feelings that inform and guide any response. In this view, it is a mistake to push distinctions between intellect and feelings very far. The Chinese term for the faculty of our inner life, x*in*—in some contexts translated "heart," in others "mind"—is in fact a holistic notion that assumes a responsive life of intelligent emotions. Therefore, in speaking of cultivation, I prefer to translate x*in* by the hyphenated "mind-and-heart." When the intelligent emotions of this responsive mind-and-heart are so attuned to the world that they longer require the hesitation and indecision marked by thought, they function with self-so appropriateness, the characteristic spontaneity of the sage.

Appropriateness

An appropriate response fits the situation. This sounds straightforward, but a little reflection reveals ample scope for the kind of wisdom we think of as ordinarily acquired only by long experience carefully attended to. In particular, we find what might be termed a wisdom of scale. After all, what is "the situation"? The people and circumstances of immediate concern? The situation as it will unfold over months, years, generations? Do I consider it narrowly, or in terms of family, of community, perhaps in terms of the whole local or global life system? Such questions have no simple or consistent answer, or to put it another way, the answer itself varies with the situation. Appropriate fit demands a lively awareness of dynamic ramifications through a relational web of varying scope. The ability or inability to consider scale and consequences would already suffice to generate a metric running from superficiality to profundity.

And then there is the question of how we recognize fit versus non-fit in the first place, at whatever scale. This asks for a wisdom of ends. Differing traditions suggest overarching goals that variously define the desirable conduct of our situated lives. Love of neighbor, alleviating suffering, finding God's will, profit, social justice—each of these readily brings to mind typically different communities, perhaps different time periods as well.

Confucian wisdom regarding appropriateness has a broad continuity of understanding, but it took on new and deeper framing as Chinese society underwent major changes. The most important for our considerations are the formative period, the Chin-Han unification of the empire, the great Confucian restoration movement in the Song Dynasty.

FORMATIVE PERIOD

Through centuries of increasingly brutal warfare, China's many small feudal states gradually consumed one another until in 221 BCE the final victors established the Chin dynasty, the first unified Chinese empire. This, the formative or classical period of Chinese thought, from Confucius (551–479) through the Warring States Period (475–221), saw the emergence of a variety of teachers and a proliferation of schools of thought. However they diverged, the schools of thought that emerged during this period were deeply imprinted by the overshadowing question of the times: how to mend and unify a fragmented and dissolving society. Unlike myths of a primordial chaos, Chinese thinkers generally assumed an original harmonious unity, a functional wholeness manifested in the familial, social, and political life of a bygone ideal age. The secrets of this unity were purveyed by the early sages, though the voice of their wisdom sounded quite different as refracted through the lenses of competing schools of thought. Mohists taught defensive warfare, universal love, and frugality; Daoists focused on responsiveness to a deep and unified patterning running through everything, Legalists on techniques of totalitarian government control aimed at economic and military might.

For his part, Confucius identified the dissolution of society with the waning of the moral qualities that make possible whole and proper relationships among people. His portrayal of the Sages told of how their wise and benevolent governance inspired life-giving relationships throughout all levels of the community, and explained how they institutionalized this especially in the form of norms of appropriate ritual and propriety, an outward manifestation of the deep reality of our relational existence. The noblesse oblige norms of an interdependent blood-related aristocracy, in the teaching of Confucius, became generalized human norms, and among Confucians the aristocratic term "Superior Man" came to mean not a nobleman but a noble man, that is, anyone cultivated as a worthy and profound human being. He taught the personal qualities and the knowledge of ritual and propriety characteristic of an earlier elite society at its ideal best, as the essential qualification for would-be officeholders. And in a milieu where trustworthy confederates in governing were hard to come by, there was indeed a market for the recipients of this idealistic education.

Confucius saw integral relationships as both the fundamental challenge of governance and the core of what it means to be a fully cultivated human being, and consequently self-cultivation in the Confucian tradition over the centuries always maintained this dual reference. As we pursue at greater length how a deepening analysis of personal inner life was accompanied by enhanced techniques for the personal cultivation of sage wisdom, we should also bear in mind that governance and social institutions cannot be separated from Confucian wisdom.

The teachings of Confucius are preserved as a loose collection of short aphorisms in the *Analects*. The more systematic exposition of his vision came with the second foundational figure of the tradition, Mencius (372–289). In the gritty milieu of the Warring States period, a debate raged regarding human nature, for the times were rife with social upheaval, treachery, and warfare. Looking at the society around them, some philosophers concluded that from birth humans are evil, others that we are a mixture of good and evil.

Mencius defended the unlikely proposition that, in spite of all indications to the contrary, human beings are fundamentally good, that is, life-giving creatures: "Look at that barren mountain outside of town," he said. "Once it was covered with trees and with grass. But people cut the trees and their animals ate the grass. Every night the life-giving force would move producing new sprouts and reviving the plants. But the next day would bring more cutting and more grazing, until finally the life-giving force could not keep up, and the mountain became bare. People think it has always been like that, but that is not so." Mencius then went on to apply this to the human case. "People are like this. Everyday they get bent out of shape and depleted by difficult social interactions. When they sleep at night, the life-giving force restores them, so at early dawn they are almost human again. But the next day brings more bending and depletion, until finally they cannot recover. They may seem evil, but that is not their original nature."[3]

This is a powerful story, in part because each of us can easily recognize ourselves and our children in it. We are not evil. But we do get bent out of shape in the dynamic interplay of distorted relationships. It has also been an exceptionally powerful story historically, for it captured essential elements of a developing worldview and gave them a shape that carried forward mightily for more than two thousand years. Mencius told this story to make a point about human beings, and this eventually became the well-known Confucian doctrine of our good "original nature." But equally important, it tells us what to think about the universe: the universe gives life. Unbalanced activity— overcutting trees, overgrazing grass, overstressed human interactions—can tilt the slope toward irreversible destruction, but that is not the deep way of things. The story thus established an "original nature" for the universe as well as an original nature for humans. In fact, our original nature is what it is only because it continues, in a human manifestation, the original nature of the entire world of nature.

Mencius himself made this connection in a second great story. To elucidate the dispositions in the depth of our mind-and-heart, he told his story of the child about to fall into the well. "Who," he asks, "will not feel alarm and an urge to save a small child about to fall into a well?" This life-giving impulse reveals our deepest nature, even though it can be blocked and distorted in many ways before we act on it. Mencius described this inborn disposition as commiseration, the beginning of humanity (ren), the seed of all proper relations. He then went on to fill out his account of human nature, not only in terms of life-giving commiseration, the beginning of humanity, but in terms of other qualities of great importance to Confucians. We have, he observed, three other deep, inborn dispositions: a sense of modesty and deference, a sense of shame and dislike, and a sense of approving and disapproving. Each of these is the beginning or seed of fundamental human qualities, namely propriety, righteousness, and wisdom.[4]

The account given by Mencius of human nature was not uncontested, even among Confucians, but it became over the centuries the dominant Confucian understanding of the constitution of our innermost life. Note that his description of human nature addresses the question in terms of deep inborn feelings, inclinations, and dispositions. That is, unlike the Western search for essences, the quest for human nature in the Confucian context aims at identifying the source and character of our deepest responsiveness. This assumption is congruent with a pursuit of wisdom in which the focus is on the profundity of deeply cultivated and responsive feelings.

UNIFICATION OF THE EMPIRE

The Confucian tradition has always maintained a strong human and social focus, but events unfolded in a way that also directed reflection to the systemic human-universe connection suggested by Mencius. The short-lived

Chin dynasty (221–206) reunified China and originated the Chinese empire with which we are familiar. Then for four centuries the Han dynasty (206 BCE–220 CE) presided over a great political and cultural civilization that made the Confucian school its sanctioned gateway to government careers and elite status. As the new dynasty attempted to ensure its longevity and prosperity, attention turned to seeking out the correspondences that weave the universe into a multilayered but unified performance. Colors, tastes, seasons, directions, and cosmic agency could be harmonized for both the beauty and the efficacy of ritual and administrative life. And in this milieu, Mencius's account of our four fundamental inborn dispositions likewise took on a cosmic dimension, being associated with the four seasons, the most fundamental of all natural phenomena for an agricultural society.

The gateway for this development was the classic *Book of Changes,* an ancient divination text, that has also long served as a major source of cosmological and metaphysical thinking. Its first hexagram describes Heaven (i.e., Nature) by four characteristics: origination, flourishing, benefiting, and firmness. Taken as a reference to the four seasons, this describes the essential cycle of the force of life and vitality. In spring, the life force begins to move and originate a new cycle of life and growth; in summer, life grows and flourishes; in autumn, there is harvest and all life is benefited and sustained; in winter, crops are stored firmly and securely, and the life force likewise is stored in the frozen earth. To the correspondence-sensitive thinkers of the Han, the unity of the deep vital dynamic of the seasons and of our inner life was self-evident. The originating life-giving dynamic of spring/commiseration/humanity runs thoughout, flourishing beautifully in propriety (summer), benefiting all by harvesting the rightness of life-giving responsiveness (fall), and storing the accumulation as wisdom in the firm quiet of age (winter).

If wisdom is taken as one quality among others, we see in this correspondence with winter some of its most conventional associations: it is a matter of accumulation over time, stored up in the quiet of reflection and becoming a rich resource, typically, late in life. But from a more holistic point of view, running through the seasons we find the cosmic centrality of a vital, relational flow of life with various manifestations. This means conducting the flow of life is the deep character of our inborn dispositions, just as it is the character of the seasons. Life-givingness thus becomes the lens through which we examine and understand the interdependent dynamic and meaning of the most profound dispositions and potentials of our minds-and-hearts.

SONG DYNASTY

Such indeed was the understanding emphasized by the leaders of a great Confucian revival movement almost a thousand years later. Daoism and especially Buddhism had predominated after the fall of the Han dynasty, so the intellectual and spiritual world of Song dynasty (960–1279) "Neo-Confucians"[5] was far different from that of the Han. Chinese Buddhist schools offered an array of cosmic imagery and a range of sophisticated techniques for cultivating the conscious life of the mind-and-heart, which was now seen as a matter of central importance. In response, Confucians deepened their approach to personal cultivation by elaborating their own account of the inner dynamics of the mind-and-heart in a way that could frame a far more sophisticated ascetical practice. Critical to this project was a careful new explication of the metaphysical framework implicit in assumptions long shared with Daoists. Within this framework traditional Confucian social concern was interwoven with a new depth of cultivation practice, and the resulting Neo-Confucian synthesis spread and in various forms and schools became the predominant intellectual and spiritual tradition throughout China, Korea, and Japan down to the modern era.

It is with the Neo-Confucians that we find the full maturity of the Confucian wisdom tradition. The great Neo-Confucian synthesizer Zhu Xi (1130–1200) took up the Han dynasty correspondence of the life-giving cycle of the seasons and the dispositions of the mind-and-heart and moved it to a new level. Now life-givingness is the central disposition of the cosmos ("Heaven and Earth") in which we participate: "Humanity is the mind-and-heart of Heaven and Earth whereby they produce and give life to creatures, and this is what man receives as his own mind-heart."[6] His classic source for this was a passage in the *Book of Changes* that describes the continual production and giving of life (*sheng-sheng*) as the fundamental character or disposition of the universe.[7] His identification of the life-giving humane disposition of our mind-and-heart as our participation in the life-giving character of universe fit with the Neo-Confucian explication of a metaphysical framework based on the broadly shared traditional view of a world that dynamically self-organizes in terms of an all-encompassing single normative pattern, the Dao. Zhang Zai (1020–1077), in his *Western Inscription*,[8] had spoken of Heaven and Earth (i.e., the universe) as our father and mother, emphasizing that our own physical bodies and our natures are an extension of their physical body and their nature, and that all life constitutes a single family. Cheng Hao (1032–1083), another founder of the Neo-Confucian revival, went further to speak of all things in the universe being as a single body; he describes lack of *ren,* compassionate humanity, as paralysis, cutting off the connection of the vital flow of life through the members of this single body.[9] Zhu Xi, the great synthesizer,[10] preferred a related image, that of a single circulatory system of veins running through everything, with lack of *ren* being like a blockage in the bloodflow.[11]

The dao of the universe, the dao of the seasons, and the dao of human beings are all simply variant manifestations of the one Dao, the Dao that above all patterns the flow of life through the network of all creatures. By emphasizing these elements long implicit in the perennial Chinese worldview, and by encompassing them in a more carefully explicated metaphysics, the Neo-Confucians were able to elaborate new and deeper dimensions in their approach to self-cultivation.

The Cultivation of Wisdom

Confucians had long held that anyone could become a sage, a conclusion implicit in the Mencian explication of the goodness of our inborn Original Nature. But over the centuries cultivation techniques remained more proportioned to the formation of ordinary good moral character: study and memorize the wise teachings of the classics, study the historical records for examples, and inculcate the habits of good character through strong self-discipline. There was no explanation or claim here that such practice would lead to the unfailing responsiveness of a sage. So for more than a thousand years sagehood in practice remained little more than a distinctive attribute of the authoritative figures who served as reference points in the tradition.

Mencius had spoken of our "original nature," but he had located the distortion of its function mainly in the way we get bent out of shape by problematic social interaction. This account was supplemented by a general Confucian consensus regarding the disrupting influence of self-centered tendencies, but in the absence of a more probing analysis of the inner life of the mind-and-heart, instruction and strict observance of rules of conduct remained the main ways of trying to shape the internal self-control to counter such tendencies.

All of this changed with the emergence of the Neo-Confucian revival of the tradition. Their metaphysics enabled a new and deeper reading of the Mencian account of human nature and a new analysis of distorted responsiveness. Ascetical theory could now describe the inner dynamics of inappropriate response and suggest forms of cultivation proportioned to the problem. With this, the perspective opened that the apprehension and possession of wisdom evident in the perfectly attuned responsiveness of the Sage could indeed be made the object of deliberate cultivation.

The entire tradition regarding the Dao, in both its Daoist and Confucian forms, assumed that we live in a world suffused in guidance. Every moment, every situation presents us with guidance: "If one can absent oneself from it, it is not the Dao."[12] Although perfect outcomes may not be available in really messed-up situations, there is always a difference between more and less life-giving responses, a guiding difference inherent in the situation itself.

In their metaphysical account of this traditional worldview, Neo-Confucians gave new prominence to the notion of *li,* a term which in many ways replicates the idea of *dao.* But where *dao* is the "way" of things, the ancient roots of the term *li* refer to the markings in jade, so the notion of "pattern" is more prominent. As one of the favorite Neo-Confucian sayings puts it, "*Li* is one but manifested diversely."[13] While this way of handling unity and diversity is in line with traditional thought regarding the Dao, the window of "pattern" opens easily and naturally onto consideration of the myriad patterns of the world about us—and not only of the exterior, but the interior world as well. Thus, the inborn tendencies Mencius had described as our "original nature" could easily be understood as *li.* And since pattern is likewise present in the nature of all things and all times and situations, that also is a matter of *li.*

Since it is the same patterning that informs both the external world and the internal dispositions of the mind-and-heart, the metaphysics of *li* becomes also an epistemology that explains the seemingly spontaneous or "self-so" responsiveness that knits the world together in a web of appropriate, life-giving and life-sustaining interaction. Insofar as there is but one Dao or all-embracing pattern (*li*), the pattern of the whole is implicit in the dynamics of the parts, and so the appropriate responsiveness to an "external" world is already patterned as the "inner" nature of creatures.

In fact, in an existence of such patterned dynamic relationship, the more difficult task is to explain inappropriate responsiveness. If guidance is patterned into every situation and responsive apprehension is pre-patterned within, what goes wrong? Other creatures in the natural world seem to do pretty well. Why do we, of all creatures, need cultivation in order to act with a wisdom already inherent in the patterning of the world and of our nature? Knowing the nature of the problem is the first step in mitigating it.

Neo-Confucians explained the blockage that impedes such wise responsiveness in social, psychological, and metaphysical terms. In some respects these are variant ways of saying the same thing, but each offers a particular perspective on the cultivation of sage wisdom. The social and psychological explications pervade the earlier tradition as well, while the metaphysical was distinctively Neo-Confucian; we shall consider each in turn.

Social Distortion

As we have already discussed, social relations were a central concern from the founding of the Confucian tradition. While Confucians saw responsive relational living as an inborn disposition, they made no assumption that people automatically grow up with a sensitive social awareness. On the contrary, deliberate and intensive effort was devoted to inculcating awareness that life and livelihood are gifts that flow to us across a relational net. We are inherently indebted to others and repay by our own reciprocal contribution.

Children grew up memorizing the *Classic of Filial Piety,* which tells us in the first chapter: "Our bodies, including every hair and bit of skin, are received by us from our parents, so we may not dare to injure or wound them." Even our most personal, physically separate bodies are not really separate, our own to dispose of as we wish! Much less do we own the nutritional and economic flows that keep these bodies alive, or the contents of our socially formed intelligences and psyches.

Thus, the young were raised with a lively consciousness of a debt of gratitude and reciprocation to parents, elders, teachers, friends, and the agencies of a stable society that make life sustainable. Inculcated as the most basic commonsense, this understanding of the fundamental interdependence of a relational existence laid the foundation and framework for the pursuit of wisdom. As a shared cultural assumption, it became the wellspring of self-identity and way of life. This prefigures and supports a personal apprehension and cultivation of a kind of wisdom that is not at all self-evident to those of us who grow up in a milieu that leads us to accept as an obvious fact the assertion, "I have my own life to lead."

Psychological Distortion

Confucians were fond of pithy phrases or sentences, plucked from classical sources, that became endowed with highly compressed meanings which were expanded and explicated in a tradition of commentaries. These were committed to memory and salted into all sorts of discourse, a practice that effectively shaped a vital core of shared values, attitudes, and priorities that informed and supported an individual's spiritual cultivation. For the psychological framework of cultivation, one of the most important of these pregnant catchphrases came from the classic *Book of Rites*: "The human mind is perilous, the mind of the *Dao* is subtle; be discerning, be undivided. Hold fast the Mean!"[14]

The Dao Mind was identified with the four strongly social feelings or instincts Mencius described as the characteristics of our life-giving original nature. Their "subtlety" has to do with their need for nurture and cultivation; though inborn and fundamental, they are not as obvious and strongly or immediately triggered as the kind of feelings that keep us intact as individual physical organisms. Those take-care-of-yourself feelings were identified rather as the Human Mind, typified by the "Seven Feelings," desire, hate, love, fear, grief, anger, and joy.[15] The Human Mind, is "perilous," for the inherent strength and easy trigger of such feelings mean they easily take over and lead to inappropriate responses that serve an individual's immediate proclivities but disrupt the flow of the life-giving web. Thus, while the socially oriented feelings identified by Mencius were regarded as inherently good, the Seven Feelings were regarded as more indeterminate, inherently likely to lead response astray, and hence in need of careful control.

This framing of the psyche led to a constant awareness of the tension between the more immediately personal and the broader social dimensions of life. We are even warned against "privating" our wife and children, that is, allowing them to become a competitive interest within the life of the extended family. One powerful technique of cultivating a habitual prioritizing of the relational was strict observance of social propriety and ritual norms, for these insert individual behavior into a larger normative framework. Confucius himself advised his students: "To overcome [your]self and return to propriety is to become humane (*ren*)."[16]

Metaphysical Distortion

Neo-Confucians assumed a concrete, everyday-real sort of universe. Thus, in addition to *li*, they made use of another traditional concept, *qi*, to account for the concrete, energizing dimension of existence. *Qi*, a character originally referring to steam, had come to refer also to the vital force of life, to the power of feelings, and in more philosophic discourse, to the stuff of the universe. Like ice, it congeals at its most turbid as the stuff of physical separateness. Like water, it flows in the lively life of the sentient feelings which relate individuals into a responsive whole. And in its pure condition, like invisible steam, it is a vital moving force that transcends separateness, as evident in the way consciousness can encompass the world.

Complementing the patterning of *li* with an energizing *qi* dimension gave Neo-Confucians a way of thinking about the sources of self-centered dynamics in ways that opened up the wisdom project to techniques of direct cultivation of the inner life of the mind-and-heart. While *li* accounts for the networked, patterned relational aspect of existence, *qi,* is at once both the stuff of individual physical existence and also the energizing component of all relational activity. Thus, the dynamic tension of our social-yet-individual existence is critically shaped in practice by the quality of the *qi* that energizes the mind-and-heart. The turbidity of *qi* is associated with the opaqueness and seeming separateness of individual existence. While this is appropriate to our diversified physical world, as degrees of such opacity affect the dynamics of our conscious life, they distort the smooth responsive interchange at the very center of relational existence.

This reframing and concretizing of self-centered tendencies opened a path to a new and vibrant psychological and spiritual cultivation. As a dynamic distortion of our conscious life, the turbidity or clarity of *qi* could be understood to manifest itself in various forms of mental tumult as opposed to the calm, self-possessed centeredness that enables appropriate responsiveness.

Mencius, more than a thousand years earlier, had observed the effects of the life-giving force that in the night restores not only stressed vegetation but stressed psyches. In the quiet hours before dawn, he tells us, we return to being "almost human," that is, almost what our inborn dispositions would have us be.[17] Now, interpreted in terms of *li* and *qi,* this ancient passage took on a broader import and a new practical application. Not the night, but its quiet must be the critical factor in restoring the mind-and-heart to its original condition. Neo-Confucians saw that meditative quiescence, familiar from Buddhist practice, would actually nurture a condition of serene unity with one's original nature, unimpeded by the distorting turbulence besetting the *qi* of ordinary conscious activity. Far from being empty, pure objectless consciousness could be understood as a condition of full integration, a quiet healing process putting us more deeply in touch with the our most profound inborn lifegiving dispositions. Such a practice itself could be expected to move us incrementally toward a more integral human responsiveness, and even more so since the quiet of meditation would gradually clarify our *qi* and spread to become a quiet, undistorted centeredness of the mind-and-heart as it actively engaged with the affairs of daily life. With this understanding, meditative practice, called "quiet sitting," became an important technique of Neo-Confucian self-cultivation.

Quiet-sitting is valuable because from such practice a calm centeredness gradually pervades every area of life. But inner turbulence is double-edged: it not only distorts the response of our feelings, it also interferes with our appraisal of the situation to which we are responding. Hence, a self-possessed focused attention on the matter at hand is the necessary correlate of inner calmness. Zhu Xi thus came to advocate the practice "mindfulness (*zhing*)"[18] as the central and inclusive practice of self-cultivation. Described as maintaining a constant state of calm and focused self-possession that would allow proper attention to the situation at hand, mindfulness also encompassed quiet-sitting, insofar as profound quiescence could be considered appropriate to times when not actively engaged with affairs.

Since an all-pervasive guiding pattern inheres in all things and also serves as the basis of our responsive consciousness, one might conclude that inner cultivation, clarifying the turbidity of consciousness, would be sufficient to lead to the kind of spontaneous life-giving responsiveness characterized as the perfection of sage wisdom. Major schools of thought in fact split over this issue, with the school of Wang Yangming (1472–1529) emphasizing the potential of spontaneous apprehension and response. The school of Zhu Xi was wary of such an approach, however. They indeed held out the hope for some such breakthrough, a Confucian version of an enlightenment experience that would fully integrate our inner responsiveness in life-giving relation to the ever-changing situation within which we exist. But short of such a breakthrough, they felt too much of a purely inward cultivation risked the pitfalls of an inappropriate quietism or delusional spontaneity. Thus, they emphasized that the deep appropriation of the pattern inscribed throughout the universe might be facilitated in many ways. The direct cultivation of the *li*-informed dynamism of the mind-and-heart by consciousness-oriented techniques such as mindfulness or quiet-sitting should be complemented with a deep study and attention to the *li*-informed affairs of the world, a cultivation practice known as the "investigation of things" or "the investigation of *li*."

The investigation of *li* could take many forms. It encompassed traditional practices such as studying the wisdom of the sages distilled in classical sources, the examples of history, and the teachings of elders. But above all, keen observation, reflection, and personal appropriation are critical to the investigation of *li*. True learning, Confucians have maintained, is learning that transforms you. And in this vein the Neo-Confucian investigation of *li* turned especially toward plumbing the depths of one's personal relational situatedness in the world. What does it mean for me to be a father? A son? A mother or daughter? An official or minister to the ruler? A teacher or member of the village? Such questions appear simple and mundane only to those who have never spent hours of reflection examining not only the ideal life-giving meaning and function of such roles, but also how to form oneself and implement them in terms of one's own capacities and situation—always a far more complex matter than ideal understanding. While we may be born with the subtle shoots of life-giving social responsiveness, they require careful nurture, and this kind of practice contributes the deeply cultivated understanding that helps bring them to a vibrant and mature sensitivity.

Summary of Practice

The self-cultivation practices common among Neo-Confucians include propriety, mindfulness, quiet-sitting, and the investigation of things. Together these form overlapping and interwoven strands of an ascetical practice aimed a perfecting our responsive participation in the interdependent web of life.

Propriety

We translate the Chinese character *li* as "propriety" in some contexts, and as "ritual" in others. Confucians needed only one character, for they saw a continuity running from the most sacred rituals down to the conventions that guide us in daily social life. Confucius instructed his disciples, "When you go abroad, behave to everyone as if you were meeting an important guest; preside over affairs as if presiding at a sacrifice."[19] The conduct of life itself is our participation in a sacred or ultimate performance, and the reverence and respect commanded by what we often separate out as "the sacred" is likewise the life-enhancing essence of the conventions of social interaction that we call propriety. Thus, Confucians identified propriety with summer's full-flourishing life, seeing it as the natural fulfillment of the feelings of empathetic humanity they associated with the origination of life in the spring.

Contemporary Western attitudes tend to emphasize the arbitrary and provisional nature of convention and thus are quick to observe that a profound person easily moves beyond convention when it does not fit the situation in a life-giving way. Confucians would agree in principle, but they focused more on the relational *reality* which emerges from and is shaped by the patterns of shared expectation (conventions) that make social life possible. It may be an arbitrary convention in any given culture whether a male or female, elder or younger goes through a door first, but the expectation is very real, and that makes observing or not observing the convention a communication of respect or the contrary.

This means that Confucian judgments were more weighted toward maintaining conventions as the appropriate way of conducting a life of reverence and respect, with a suspicion that failure to do so is more often than not motivated by feelings of personal inconvenience rather than by feelings of concern for others. Confucian cultivation sought to inculcate a habitual prioritizing of the relational or social conducting of life over our more self-regarding personal inclinations. Even as they developed more sophisticated techniques of cultivating the mind-and-heart, "Regulate the external in order to nurture the interior" remained a favored and an oft-repeated dictum, for they understood that adherence to propriety offered a concrete, easily understood external approach to this deep inner formation.

Mindfulness

Mindfulness is above all a matter of maintaining a centered, alert, and focused state of mind. It includes propriety as its most external practice and quiet-sitting as its most internal, for both of these contribute to inculcating the calm self-possession that is the heart of this practice. Mindfulness is the antidote to inner turmoil, distraction, stress—all the conditions Neo-Confucians lumped together as the "turbidity" that disrupts the natural and appropriate responsiveness of the heart-and-mind. It is difficult to try to directly grasp and control the mind-and-heart, and questions and warnings about misdirected or excessive efforts in this regard are frequent in the correspondence between masters and students. The trick is to find the happy medium between trying too hard to control one's state of mind and neglecting to make any special effort in that direction. Often, students are directed to the practice of propriety, for the mental condition of respect and reverence nurtured by propriety is just the kind of responsive attentiveness meant by mindfulness. In general, attempts to quiet and recollect the inner life are greatly helped by controlling circumstances, such as deliberately slowing the pace of one's activities and avoiding a lifestyle that demands or seeks out constant multitasking.

Quiet-Sitting

As mentioned above, quiet-sitting could be considered an ancillary form of mindfulness, for the quietness and centeredness of a practiced meditator spreads to all areas of life. Following their turbidity metaphor, Neo-Confucians likened the meditation process to the way clouded water naturally settles and clears when stilled. Such a stilled mind presents a healing and nurturing environment in which we become attuned to the profound inclinations and responsiveness of our feelings, and as we emerge back into activity we have a clearer grasp of the situations we encounter. Again, we find that appropriate, life-giving responsiveness to the world with which we are constantly engaged forms the rationale for Neo-Confucian meditative practice.

Neo-Confucians saw appropriate responsiveness as already inherent in the nature of the world and the constitution of the mind-and-heart. Thus, they preferred to frame quiet-sitting as a natural occurrence, the quiet of *yin* alternating with the activity of *yang*. Neo-Confucian quiet-sitters readily borrowed concentration techniques from Buddhist or Taoist sources. They used an ordinary sitting posture rather than the lotus or other yoga positions, and readily borrowed basic concentration exercises such as following the breath from Buddhist and Taoist sources. Such meditation would release the mind from active engagement and allow it to settle into a natural profound objectless quiescence.

Familiarity with Buddhist practice made objectless consciousness a plausible way to think of inner quiescence, but Neo-Confucians urged caution about making such meditative quiescence a goal in itself. If one keeps a clear view of quieting and clearing consciousness in order to enhance a finely tuned responsiveness, it is evident that not just objectless consciousness but any measure of quieting one is able to achieve by this practice can be a significant contribution to this spiritual cultivation.

The Investigation of Things

This classic phrase covers all aspects acquiring and deepening understanding. Our comprehension of the world critically shapes our responsiveness to all sorts of situations, so any path of study and investigation can become a key component of self-cultivation. Neo-Confucians understood investigative activities as an apprehension of *li,* the patterning component of the way things are and of the dynamics of their relational behavior. While the multiple manifestations of *li* and its ever-changing nuances in any particular situation calls for careful observation and broad learning, the unity of *li* as a holistic all-encompassing pattern means that everything learned ultimately fits into a whole. This holds out the possibility of sage wisdom, in which the accumulation of many sorts of experience and understanding coalesces into an emergent understanding of the dynamic whole to which every new item or situation belongs. When manifold *li* thus coalesce in a single apprehension, one *sees more* in any particular situation by grasping the broad relational matrix in which it is encompassed, and thus can respond with the deeper appropriateness that is the mark of wisdom.

Experiences rain upon us continually, and the experience of ages is available through reading and now through an ever-expanding range of audio and visual resources. But much of this experience runs off us like rain off a roof. The practice of mindfulness is meant to provide a context not only for more alert responsiveness, but for the cumulative soaking in of understanding, like rain on good soil. The investigation of things looks to this cumulative process, which Neo-Confucian literature often refers to as "ripening."

Ripening is achieved through the understanding that emerges from habitual reflection. Just as learning can take place in many ways, the reflective process that turns it into a deepening and cumulative apprehension takes many forms. We learn to be reflective even in the midst of the rain of experience. Slowing down, becoming more attentive, that is, mindfulness, allows this reflective dimension to gain a greater depth. And mindfully slowing down and focusing attention segues into meditative forms of reflection, a practice that overlaps quiet-sitting but is on a vector of more profound apprehension and understanding rather than quiescence.

This range of reflective dimensions applies likewise to reading, the most common mode of expanding our investigation of things. The wide variety of texts invites a corresponding variety of reflective processes. Reading for information just scratches the surface of inquiry as a ripening process, though there is increasing potential for reflective depth as more and more is accumulated. Reading that slows us down to savor the words and thoughts also starts to transform and shape us in the very reading process. And again, this segues into meditative forms of reading. In East Asia, texts were often read aloud with a chanting mode of intonation. Highly revered texts were committed to memory and read very slowly in this manner, the object being to have one's consciousness entirely absorbed in the words and meaning of the reading, recreating the very presence of their sage authors.

Such meditative extensions of modes of inquiry highlight the purpose of the investigation of things as a critical dimension of spiritual self-cultivation. The meaning of words such as "learning," "study," or "apprehension" in this context point to the cultivation of a transformative understanding of the patterned workings of self and world. Such understanding ripens into wisdom as it informs the mind-and-heart with a life-conducing resonance across scales of context as we participate in the sacred ritual of the world's affairs.

Implications

Understanding of Human Nature

The interiority of conscious life is the center of responsive relational activity with the world. Activity is always motivated: we are primed to care for ourselves, primed to care for others, and feelings informed by thought and reflection move and guide us. As creatures who survive and thrive only through a shared flow of life, we are born with a life-giving, nurturing disposition as well as with the instincts that equip us to take care of our immediate well-being. In the big picture, these are not two things: we flourish most deeply by attending to the flourishing of others. In day-to-day life, however, self may be experienced as a center of care and concern that distorts and obscures our responsiveness to the wider community of life.

As social beings who exist only as physical individuals, this tension is inevitable. Confucians have seen that without attention and cultivation of the social, the strength and pull of our individuality becomes a distortion of personal character that deadens our life-giving responsiveness to the world about us. Awareness, sensitivity, and even priorities are always subject to shaping and habituation, whether it be by deliberate and reflective cultivation or by the formative pressures of a pervasive consumer culture. A deep, habituated inner shaping guides the way we move through life. Sage wisdom would manifest that shaping as an on-going sensitive and life-giving responsiveness that makes the community whole.

Social Implications

The Confucian tradition originated as a response to a disintegrating society. In formulating their response as a personal and social search for modes of life-giving relationship, Confucians identified a problematique as broad and as lasting as the community of life itself. They observe that life emerges from and is maintained within a matrix of interdependent systemic relationships, and they identified inappropriate self-maximizing dynamics as the critical factor distorting the life and the life-supporting functions of society. The personal and the social form a dynamic feedback loop; ideally, wise and life-giving individuals foster wise and life-giving families and communities, and wise and life-giving communities and families foster wise and life-giving individuals. But this also means that problematic cultural distortions become personal distortions, and Confucians sought life-giving wisdom in government and social institutions to create a context where personal cultivation would work with, not against the social current.

Contemporary society thinks of the essential flow of life mainly in terms of economic flows of goods and services, with feedback between a healthy, job-producing economy supported by a vigorously consuming population. This calls to mind the Confucian wariness of our dispositions to put a priority on taking care of ourselves. An entire industry, advertising, dedicates itself to saturating society with the most sophisticated and powerful messages to foster exactly the personal consumptive urges Confucians feared would distort our life-giving relational responsiveness. And as the consumer mindset circles in dynamic feedback through individuals, communities, and societies, it has become the common, continually self-reinforcing human identity in a now global market system.

Confucians worried about self-centered dynamics distorting the life-giving character of interpersonal relationships. Our contemporary sustainability issues are simply their issue on a larger systemic scale. In terms of the systemic flow of life, the human community and other species-centered communities are but individual subunits of the inclusive community of life. Life-giving wisdom navigates the inevitable tension between the individual and the larger communal matrix, knowing that the notion of maximizing anything belies the very nature of an interdependent existence. The idea of a human economy flourishing independently of the well-being of the larger economy of the community of life shares the impossible myopia of the individual person trying to maximize their own well-being with no regard for family, community, or society. Insofar as they challenged themselves to cultivate a wisdom that could maintain and bring about life-giving relationship in the web of interdependent existence, Confucian insights and their entire cultivation project of maintaining or bringing about life-giving relationships remain critically relevant today.

Implications for the Individual

In keeping with their understanding of individuals as relational beings supported by and shaped within a social matrix, Confucians addressed themselves to the wisdom of governance and social institutions as much as to a life-giving wisdom that might be cultivated in one's personal life. A society that pays keen attention to the life-supporting quality of relationships fosters individuals who grow up with such an awareness and likewise supports focused and intense personal cultivation practices aligned with such values.

Our society has attained unprecedented levels of material well-being accompanied with high levels of personal psychological and spiritual distress and a wave of destructive transformation rolling through the biosphere. The values informing our social matrix shape us to become comfort, pleasure, and stimulus-maximizing individuals accustomed to a fast pace of life and instant gratification. In other words, serious pursuit of the path to wisdom as envisioned in the Confucian tradition will be a profoundly countercultural project, one that runs contrary to the ingrained shape and expectation of our society.

On a superficial level, everyone wants life-giving relationships. But a society that tends to assume self-interest as the essential dynamic of life is subject to deep distortions and remarkable shortsightedness in understanding what life-giving means. Confucians saw a disposition not just to receive, but to support and convey life as fundamental to human nature. Rediscovering what this means, both in oneself and in others, would be a necessary first step toward wisdom. Having discovered the living sprout of life-giving instinct within ourselves is key both to undertaking its nurture and contemplating its potentials.

The potentials, as evidenced in the heritage of Confucian thought, are evident in individual maturation and encompass one's view of the entire universe. In the contemporary world, consideration of the dynamic inter-dependent flow of life would take one easily to reflection on ecosystems as well as social systems, or holistically, to the entire earth-environed community of life. But nurturing these dynamics within oneself begins with personal observation and reflection. Granted this life-giving dynamic is within me, something that wants to happen, what gets in the way? This is the Confucian question, and answers today would resonate with texts a thousand years old: too busy, too distracted, moving too fast, too self-absorbed, worried, stressed out.

Addressing these obstacles requires no arcane lore. Our consumer society is already replete with techniques and spiritual centering methods geared to remedy our discomfort. The path to life-giving wisdom simply reframes already common recommendations. Slow down. Simplify. Quiet. Center. Not only because it feels better (it does), but because it enables a more life-giving participation in the community of being. This would be the path of Confucian wisdom.

Summary and Conclusion

In seeking to mend their own torn social fabric, Confucians focused on distorted relationships as the essential problem, with the assumption that life flows freely and flourishes when relationships are proper. They likewise assumed that, like a living body's inherent dynamic to maintain or recover a healthy condition, the world of life possesses an inherent dynamic that informs and guides a life-giving responsiveness. The task and measure of sage wisdom is the fullness of participation in that dynamic.

The sage is the paradigmatic symbol of such wisdom, but the dynamic of life-givingness is inherent in all, not the exclusive property of the uniquely profound. Or to put it another way, this is a profundity open to everyone, largely invisible because it is the ordinary way things work when they work well, that is, when they work in a life-giving way. Of course, things often do not work so well, a condition that also is so ordinary that we come to take it for granted. Confucians identify the problem here as an overly self-centered dynamic distorting our response to many situations from its appropriate or full life-giving potential. Taking care of oneself is an inherent and appropriate part of a life-giving dynamic, but Confucians part company with profit-maximizers and selfish-gene theorists in insisting on a complementary inherent dynamic to care for and support others. When this dynamic gets overridden by self-care, society feels the pain.

Or the earth feels the pain, for this dynamic tension pervades all systemic levels. Though Confucians concentrated mainly on human relationships, the network of the interdependent flow of life knows no species boundaries. When personal fulfillment is misconceived as in opposition to taking care of a family, when national well-being seems to demand the subordination of other nations, or when human economic flourishing carries a debit of geophysical transformation and species extinction, the unsustainability of the condition signals itself by varieties of manifest pain. Wisdom recognizes the warning and rectifies the distorted flow of life; that is what pain is for.

The Confucian wisdom of life-giving responsiveness contains no great surprise, no hidden truth awaiting only the most gifted and insightful. What it tells us about our globalized market, consumer mentality, and personal relationships is echoed in manifold modalities by a chorus of voices alarmed about unsustainable trajectories. This is as one might expect of a matter that indeed is fundamental to the function of a living system: really important understandings must be evident and available for the conduct of daily life. Such wisdom is more, not less, profound for being close at hand.

Endnotes

1. *Analects,* xi, 11.
2. *Mencius,* 3A, 4.
3. Paraphrase of *Mencius,* 6A, 8.
4. *Mencius,* 2A, 6.
5. They simply thought of themselves and referred to themselves as Confucians. Twentieth-century Western scholars, observing the new metaphysical and ascetical dimensions of the renewed tradition, have dubbed Song and subsequent Confucianism "neo" Confucianism, and scholars in East Asia have now picked up this terminology.

6. *Yü-lei,* 105.71a.

7. *Book of Changes,* Appended Remarks, pt. 2, ch. 1.

8. Translated in Michael Kalton, *To Become a Sage,* pp. 51–52.

9. *I-shu,* 2A.2a.

10. His name, along with the two Cheng brothers, is attached to the "Cheng-Zhu school" of thought, the major or "orthodox" Song school of Confucian thought.

11. *Yü-lei,* 95.8b, 9a.

12. *Doctrine of the Mean,* ch. 1.

13. Cf. Wing-tsit Chan, *Source Book in Chinese Philosophy,* pp. 550–551.

14. *Book of Documents,* pt. 2, 2.15.

15. Known as the "seven feelings," derived from another passage.

16. *Analects,* 12, 1.

17. *Mencius,* 6A, 8.

18. I prefer the translation of this term as "mindfulness," rather than other common translations such as "reverence" or "seriousness," because texts carefully define the practice as maintaining a state of constant self-possession and focus. Translators may avoid using "mindfulness" because of its use in texts dealing with Buddhist meditative practice, but that does not preclude Confucians having their distinctive form of mindful practice.

19. *Analects,* 12, 2.

Endnote References

Analects. A number of translations. James Legge (1815–1897) was the original and very capable translator of all the Confucian classics. His bilingual Chinese and English edition of the classics, *The Chinese Classics,* is now available for free download online (cf. below). The translation by Arthur Waley (New York: Vintage Books, 1989) is very good. For a good scholarly and philosophical translation, see Roger Ames and Henry Rosemont's translation (New York: Ballantine, 1998).

Mencius, James Legge translation (cf. *Analects,* above); D. C. Lau (Hong Kong: Chinese University Press, 2003); and Irene Bloom with P. J. Ivanhoe (Columbia University Press, 2009) are good contemporary translations.

Yü-lei. Zhu-zi yü-lei (The classified conversations of Master Zhu Xi), not available in translation.

Book of Changes, James Legge translation (cf. *Analects,* above). See John Blofeld (London: George Allen & Unwin, 1965) for a more contemporary translation.

To Become a Sage: The Ten Diagrams on Sage Learning by Yi T'oegye, Michael C. Kalton (Trans., Ed., and Commentaries) (New York: Columbia University Press, 1988).

I-shu. (Surviving Works of Cheng Hao and Cheng I), in *Er Cheng chüan-shu,* not available in translation.

Doctrine of the Mean. Zhung yong, James Legge translation (cf. *Analects,* above). See also translation in Chan, *Source Book in Chinese Philosophy.*

Source Book in Chinese Philosophy, Wing-tsit Chan (Princeton: Princeton University Press, 1963).

Book of Rites. Li zhi, James Legge translation (cf. *Analects*, above).

Book of Documents. Shu zhing, James Legge translation (cf. *Analects*, above).

Bibliography

Berthrong, J., and Tucker, M. E., eds. (1998). *Confucianism and ecology: The interrelation of heaven, earth, and humans.* Cambridge: Harvard University Press. This volume explores Confucian perspectives and potential contributions to the vexed issue of how humans fit and fail to fit with the life-giving dynamics of the earth.

Mencius. (Irene Bloom, Trans.). Philip J. Ivanhoe (Ed. and Introduction). For Neo-Confucians seeking to understand and cultivate sage wisdom, *Mencius* was the classical source without equal. This new translation by Irene Bloom recaptures his voice for the contemporary reader, and P. J. Ivanhoe is a leading interpreter of Mencius's relevance to contemporary ethical thought.

Tu Wei-ming. (1989). *Centrality and commonality: An essay on Confucian religiousness* (A revised and enlarged edition of *Centrality and Commonality: An Essay on Chung-yung*). Albany: State University of New York Press. The *Chung-yung* or *Doctrine of the Mean* became one of the most important sources of Neo-Confucian spiritual reflection and practice. Tu Wei-ming's reflections on this text reveal a Confucian understanding of what it means to be a profound human being that speaks incisively to the contemporary world.

————, ed., with Tucker, M. E. (2002). *Confucian spirituality*, Volume 11 of "World Spirituality: An Encyclopedic History of the Religious Quest" Series. New York: Crossroad. This volume is the product of a Harvard conference that assembled the best contemporary scholars on the topic. The compiled articles cover a broad range of topics and perspectives and furnish a unique overview of a rich spiritual tradition that is very thinly represented in English works.

Yi T'oegye (1988). *To become a sage: The ten diagrams on sage learning.* Michael C. Kalton (Trans., Ed., and Commentary). New York: Columbia University Press. T'oegye (1501–1570), Korea's most famous Neo-Confucian thinker, composed this work to instruct the king in sage wisdom. Its ten diagrams begin with metaphysics, proceed though ethics, learning, and self-cultivation, and conclude with how to live a single day. It is perhaps the most thorough overview of Neo-Confucian understanding of world, self, and self-cultivation available in English.

Internet Resources

http://ia700200.us.archive.org/21/items/fourbooksconfuci00leggiala/fourbooksconfuci00leggiala.pdf. One of a number of sites offering free downloads of the

Chinese Classics by James Legge. Various formats available. PDF reproduces the original, which is an advantage in that it is accompanied by a handsome copy of the Chinese text and copious notes on every page.

http://faculty.washington.edu/mkalton/. This site offers a free download of *To Become a Sage,* as well as a number of papers by Michael C. Kalton dealing with a a variety of topics relating Neo-Confucian thought and spirituality to contemporary concerns.

http://terpconnect.umd.edu/~tkang/. This site offers a good selection of reading suggestions from among the best scholarly works on Confucian thought and spirituality.

9

Wisdom in Western Philosophy

Robert McDermott

This essay concerns the concept, history, and practice of wisdom in the Western philosophical tradition. It issues from its author's conviction that the ideal of wisdom was prominent at the dawn of Western philosophy but modern and contemporary philosophers have generally denied its significance. Despite this neglect, this essay claims that the ideal of wisdom is nevertheless worthy to be reestablished as the source and goal of philosophy. This retrieval can be accomplished by a clear characterization of wisdom, by exemplars of wisdom throughout the history of Western philosophy, and by affirming philosophical practices that can lead to wisdom.

The Concept of Wisdom

The concept of wisdom is complex and controversial both because it has evolved over many centuries and because wisdom itself is probably not accessible at ordinary levels of inquiry and discourse. Like drivers, teachers, and lovers who claim to perform above average, not all claimants to wisdom deserve to be so regarded. Nor is it obvious that wisdom resides primarily in philosophy—though given its name (*philo* meaning love and *sophia* meaning wisdom), as well as its origin and early history, it clearly ought to be wisdom's primary source and exemplar. The last section of this essay discusses some wise thinkers who are not counted as philosophers by mainstream philosophy.

This essay is a rather traditional endeavor—neither analytic nor postmodern. It finds wisdom most convincingly when Platonic and Aristotelian, European and American, idealist and practical, religious and secular elements, and other philosophical polarities are rendered complementary.

The effort to find wisdom in Western philosophy requires some initial agreement as to what to look for. On the basis of select philosophers and the overall history of Western philosophy, this essay proposes that wisdom holds in harmony the three primary components of philosophy—metaphysics, epistemology, and ethics—and further that it manifests a mutuality among them. To the extent that each leads to the other two, wisdom can be realized regardless with which component one begins—depending, of course, on the value (whether truth, ethical, aesthetic) of each of the three strands. These three disciplines are essential for a full philosophy, that is, for a complete articulation of a loving (*philo*) relationship to wisdom (*sophia*). These three components of philosophy, and of wisdom, warrant a characterization:

- *Metaphysics*, the study of what exists, both as one reality (fundamental and ultimate) and many realities (single thoughts, cells, grains of sand). It includes the relations among unity and particularity, the ways that whatever exists (whether one or many) comes to be and passes away, and whether such processes have a meaning and a goal. The primary content of metaphysics is ontology (*ontos,* being; *logy,* study, knowledge).

- *Epistemology* (*episteme,* knowledge), or how one knows, and the criteria by which persons and groups know whatever they claim to know; if there are various ways of knowing, might some be more reliable than others?

- *Ethics*, the study of morality; which thoughts and actions are moral, and by what criteria; how might philosophy evaluate human behavior?

Here is the working characterization of wisdom for this essay:

Wisdom is knowledge that is derived from a deep source and leads to right action. Right action in turn leads to a deeper ontological experience and the advancement of knowledge. All three components are mutually implicating.

Metaphysics / Ontology

"Deep source" is deliberately vague because philosophers do not at all agree on the nature or description of a source that serves, or might serve, as a foundation for wisdom. Claims for this foundational reality include the Good according to Plato, Being (as well as Uncaused Cause) according to Aristotle, the One according to Plotinus, God according to Christian thinkers such as Augustine, Boethius, and Aquinas, and the Absolute as variously affirmed by a series of ontological monists, including Spinoza (seventeenth century), Hegel and Emerson (nineteenth century), and Josiah Royce (twentieth century). In the Indian/Hindu tradition the fundamental reality is called Brahman; in Buddhism, Buddha nature; in the Chinese tradition (for both Daoism and Confucianism), Dao. Some philosophers, such as William James and John Dewey, insist that there is no single substance or absolute unity but rather a radical pluralism or network of relations, all in process, each relating to all of the other relations but with no unifying or encompassing reality.[1] This essay presupposes that these diverse metaphysical/ontological claims do not eliminate each other but rather point to an ultimate reality irrespective of which names most adequately describe it.

Epistemology

Wisdom clearly has to do with knowledge, and particularly extraordinary knowledge, or knowledge attained by an extraordinary capacity. By definition, it is not commonly shared. Philosophical statements sometimes resemble proverbs in that they appear at first view to be wise until they are contradicted by an equally attractive perspective, by which process both philosophies reveal their incompleteness. In the face of contradiction, a deeper knowing is needed. Plato's entire philosophy, especially in his early and middle dialogues, argues for and exemplifies a deeper and broader kind of knowing, the kind that, if sustained, could qualify as wisdom.

Remarkably, Plato himself, in his later dialogues, powerfully critiqued his own earlier knowledge claims. In the end, he showed himself to be wise in two respects, for the intuitions in the early and middle dialogues and for brilliant scrutiny of those intuitions in his later dialogues. Both metaphysics and epistemology are needed for wisdom, and ideally lead in tandem to ethics. A moral decision, or deed, presupposes, enlists, and helps to fashion and refine both metaphysics and epistemology. The entire Anglo-American analytic movement that has dominated philosophy since the 1920s has specialized in criticism. Philosophic wisdom, however, also depends on speculation. Both criticism and speculation are necessary for wisdom, ideally in balance.

While scientific knowledge might be important on the way to wisdom, it does not constitute wisdom itself because without the collaboration of philosophy it does not typically offer a comprehensive account of metaphysics or ethics. The great scientific-philosophic geniuses of the seventeenth and eighteenth centuries, Galileo, Descartes, Newton, and Leibniz, are intellectually brilliant but because they did not develop the ethical dimension they are less likely to be considered wise than philosophers whose contributions include ethics. Einstein surely seems wise but mostly because in addition to being considered the greatest scientist since Newton, he pronounced brilliantly on human nature, society, and peace. The greatest scientist since Einstein, Steven Hawking, is clearly in a class by himself as a physicist, with an amazing knowledge of the cosmos (and applauded for his ability to cope with an extremely debilitating illness), but because he does not advance systematic ethical thinking, he is not a prime example of wisdom.

Alfred North Whitehead exemplifies wisdom not particularly on the basis of his mathematical or scientific knowledge but because of his philosophical knowledge, and specifically his learned and eloquent philosophical imagination. Like Whitehead, Karl Jaspers qualifies as a wise philosopher precisely because his philosophy includes but is not limited to science. Whitehead and Jaspers, like James and Dewey, speculate but not without criticism, and also have a constant eye on the relevance of their critical-speculative philosophy for individuals, groups, cultures, civilizations, and the future of humanity.

Ethics/Right Action/Virtue

Wisdom is here defined in terms of scope and depth of knowledge and truth, and of equal importance, on the side of virtue, practical relevance, as well as social and historical significance. Wisdom is precisely the knowledge most worth having, often after a lifelong search, and consequently extremely valuable. In this sense, wisdom is deep or uncommon knowledge essential for living and a foundation for right action. A wise virtuous person[2] knows right action from wrong, and further, is able to act on the side of right. However, contrary to Plato who thought that true knowledge leads automatically to right or moral action, there is often a split between knowing what is right and doing it. A person who seems to know and to espouse right action but does not act accordingly is rightly accused of inconsistency, or worse, of hypocrisy, or caught in a psychological limitation such as fear or a complex. The Christian tradition, following St. Paul and Augustine, admits of internal conflicts between knowledge and virtue. Shakespeare's characters put dramatic, and tragic, flesh on these theological bones. Then Freud showed that instincts, unconscious drives, and fears often overwhelm fragile knowledge, even knowledge considered wise. Since Freud, wisdom must include psychological insight, or knowledge of one's many layers of motivation. This, of course, requires a person to possess deep knowledge of the unconscious. C. G. Jung's concept of individuation refers to the ideal integration of conscious and unconscious dimensions of the self.

Josiah Royce, William James's younger colleague at Harvard, and a great historian of philosophy as well as the creator of a vast metaphysical system, emphasized the practical import of even the most contemplative metaphysical speculation:

> The reflective play of one age becomes the passion of another. Plato creates utopias and the Christian faith of Europe afterwards gives them meaning. Contemplation gives birth to future conduct, and so the philosopher also becomes, in his own fashion, a world-builder.[3]

The History of Wisdom

Philosophic wisdom is perhaps most frequently associated with Greek and Roman philosophy, and secondly with medieval Christian philosophy and theology, and with the exception of German idealism, scarcely at all with modern or contemporary philosophy. In this light, it would almost be accurate to have entitled this essay, "the loss of the love of wisdom in Western philosophy."[4] Fortunately, this loss, though significant, is not total: there are some genuinely wise modern Western philosophers, including a few explicitly committed to the ideal of wisdom.

From the perspective of originality and complexity, the history of wisdom in the West can be seen as an evolutionary process, from broad generalizations seen to be naive from later perspectives, to highly nuanced, self-conscious, well-argued positions. With respect to the ideal of intelligence, argumentation, and clarity, Western philosophy is surely progressive. In important (though not all) respects, Whitehead is an advance on Plato, Dewey is similarly an advance on Aristotle, Aquinas an advance on Augustine, and Steiner and Teilhard an advance on Aquinas. In each comparison, the later philosophers are more informed concerning history and science, and more efficacious in application. This is progress. By other criteria, specifically concerning wisdom, however, modern Western philosophers, and thinkers generally, might not be wiser and they might be less devoted to wisdom.

If this perspective, and approach, is at all valid, and illuminating of wisdom, then it would seem right to proceed to the beginning of philosophy, when it was, or certainly was understood to be, the love of wisdom. For Plato, wisdom is the object of the lifelong desire of the philosopher.[5] Before

Plato, there was Socrates, and before Socrates there was cosmological thinking mixed with mythic figures such as Apollo, the god of reason.[6]

Prior to Socrates, Wisdom/Sophia in the Greek tradition, and Hokhma in the Hebraic tradition, were assumed to be real beings, with an existence independent of whether human beings ever thought of them. By his insistent thinking and inquiring, Socrates successfully challenged that assumption. He started his career by a consultation with the Delphic Oracle, a source of wise advice, and finished his career, as he was about to drink the hemlock ordered by a politically corrupt jury, by affirming the value of thinking but little else in the way of conclusions. It was Socrates who introduced this kind of questioning as an ultimate value and the core meaning thereafter of philo-sophia in the West.

As a result of the depiction of Socrates in Plato's *Apology, Crito,* and *Phaedo,* Socrates is regarded as the primary source of philosophic wisdom in the West. Pythagoras and Parmenides, of course, are important precursors of Socrates, but note that Socrates is never referred to as a Pythagorean or a Parmenidean; they are referred to as Presocratic. Since the time of Plato's dialogues, Socrates has been seen as the model of calm in the defense of reason and of integrity in the face of life-threatening danger (in his case, impending unjust execution). In this specific respect, he is the precursor of Boethius in the Christian Middle Ages—as well as Simone Weil who died of tuberculosis and malnutrition during World War II, and Karl Jaspers who calmly resolved to face death should his Jewish wife be a victim of the Holocaust.

The narrative of Western philosophy typically begins with Socrates the dialogical questioner, followed by his student Plato, the dramatist of ideas, and then by Plato's student Aristotle, the systematizer of all knowledge at that time into disciplines, methods, guiding principles, and brilliant outcomes. Although there are several subsequent periods of explosive genius in the West, particularly the 130 years that includes the scientific achievements of Copernicus, Kepler, Galileo, Descartes, Newton, and Leibniz, as well as the emergence of German genius in the early nineteenth century that includes Kant, Goethe, Schiller, Fichte, Schelling, and Hegel, it is the combination of Socrates, Plato, and Aristotle that clearly stands out for its philosophical originality and comprehensive influence.

Many introductory lectures on the history of Western philosophy introduce the importance of Plato by quoting the comment of Alfred North Whitehead, "The safest general characterization of the European philosophical tradition is that it consists of a series of footnotes to Plato."[7] The reply of Aristotelians is less well known but equally apt: "Yes, and Aristotle wrote all of the footnotes." This history is more complicated and interesting in that Plato reemerged through Plotinus and Neoplatonism, through Augustine and the entire arc of Christian thought, and the modern Western idealist and Romantic traditions. Each subsequent version of Platonism strives to advance Plato's verticality while variously trying to manage Aristotle's more horizontal, empirical approach. Appropriately, in Raphael's "School of Athens," Plato points up, Aristotle down, and both are in the center, the indispensable alternatives. Together they represent the two halves of Western philosophic wisdom, and behind them both, Socrates, the embodiment of the philosophical ideal of honest questioning and persistent dialogue.

It takes a significant effort, and help from historians of Greek philosophy such as W. C. K. Guthrie and F. M. Cornford, for a modern, and particularly postmodern person to take seriously the reality of Apollo or Sophia—or Isis, the dominant divine figure in the Mediterranean world for three thousand years. It would be equally implausible to a contemporary educated person to consider that Socrates, the progenitor of Western philosophy, and Plato, the first to create sophisticated methods of argument, could have regarded Sophia, the concept of wisdom, as anything but a metaphor, and certainly not as a real being, an active source of insight. Yet in the *Symposium*—a masterful dialogue from the middle, i.e., the peak, of Plato's philosophic powers—we read that a wise woman, Diotima of Miletus, revealed to Socrates the most profound meaning of love.[8] What was behind this device, and what did Plato's contemporaries make of it?

The difference between regarding Isis or Sophia as a being or a concept can be considered the difference between mythos and logos, or the difference between mythic and rational thinking. After more than three hundred pages of careful argumentation on the nature of the self and the state, Plato concludes his *Republic,* his most ambitious and most confident dialogue, with "The Myth of Er," an account of justice in the afterlife. In all subsequent dialogues, however, the mythic is absent. The transition from mythos to logos was realized in the course of several of Plato's dialogues. In three generations, Western philosophy evolved from a Socratic mix of myth and inquiry to Platonic dialectic with only occasional appearances of myth, to Aristotelian analysis and argument without myth.

If this essay were focused on wisdom in the West without a specific focus on philosophy, a substantial portion would be given to the Abrahamic religions. However, as this volume includes essays on wisdom in Judaism, Christianity, and Islam, this essay, except for its final brief section, focuses on wisdom in Western philosophy. Philosophy and religion in the early centuries of the West, as in all other traditional cultures, were entwined. The Hebraic tradition gives the West some of its most beautiful descriptions of Wisdom as the source of divinely inspired human knowledge and virtue. These texts are generally in contrast with Socratic dialogue, Plato's unrestrained inquiry, and Aristotle's disciplined pursuit of core principles and their rightful application. At approximately the same time as Socrates, in the Hebraic tradition, an entirely different idea of wisdom emerges, one that is mythic rather than philosophical, closer to the Greek idea of Sophia than to the ideal of wisdom according to Plato and Aristotle.

As with the entire Judaic tradition, the relation between the human and divine is intensely personal. And so it is with Wisdom, particularly in the five Wisdom books: Job, Proverbs, Ecclesiastes, Ecclesiasticus, and Wisdom. The Book of Wisdom, which was written in Greek during the last century BCE, uses the name *Sophia* instead of the Hebrew term *Chokhmah*. Subsequently, in the first century CE, Philo Judaeus wrote on, and to some extent fused, the Logos of the Greek tradition and Sophia of the Hebraic tradition.[9]

Following Philo as well as the New Testament writers, the early Christian tradition developed a variety of theological explanations concerning the relationship between Logos who is one with the Father/Creator, and Sophia, the mediator between the Logos/Christ and humanity. For the Christian tradition generally, the Incarnation of Christ and Wisdom/Sophia are entwined, as are the Love that is Christ and the Wisdom that is Sophia.[10]

Wisdom of the Stoics

Histories of Western philosophy tend to proceed from Aristotle to Descartes and the seventeenth century. They usually give only fleeting attention to Roman, and specifically Stoic philosophy, as well as to the entire history of Christian ethics which can be characterized as a creative blend of Stoicism with the Incarnation of Christ as depicted in the New Testament. By so doing, they neglect one of the world views that forms, along with Plato and Aristotle, the foundations of Christian, and more broadly, Western thought and culture.[11] Stoicism, and particularly their conceptions of wisdom and virtue, exercised a profound influence on the major thinkers of the Roman empire, including: Epictetus (ca.50–135 CE), a former slave who founded and directed a school for Stoic ethics; Seneca (4 BCE–63 CE), a tutor of Nero and a high official in Nero's administration (it was at Nero's direction that he committed suicide); Cicero (106–143 BCE), a Roman senator; and Marcus Aurelius (121–180 CE) the Roman emperor from 169–180 CE, during which time he was frequently in battle throughout Europe, and during which time he wrote his enduring *Meditations*.

By the definition of wisdom guiding this essay—the commingling of epistemology, metaphysics, and ethics—the Stoics are surely contributors to the lineage of Western philosophical wisdom. In contrast to most Western philosophies, however, Stoicism contributed more significantly to ethics than to either epistemology or metaphysics. Briefly, the core claim of the Stoics is both profound and slightly unclear. Starting with Zeno (334–362 BCE), the founder of the early Stoa (paths for walking between two rows of columns while philosophizing), and continuing until the death of Marcus Aurelius more than five centuries later, the Stoics based their ethics on a conception of Nature that was both fundamental and epistemologically vague. More importantly, the same can be said of Stoic ethics: it is difficult to establish just what the Stoic philosophers meant by their two essential terms, Nature and human nature. A lack of clarity concerning these complementary terms makes it difficult to know the extent to which and ways in which one is (or is not) cooperating with Nature or realizing (or not) what is best in human nature.

One characteristic of the Stoic conception of Nature is absolutely clear: it is deterministic. All natural events are determined—while at the same time, in a decisive claim, human beings are not determined in how they might react to determined events. In effect, *amor fati,* to be found in so many religious documents, is precisely this Stoic conviction: love what you cannot change. It is also at the core of the life and writings of Simone Weil, the mid-twentieth-century pacifist philosopher, and the essential point of the triad known as the Serenity Prayer first formulated by Reinhold Niebuhr, mid-twentieth-century American protestant theologian: "Lord grant me the serenity to accept the things I cannot change, the courage to change the things I can, and the wisdom to know the difference."

By way of summary, the inspiring writings of the most prominent Stoics, Seneca and Cicero in Latin, and Epictetus and Marcus Aurelius in Greek, offer a deep and compelling case for serenity in the face of pain and death. Wisdom is virtue, and virtue is wisdom, both based on the knowledge of the perfect unity of Nature and human nature, both revealed by the virtuous person. The difficulty, of course, lies in the circularity of these terms which can be broken only by locating a model virtuous person. Seneca was calm in the face of adversity, including his *amor fati* suicide, but in other respects, particularly his wealth, he seems to have lived at variance with his Stoic ideals. Fortunately, Zeno, Epictetus, Cicero, and Marcus appear to have been candidates for this status. As Stoicism was taken up very significantly by Christianity, particularly once it united with Rome, the life of Christ and the early saints assumed this function, so that wisdom and virtue were identified with the life depicted in the New Testament and in the individuals whose lives were devoted to the imitation of that singular life.

Christian Wisdom

If Wisdom lost some, or perhaps all, of its transcendent status as the source of knowledge after Aristotle, it was restored and enhanced by the Christian revelation, especially in the Gospel of John and the Epistles of Paul. The Prologue to John's Gospel reads:

> In the beginning was the Word and the Word was with God, and the Word was God. He was in the beginning with God, all things were made through Him and without Him not anything was made that was made.[12]

This text claims that the Word (the English word for the Greek word *logos*) is one with God the Father and as such was and is the instrument of all creation. The Logos of John's Gospel presents Light, Love, and Wisdom as synonymous, rather like the eternal Ideas—Truth, Beauty, the Good—that Plato affirmed in his *Republic*. Logos represents a new law characterized by love (*agape*). John writes: "For the law was given through Moses; grace and truth came through Jesus Christ."[13]

Paul, a Jew, a Roman citizen, and a convert to Christianity, contrasted the wisdom of both Jews and Greeks with the wisdom bestowed on believers by Christ:

> For the word of the cross is folly to those who are perishing, but to us who are being saved it is the power of God. For it is written,
> I will destroy the wisdom of the wise,
> And the cleverness of the clever I will thwart. (Isaiah, 29:14)
> Where is the wise man? Where is the scribe? Where is the debater of this age? Has not God made foolish the wisdom of the world? For since, in the wisdom of God, the world did not know God through the folly of what we preach to save those who believe. For Jews demand signs and Greeks seek wisdom, but we preach Christ crucified, a stumbling block to the Jews and folly to the Gentiles, but to those who are called, both Jews and Greeks, Christ is the power of God and wisdom of God. For the foolishness of God is wiser than men, and the weakness of God is stronger than men.[14]

If one wishes to find wisdom in the Christian tradition it is well to call on guides such as Bruno Barnhart,[15] a Benedictine monk and expert of Sapiential Christianity, or William Johnston,[16] expert on Christian and Buddhist spirituality, or Raimon Panikkar,[17] philosopher and theologian of Asian and Western traditions, all authors of important writings on Christian wisdom. Bruno Barnhart writes:

> Central to the experience of Christians was a new consciousness, a new understanding. Jesus himself was the divine Wisdom come into the world, a fullness of light now shared by the believer. Christian writers of the early centuries, on the basis of the Johannine Prologue, developed a theological vision centered in Christ as the divine Logos. This incarnate Word was understood as the Bridegroom of the Church, participated in through a unitive knowledge (an intimate personal relationship with Christ), and was seen as the sun of understanding. This Logos was recognized as the one key to penetrating the mysteries both of the cosmos and of the biblical history of salvation. In the Greek patristic tradition, it is Jesus Christ as Logos that illuminates the whole of reality.[18]

With wisdom identified with Christ, who in turn is identified with the Father, the infinite and eternal Creator, the challenge for Christian theologians and philosophers was to restore some of the prestige of reason. To the extent that they were able to do so, it was significantly with the works of Plato and Aristotle. In general, Augustine in the fifth century absorbed the Platonism of Neoplatonic philosophers, especially Plotinus and Porphyry. In the thirteenth century Thomas Aquinas absorbed and Christianized the philosophy of Aristotle.

Early in his career as a professor of rhetoric in North Africa, Augustine was influenced by Cicero's *Hortensius,* an exhortation to philosophical wisdom. He then studied Manichaeism, and as he narrated in his *Confessions,* his classic autobiography—which is also the first autobiography in world literature—he converted to Christianity and emerged as the single most influential thinker of the early Christian centuries. Augustine identified wisdom with the divine archetypes, or the ideas in God's mind. He developed an epistemology of two levels of knowledge, intellect and intuition, a distinction characteristic of Romantic thinkers. According to Augustine, it is only by intuition, by an illumined mind, that one can know the divine. Such knowledge requires a combination of epistemological effort and the grace of Christ dwelling in the human soul.

True happiness is to rejoice in the truth, for to rejoice in the
truth is to rejoice in you, O God, who are the Truth, you my
God, my true Light, to whom I look for salvation. This is the
happiness that all desire.[19]

Thomas Aquinas defined wisdom as the source of all true knowledge
and of moral action.[20] Similarly, for the fourteenth-century German mystic,
Meister Eckhart, wisdom is the basis of the knowledge of God and "the
'birth' of God in the soul." Nicholas of Cusa, a Roman Catholic Cardinal
and diplomat as well as a mathematician, theologian, and philosopher, saw
wisdom "on all levels of spiritual being and as the principle and goal of all
spiritual activity."[21]

In the middle of this survey of theological statements concerning wisdom is the inspiring figure of Boethius, a devoted student of Plato, Aristotle,
and the Stoics, imprisoned after being falsely accused of treason. By his lone
work, *The Consolation of Philosophy,* which he wrote in prison awaiting execution, he bequeathed to his contemporaries and all interested in wisdom and
justice thereafter a remarkably dramatic affirmation of the Christian love of
wisdom. With echoes of Job's experience of the Voice from the Whirlwind
that reveals the wisdom of God's ways, and the calm, resolute embrace of
falsely accused Socrates when forced to drink hemlock, or the suicide of
Seneca under pressure from the emperor Nero, Lady Philosophy convinces
the ill-fated—and increasingly equanimous—Boethius that even his execution
can be understood in the light of divine wisdom. Petitioned by Boethius,
Lady Philosophy vividly revealed herself to be an inspiring image and presence in the mind and heart of the imprisoned and doomed Boethius. She
provided wise consolation that Boethius would presumably not have been
able to generate without her influence. Boethius in conversation with Lady
Philosophy would seem to provide a convincing example of Wisdom—
knowledge from a deep source—Lady Philo-Sophia Herself—leading to right
action—calm in the face of death.

The Enlightenment and Romanticism

While no sensible modern Western person would want to live in a culture
not yet transformed by the humanistic genius of the eighteenth-century
European Enlightenment, neither would we want to live in a culture guided
solely be Enlightenment ideals. It is right to bow to the genius of Locke,
Hume, Diderot, and Kant, and other Enlightenment thinkers. It might be
even more obvious to bow to their American followers, the Founders—

Washington, Franklin, Jefferson, Adams, Hamilton, and Madison—but the history of thought is sufficiently progressive that even they were surpassed three-quarters of a century later by Emerson and Lincoln, and they in turn were surpassed in enlightened thinking by John Dewey and the Rev. Dr. Martin Luther King Jr.

Such intellectual progress is due at least in part to critique and opposition, to vigorous dialectic. The dialogical opposition to the Enlightenment is Romanticism. Both of these worldviews have contributed many positive influences, but only the Romantic worldview honored and aspired to wisdom as such. We might say that the Enlightenment offered a great advance in the use of intelligence, particularly in science and social sciences, namely, instrumental reason; the philosophical Romantics, including Goethe, Coleridge, and Emerson, advanced the use of intuition in science and social science, and particularly in relation to the arts.[22] In the context of this essay, it would seem justified to view Romanticism as dedicated to wisdom, that is, to an experience of a deep source, whether Nature or the Absolute, or in the twentieth century, the unconscious, by a deep way of knowing, usually imagination or intuition, and leading to right and creative action. In general, twentieth-century philosophy is closer to science than to art, and so relies on rational argument, shunning the possibility of knowledge from a deep source and the method of imagination/intuition that might lead to it.

The Cultivation and Significance of Philosophic Wisdom in the Twentieth Century

This section offers very brief introductions to philosophers whose works are examples of wise thinking and thinking as a way to wisdom. The first part briefly introduces the classic American philosophical tradition during the nineteenth century and the first half of the twentieth century: Ralph Waldo Emerson, William James, Josiah Royce, John Dewey, and Alfred North Whitehead. The second part discusses the contributions of three European philosophers at mid-twentieth century: Simone Weil, Martin Buber, and Karl Jaspers.

Classical American Philosophy

Wisdom with an American accent tends to be very practical as evidenced by the predominance of American philosophy generated in lectures and essays written in response to pressing social and cultural concerns. James was a sophisticated thinker and writer in several disciplines and several languages but in *Pragmatism* his purpose was to make it possible for the nonphilosopher to make sense of his or her own experience. Similarly, Josiah Royce explained that in his teaching and writing philosophy he sought to give his students a place to stand.[23] John Dewey's philosophy of democracy is explicitly a philosophy of "the common man." As Dewey wrote:

> Philosophy recovers itself when it ceases to be a device for deal-
> ing with the problems of philosophers and become a method,
> cultivated by philosophers, for the problems of men.[24]

Given the history of the twentieth century, what could be more impor-tant than Dewey's philosophy of democracy, the enemy of National Socialism and other expressions of totalitarianism? From the Founders to Lincoln to James and Dewey, to Rev. Dr. Martin Luther King Jr., the American reli-gious, political, and philosophical traditions represent a commitment to the integration of metaphysics, epistemology, and especially ethics. "We hold these truths to be self-evident, that all men are created equal" was not applied when articulated, nor was it intended to be, but in its depth and clarity, in its ability to raise consciousness and to exercise practical cultural and politi-cal behavior, it stands at the base of American wisdom, the fruit of the first cluster of wise Americans.

A broad review of the philosophic wisdom of the classical American philosophical tradition must begin with Ralph Waldo Emerson, America's sage, for it is Emerson who provides the richest language, and most exem-plifies the transformative power of philosophical reflection. In language that is later echoed in the writings of the pragmatists (Peirce, James, Royce, and Dewey), and religious philosophers such as Weil, Buber, and Jaspers, Emer-son proclaims the transformative power of the active soul, the person who thinks freshly and honestly, with devotion to the challenges of individual and social life. He wrote: "Why should not we also enjoy an original rela-tion to the universe?"[25] This relationship involves both the individual and the Absolute: "I could not be, but that absolute life circulated in me, and I could not think this without being that absolute life."[26] Emerson's ethical judgments and moral behavior follow typically from his solitary reflection and his conversations with past representatives of wisdom and with contem-poraries equally devoted to "an original relation to the Universe." His essays and journals stand out as an inexhaustible source of wisdom. His life and his writings exemplify his conviction that "The one thing in the world, of value, is the active soul."[27]

As the Founders represent the first American convergence of political genius (as well as courage and vision that proved historically momentous), a second cluster of genius emerged three-quarters of a century after the Founders, in the Concord of Ralph Waldo Emerson and in the presidency of Abraham Lincoln. In his essay, "Self Reliance" (1836), Emerson declared a second declaration of independence from England and Europe—not political independence, but intellectual. In his Gettysburg Address and Second Inaugural Address, Lincoln in effect joined deep insight, eloquent argument, and inestimable practical historical import, each an integral component of wisdom. Emerson and Lincoln, each of whom suffered the death of a child, acknowledged divine immanence and transcendence, both exhibited epistemological clarity and caution, and both spoke with impressive insight concerning the moral claims needed at that time, and at the present.

A third such cluster of genius occurred in the early twentieth century Harvard philosophy department of William James, Josiah Royce, and Alfred North Whitehead, and the mid-twentieth century Columbia philosophy department of John Dewey.

In psychology, philosophy, and the study of religion, as well as three decades of research concerning psychical experience,[28] James showed a genius for original insight. He practiced philosophy as "a habit of always seeing an alternative."[29] From beginning to end, James's convictions remained open to revision.

One of Josiah Royce's many original, wise insights is his ethical theory, "loyalty to loyalty."[30] We might approach this contribution by noticing that contemporary writers on wisdom, most of whom are psychologists, seem to offer characterizations of wisdom that include some wise individuals but they do not exclude scoundrels and truly evil individuals such as Hitler.[31] Royce's loyalty to loyalty would seem to offer an ingenious solution to this stubborn problem. By being loyal to Hitler's genocidal "final solution," Germans, Austrians, and others were disloyal to the loyalties of the Jews, Gypsies, gays, and others whom the Nazis considered unworthy to participate in the Third Reich. Hitler's absolutely evil project deliberately denied these others the opportunity to practice their own loyalties. Jesus and Buddha certainly did not violate the loyalties of their intellectual opponents and political enemies, nor did the actions of Gandhi, King, and the Dalai Lama, but the actions of Hitler and all tyrants, as well as the actions of intolerant religious leaders, clearly do violate the loyalties of their enemies. Royce's loyalty to loyalty, based on the reality of the Beloved Community as the holder of all ideals (including lost causes) as well as individual responsibility, would seem to be a strong candidate for wisdom.

While the classical American philosophical tradition does not end with Dewey and Whitehead, the two major philosophers working primarily from the original insights of William James, it does climax with them. Alfred North Whitehead had three great careers: as a mathematician at Cambridge University; as a philosopher of science at University of London; and as a comprehensive philosopher at Harvard, where he built on the philosophy of William James. In response to the deepest ontological question—How did the Universe come about?—Whitehead introduced and expanded the concept of creativity as the source of the universe. He also contributed an ingenious solution to the problem of theodicy: How can an all-knowing and all-powerful God be the creator and guide of so much evil and suffering? Extending, and rendering systematic, James's conception of God as finite,[32] Whitehead proposes that God should be understood to have two natures, Primordial, or the pure potential of existence, and Consequent, or the history of the Cosmos. Within the context of this solution, Whitehead proposes that the Primordial nature of God is all good but, as evidenced by God's Consequent nature, neither all-knowing nor all-powerful. According to Whitehead, God does not directly control human events and does not know the future. For traditional adherents of any one of the three Abrahamic religions it might seem painful, and a contradiction of the nature of God, to deny God's foreknowledge, but to do so would seem to be an example of philosophical wisdom.

John Dewey, the philosopher of common knowledge and "the common man," entitled his one book on religion "A Common Faith."[33] Thoroughly Aristotelian, Dewey's philosophy runs in reverse order from Plato's: he focuses primarily on social and ethical problems and works back to metaphysics, to the extent possible. His great strength is in his epistemology, methodology, and ethics, specifically his development of the method of scientific rationality and shared intelligence, and their application to "the problems of men," including education, social justice, institutions, and peace among nations. Compared to philosophers such as Plato and Aristotle, or Spinoza and Hegel, Dewey's metaphysics might appear flat and restrained. He preferred, and clearly trusted, practical intelligence over metaphysics because he was convinced that claims for and against a particular metaphysics have often led (and continue to lead) to all manner of misdeed. For this reason, he begins with the crises and precariousness of daily life and proceeds to an appropriate epistemology, and then, as he deems possible, he articulates an ontology—not of the Absolute, or the One, or God, or the Unconscious, but of nature and experience.[34]

Dewey's devotion to solving the major problems of his day, and the extraordinary versatility of his thinking, enabled him to generate a philosophy that is vast, deep, honest, and helpful—not at all common. For Dewey—who was wise in his ability to protect, reconcile, and advance the worthy causes of individuals and groups—wisdom consists in reasoning together, rather like the free debate typical of the town hall meeting of his native Vermont. Given the violent horrors of the last century, and the ecological horrors almost certainly awaiting humanity and Earth in the twenty-first century, Dewey's method of intelligence might be as close to wisdom as philosophy in the West, on its own, can attain at the present time.

Simone Weil (1909–1943)

Albert Camus referred to Simone Weil as "The only great spirit of our time."[35] Andre Gide referred to her as "the most important spiritual writer of this century."[36] T. S. Eliot referred to her as "a kind of genius akin to that of a saint."[37] In fact, Weil is equally genius and saint. Although a German name, Weil is pronounced *Veh* because she lived in the French section of Alsace and definitely considered herself French above all. Clearly a pure soul who inspired deep admiration, Weil was also frustrating. Of course, the combination of genius and saint, as well as self-proclaimed outsider, could not have been otherwise than confusing, and occasionally infuriating, for her colleagues and friends. It is no easier for us to understand her now.

Although Weil was Jewish by birth, she was fiercely anti-Hebraic. Intellectually, she was devoted to classical Greek thought and culture, and fiercely opposed to everything Roman. She referred to Hebraism and Romanism as "the beast." Spiritually, Weil converted to Catholicism in its French expression but because of its association with the Roman Empire she vigorously criticized and refuse to join the Roman Catholic Church. Perhaps it would be most accurate to classify her as a gnostic: she was entirely independent in her method of attaining and her mode of explaining her spiritual knowledge. More precisely, she was in the tradition of the Cathars, a community, or movement of gnostics, mostly women, in twelfth and thirteenth-century France who were persecuted by the Catholic Church as heretics for their anti-institutional teachings and for their opposition to matter, including the human body, both in general and their own bodies in particular.

In terms of her contribution to wisdom, Simone Weil contributed a profound body of thought perfectly fused with a brief but remarkable life, both developed very deliberately in service of integrity and nonviolence. As with Socrates and Boethius, her manner of facing death crystalized the union of her life and thought. As her solidarity with all outsiders kept her from baptism as a Catholic, her devotion to the French soldiers behind enemy lines during World War II led her to eat no more than they did, which, in combination with tuberculosis, led to her starvation and death. Her life-defining solidarity plus *amor fati* (love of fate) led to her death, less as an intentional suicide than as a result of her fundamental commitment to those who suffered.

Epistemologically, Weil learned by intense introspection, study, work (including work in a Renault factory and in a vineyard), prayer, and strenuous opposition to her own ego; metaphysically, she affirmed divinity as love. She experienced human love as a process of returning to God what God gives as existence and expects in return from human beings. Ethically, she was devoted to peace and love as the way of uniting with both God and humanity. She taught and exemplified the Christian way, and wisdom, of the cross.

Whether despite or because of her opposition to the Catholic Church, to dogma and to prescriptions, she was profoundly Christian, a new kind of saint, a patron of all outsiders. Her wisdom issues from and returns us to suffering and love. Her wisdom cannot and should not be ignored and yet is too radical, too demanding to endure. Only a few of us, or perhaps not even a few of us, can accommodate the way of this new kind of saint.

Martin Buber (1878–1965)

Although Martin Buber was seldom antagonistic, he was certainly opposed to Gandhi's opinion that the Jews should respond nonviolently to the Nazis. Not surprisingly, he was equally opposed to Simone Weil's detestation of everything Hebraic. Clearly, wisdom comes in many forms, especially when generated and embodied by highly evolved singular personalities. Simone Weil's wisdom focuses on interiority and living as an outsider in an alienated culture; Buber's wisdom focuses on dialogue and relations. Although they both aspire to love, Weil writes of love between lonely individuals. For Weil as for Kierkegaard, only the individual is authentic; the crowd is a lie.[38] For Buber, truth lives in community, the ideal between Kierkegaard's (and Weil's) individualism and Marx's collectivism.

Buber's and Weil's Jewishness is completely opposite: Buber was assimilated in nineteenth and twentieth-century German and largely Christian thought and culture; although Weil was born Jewish, and faced extermination by the Nazis on that account, she considered herself intellectually Greek and spiritually Christian (in accordance with the New Testament, and not with the Catholic Church). They were both sympathetic to the life and teachings of Jesus, but for Weil this influence led inexorably to sacrifice, suffering, and "the way of the cross"; for Buber it led indirectly to the ideal of dialogue and relationship between the humanity and a personal God.

Martin Buber's *I and Thou* is a masterpiece of philosophic prose, and very nearly philosophic poetry, filled with insight about human relations. It essentially articulates the preconditions for an individual person to attain personhood, a task that, in Buber's view, is not easily achieved or sustained. It is not only possible but usual for a person to fail in this one essential endeavor. In terms developed by mid-twentieth-century existentialist philosophers, especially Jean-Paul Sartre, a person can exist and not realize his or her potential personhood. Only an "I" can achieve a unique and authentic nature, or individual human essence—which, significantly, is temporary until the next self-defining moment, the next response, relation, or affirmation.

Buber's epistemology, metaphysics, and ethics are all based on his conception of relation, and more precisely, the "between." In his classic text, *I and Thou,* all reality, and especially human reality, is represented by the hyphen, whether between I and Thou or between I and It. Reality is between God and humanity (particularly the individual human), between person and person, person and community, and between person and nature. Accordingly, his epistemology—and his contribution to philosophic wisdom—focuses on knowing the terms of "betweenness," the conditions and effect of genuine or authentic relations, by affirming another without preconditions, without boundaries, and without a reduction of the other's mystery.

Karl Jaspers (1883–1969)

In a way comparable to Simone Weil and Martin Buber, Karl Jaspers generated a large body of wise thought and also practiced wisdom, though like Buber's middle way of wisdom and not at all like Weil's radical way. Weil, Buber, and Jaspers share a conviction similar to the medieval concept *adaequatio,* namely, that the apprehension of reality (or divinity, which is true reality) requires that the knower be adequate to this task, that is to say, to think with a pure, selfless, loving mind, capable of transcending the rational intellect. Jaspers makes this point very clearly in his *Way to Wisdom:*

> Philosophical thought begins at the limits of this rational knowl-
> edge. Rationality cannot help us in the essentials: it cannot help
> us to posit aims and ultimate ends, to know the highest good, to
> know God and human freedom; this inadequacy of the rational
> gives rise to a kind of thinking which, while working with the
> tools of understanding, is more than understanding. Philosophy
> presses to the limits of rational knowledge and there takes fire.[39]

Karl Jaspers is both an expert interpreter of many significant philosophers and an original philosopher whose scholarly rationality led him to "take fire." Jaspers is the author of *The Great Philosophers,* the magisterial four-volume study of approximately twenty great philosophers, ancient to modern, Asian and Western. In a philosophical tour de force, *The Great Philosophers* offers Jaspers's interpretations of, and perhaps more accurately, inspiring dialogues with, several Presocratic cosmologists, four paradigmatic figures (Confucius, Buddha, Socrates, Jesus), Plato, Aristotle, Augustine, Cusa, Descartes, Kant, Hegel, Kierkegaard, Nietzsche, and Weber. Jasper also wrote several volumes on the practice of philosophy.

His *Way to Wisdom* argues that philosophic wisdom can and should serve as the foundation of the individual lives of philosophers and nonphilosophers alike, as well as the source of defining cultural ideals. Jaspers aims to restore philosophy, and particularly philosophical wisdom, to metaphysical depth, epistemological clarity, and virtuous action. For such knowledge to be possible, the philosopher must serve both the source and goal of philosophy. Furthermore, Jaspers insists that one's philosophy, including its validity and significance, are inseparable from one's character and one's way in the world. One can imagine that in writing the following passage in 1952, Jaspers, whose wife was Jewish, might have had in mind his former friend Martin Heidegger, a notoriously unapologetic Nazi:

> Philosophical ideas cannot be applied; they are a reality in themselves, so that we may say: in the fulfillment of these thoughts the man himself lives; or life is permeated with thought. That is why the philosopher and the man are inseparable (while man can be considered apart from scientific knowledge); and that is why we cannot explore philosophical ideas in themselves but must at the same time gain awareness of the philosophical humanity which conceived them.[40]

The philosopher's character, for good and ill, will unavoidably affect both the acquisition and expression of ordinary (mainstream) knowledge, and perhaps more decisively influence a philosopher's relation to a deep ontological source and the service to which insight is applied. Should anyone suspect that Jaspers, the author of highly sophisticated technical philosophical texts, would be unable to enter decisively into the press of a historical situation, the following 1942 journal entry should offer adequate evidence to the contrary:

May 2. If I cannot protect Gertrude [his wife] against brute force, I, too, have to die—this is simple human dignity. But that is not decisive and not enough.

My heart speaks quietly and reliably from its depths: I belong to her. It is God's will that if the will of man (and not nature) strikes one of the two of us with destructive force, both are struck together. One cannot separate in life by force those who are bound together for eternity, who are born for each other from one source. . . .

To become one in death is the fulfillment of love—it is like a kindly fate[41] that permits us to die together, while mere nature, when it causes death, forces the survivor to go on living.

My philosophy would be nothing if it were to fail at this decisive point. Somewhere, fidelity is absolute or it is not at all. . . .

Each of us will always want to protect the other's life until the moment when—so I hope—worthy of each other and fundamentally at one—wedded to each other for eternity—we shall die calmly. . . .[42]

Clearly, Socrates, Boethius, and Weil survived in Jaspers.

As this ideal in our postmodern culture is obviously daunting, and to some extent dangerous, it is small wonder that the quest for wisdom is infrequently undertaken and even less frequently considered successful. As the last line of Spinoza's *Ethics* wisely states, "All things excellent are as difficult as they are rare." This is especially so of the excellence that is wisdom: it is difficult because it must issue from a personal relationship with a deep ontological source and must overcome psychological and ethical challenges in a world shot through with confusion and complexity. Karl Jaspers is exemplary in all of these respects: his life and writings reveal moral character, sound judgment, deep learning, and intense attention to the affairs of the world, including the horror of National Socialism.

Sources of Wisdom on the Periphery of Philosophy: Rudolf Steiner, Pierre Teilhard de Chardin, C. G. Jung, His Holiness the Dalai Lama

Beginning in the twentieth century, philosophizing has required knowledge of diverse cultures, many personality types, cosmic and atomic processes, and a variety of disciplines, but the profession of philosophy itself represents an additional challenge to philosophic wisdom. By its control of appointments and research opportunities, professional philosophers impose a flatland and alienated paradigm, one in which the human is separated from the divine, from the cosmos, and from inner realities. Philosophers who actively oppose this paradigm, or try to work outside of it, are generally considered irrelevant. Except for James, classical American philosophers tend to be ignored by European philosophers—and more incredibly but incontestably, by American philosophers who teach primarily European and British philosophers. The few philosophical positions, schools, or approaches in which wisdom appears to be both a value and a goal are associated with religious commitments, and consequently not "real" philosophy. In short, in the modern and contemporary Western philosophical tradition, wisdom is considered an illegitimate, or not serious, philosophical presupposition, assumption, focus, and goal.

Although philosophy courses continue to be an essential component in college curricula, shelves in bookstores, online book sales, and periodical book reviews all suggest that the American public reads less and less philosophy. There are, however, at least a half-dozen spiritually impressive individuals whose books continue to sell, and whose ideas are widely admired and discussed as examples of wisdom. The thought of Rudolf Steiner, Teilhard de Chardin, C. G. Jung, and the Dalai Lama reach far beyond their respective communities. Each of these four religious thinkers warrants a brief introduction.

At age twenty-one, Rudolf Steiner was appointed editor of the national edition of Goethe's scientific writing. At twenty-five, he published a book on Nietzsche. He subsequently created the Waldorf approach to education, biodynamic agriculture, and extensive contributions to various arts (including the new art form of eurythmy), sciences, research concerning Krishna, Buddha, and Christ, economics, and psychology.

The most important contribution of Rudolf Steiner toward wisdom would seem to be the directions he left for others to develop his intuitions—and their own. Steiner wrote his primary philosophy book, *Intuitive Thinking as a Spiritual Path*,[43] in 1894, six years before beginning his esoteric career. His basic esoteric book is entitled *How to Know Higher Worlds*.[44] We might note that his work exemplifies wisdom's three components: he drew from high and deep realms of spirit, he practiced and taught advanced stages of intuition, and he addressed his powers to the ethical concerns of contemporary thought and culture. He called his spiritual discipline anthroposophy: *anthropos,* the ideal human, and *sophia,* divine feminine wisdom.

Pierre Teilhard de Chardin, a French Jesuit priest, was a world-class paleontologist and Catholic mystic. Teilhard joined his two commitments, science and spirituality, in an exquisite synthesis so that his study of the Earth and evolution was simultaneously for him an act of adoration. He brought to both endeavors an unfailing optimism concerning Christendom and the goal of human evolution that he referred to as the Omega Point. Following our three-part conception of wisdom, Teilhard drew deeply from the Christian conception of divinity, and most particularly from his humble yet confident experience of Christ. By his active prayer and meditative life, and his devotion to the Roman Catholic sacraments, especially the Eucharist, he felt that he was able to see deeper into the natural world than would otherwise have been possible. Teilhard did not develop a philosophical ethics but his entire life, thought, and writings reveal an inspiring life of the highest moral ideals. Clearly, by any measure, Teilhard is an exemplar of wisdom.[45]

By virtue of his ability to access the deep levels of the psyche and intuitive powers in service of the conscious and unconscious dimensions of both self and society, Carl Gustav (C. G.) Jung would seem to be among the foremost candidates for a wisdom award. Ironically, Jung's courageous work with archetypes and symbols, and his many contributions to spiritual and esoteric research, run counter to his apparent commitment to the limits to knowledge set by Kant. He frequently insisted that he was not writing philosophy, but it might have been better if he had assumed responsibility for a coherent philosophical position, one consistent with the level of knowledge which he attained, particularly in the last decades of his life.

Although he consistently eschewed philosophy as such, he ingeniously exhibits the three components of wisdom, namely, ontology, epistemology, and ethics. In that many of his most original and significant insights focus on the wise and powerful activity of archetypes that he considered to be the foundational structure and activity of consciousness, Jung's analytic psychology could as accurately be called archetypal psychology. In countless examples drawn from his therapy sessions, sacred texts, and arts from many traditions, Jung showed that archetypes such as the Mother, Wise Old Man, Descent into Hell, Mandala, Self, and Shadow are active in the unconscious. In Jung's view, it is essential that individuals and cultures come to know the ways of myths, archetypes, symbols, and images.

Using the definition of wisdom introduced in this essay, His Holiness the Dalai Lama would seem to the very essence of wisdom. He lives in relation to Buddha-nature, the deepest Buddhist conception of reality as Emptiness/Fullness, and beyond this dichotomy and all other dichotomies. He knows this level of existence by a direct intuitive awareness made possible by rigorous training in Tibetan Buddhist philosophy and hours of daily meditation. In the ethical realm, the Dalai Lama stands out in the contemporary world as the foremost exponent and exemplar of nonviolence and peace, not in a general or vague sense but in detailed response to the Chinese government that continues to destroy Tibetan land, language, culture, and religion. Anyone who has studied the Dalai Lama's life, writings, and influence, or has had the privilege of his presence, is inclined to regard him as not only wise but as the embodiment of wisdom. As the fourteenth Dalai Lama, Tenzin Gyatso mysteriously embodies the bodhisattva *Avalokiteswara,* the spiritual being that endures as wisdom and compassion over many life times, perhaps eternally.

Conclusion

Philosophical Wisdom—knowledge from a deep source that leads to right action, and back again—seems to require that a philosopher work these three fields in harmony. Whether one begins with Platonic or Christian metaphysical conviction and works toward applications, or an Aristotelian-Deweyan cautious attention to the specifics of experience back to generalized conviction, both are needed complementarily. The Platonic approach is more bold and more prone to error; the Aristotelian approach tends to be safer in practice but limited in metaphysical assertion. Whichever of these approaches, or combination of approaches, a philosopher follows, it is important for him or her to work in collaboration with other disciplines. In this regard, Jaspers and the classical American philosophical tradition are especially successful, and the insights of spiritually efficacious, deep-thinking individuals such as Steiner, Teilhard de Chardin. C. G. Jung, and His Holiness the Dalai Lama are especially important at this time.

In sum, we have worked with the components of wisdom: metaphysics, epistemology, and ethics, and we have seen the importance of these three in mutuality. We have also seen that wisdom resides in Socrates, Plato, and Aristotle, in Augustine, Boethius, and Aquinas, in the nineteenth-century Romantic tradition, in the classical American philosophical tradition, and some twentieth-century European philosophers such as Karl Jaspers. With all of this before us we might venture an answer to question, in the terms made famous by William James, "What difference does it make?" The difference would seem to be, in another Jamesian concept, relationality: thinking is a way of relating, and thinking wisely is a way of realizing a life-sustaining relationship, offsetting the pain of opposition, loss, fear, and death. Socrates, Boethius, and Jaspers calmly facing death is a sign of wisdom, as is the courage of Washington, Lincoln, and King. There is also wisdom in the courage of thinking a new thought—Plato reaching for true Ideas, Augustine seeking to illumine his mind so as to grasp the nature of the divine revealed in Christ. As Bertrand Russell noted, philosophy renders the mind great.

> Through the greatness of the universe which philosophy contemplates, the mind also is rendered great, and becomes capable of that union with the universe which constitutes its highest good.[46]

What Russell refers to here as the Universe, Plato refers to as the Good, which is "the cause both of truth in speculation and rectitude in action."[47] Philosophical thinking, and wisdom, which is its fruit, restores us to the cosmos, to the Earth, and to the entire human community. By studying, contemplating, and imitating the wisdom of Plato and Aristotle, Emerson and Jaspers, we too can think wisely. We begin by thinking their thoughts, and eventually by thinking as they did, and then by thinking our own wise thoughts, until wisdom becomes a habit. We can habitually apprehend sources of meaning and truth, see deeper than the senses can reveal, and realize our oneness with all other realities—human, earthly, and divine. By this practice, we too can have a wise original relation to the Universe.

Endnotes

The author is grateful to Roger Walsh and Matthew David Segall, as well as to two anonymous reviewers, for suggesting improvements to this essay.

1. Irrespective of what his final ontological perspective might be, James does affirm a transcendence "through which saving experiences come," but he steadfastly resists a unity that might diminish the significance of the many. See William James, *The Varieties of Religious Experience: A Study in Human Nature,* intro. Martin E. Marty (New York: Penguin, 1982), pp. 508 and 515.

2. According to virtue ethics, a virtuous person is wise by definition and, less convincingly, a wise person is virtuous by definition.

3. Josiah Royce, *The Spirit of Modern Philosophy* (Boston: Houghton Mifflin/ Riverside Press, 1892), p. 12.

4. My reading of the history of philosophy has been deeply influenced by Rudolf Steiner's and Owen Barfield's account of the gradual separation of the human from the divine, and the corresponding evolutionary increase in human intellect and individuality.

5. *Phaedo,* 68a, trans. Hugh Tredennick, in *The Collected Dialogues of Plato,* ed. Edith Hamilton and Huntington Cairns (New York: Random House/Bollingen Foundation, 1961).

6. See F. M. Cornford, *Principium Sapientiae: A Study of the Origins of Greek Philosophical Thought,* ed., W. K. C. Guthrie (New York: Harper & Row/Harper Torchbooks, 1965).

7. A. N. Whitehead, *Process and Reality, Corrected Edition,* ed. David Ray Griffin and Donald W. Sherburne (New York: Macmillan/Free Press, 1978), p. 39.

8. For Diotima, see Plato, *Symposium* 201–212, in Hamilton and Cairns.

9. See Thomas Schipflinger, *Sophia-Maria: A Holistic Vision of Creation,* trans. James Morgante (York Beach, Me.: Samuel Weiser, 1998), pp. 1–45.

10. See Jean Leclerq, O.S.B., *The Love of Learning and the Desire for God: A Study of Monastic Culture,* trans. Catherine Misrahi (New York: Fordham University Press, 1971); see also William Johnston, *Mystical Theology: The Science of Love* (Maryknoll, N.Y.: Orbis Books, 1975), ch. 6: "Wisdom through Love."

11. The author is grateful to one of the volume's anonymous reviewers who recommended that I include Stoicism in this essay.

12. John 1:1 (RSV).

13. John 1:17 (RSV).

14. I Corinthians 1:18–25.

15. Bruno Barnhart, *The Future of Wisdom: Toward a Rebirth of Sapiential Christianity* (New York: Continuum, 2007).

16. William Johnston, *Mystical Theology: The Science of Love* (Maryknoll, N.Y.: Orbis Books, 2000).

17. Raimon Panikkar, *The Rhythm of Being: The Gifford Lectures* (Maryknoll, N.Y.: Orbis Books, 2010).

18. Bruno Barnhart, O.S.B., *Second Simplicity; The Inner Shape of Christianity* (New York: Paulist Press, 1999), p. 51.

19. Augustine, *Confessions,* trans. & intro. R. S. Pine-Coffin (New York: Penguin, 1961), X, 23, p. 229.

20. For well-chosen texts on wisdom according to Christian theologians, see Eugen Biser, "Wisdom," in *Encyclopedia of Theology: The Concise Sacramendum Mundi,* ed. Karl Rahner (New York: Seabury, 1975), p. 1819. Another excellent survey of the Medieval Christian worldview is in Richard Tarnas, *The Passion of the Western Mind* (New York: Harmony Books, 1991), pp. 89–190.

21. Ibid.

22. For an insightful comparison of the Enlightenment and the Romantic reaction, see Richard Tarnas, *Passion of the Western Mind,* p. 366, and several books by Isaiah Berlin.

23. H. T. Costello, "Recollections of Royce's Seminar on Comparative Methodology," *The Journal of Philosophy,* LVIII, no. 3 (February 2, 1956): 72–73.

24. John J. McDermott, ed., *The Philosophy of John Dewey, vol. 1: The Structure of Experience* (New York: G. P. Putnam Sons, 1973), p. 95; and in Joseph Ratner, ed., *Creative Intelligence* (New York: Modern Library, 1915), p. 65.

25. Ralph Waldo Emerson, *Nature,* Introduction, first paragraph.

26. Ralph Waldo Emerson, quoted in Gertrude Reif Hughes, *Emerson's Demanding Optimism* (Baton Rouge, La.: Louisiana State University Press, 1984), from *Journals and Miscellaneous Notebooks of Ralph Waldo Emerson,* V, 391.

27. Ralph Waldo Emerson, "The American Scholar," in *Emerson: Essays and Lectures,* p. 57.

28. See William James, *Essays in Psychical Research,* intro. Robert McDermott (Cambridge: Harvard University Press, 1986).

29. John J. McDermott, ed., *The Writings of William James* (New York: Random House, 1967), xi; from Henry James Jr., *The Letters of William James,* 2 vols. (Boston: Atlantic Monthly Press, 1920), I, 190.

30. Josiah Royce, *Loyalty to Loyalty,* intro., John J. McDermott (Nashville: Vanderbilt University Press, 1995).

31. See Robert J. Sternberg, ed., *Wisdom: Its Nature, Origins, and Development* (New Haven: Yale University Press, 1990; and Warren S. Brown, ed., *Understanding Wisdom: Sources, Science, and Society* (Philadelphia: Templeton Foundation Press, 2000).

32. "[T]he only God worthy of the name must be finite." William James, *A Pluralistic Universe* (Lincoln: University of Nebraska Press, 1996; orig., 1909), p. 125.

33. John Dewey, *A Common Faith* (New Haven: Yale University Press, 1934).

34. See John Dewey, *Nature and Experience* (New York: W. W. Norton, 1929).

35. Quoted in John Hellman, *Simone Weil: An Introduction to Her Thought* (Philadelphia: Fortress Press, 1984), p. 1; from *L'Express,* February 11, 1961.

36. Quoted in George A. Panichas, ed., *The Simone Weil Reader* (New York: David McKay, 1977), xvii.

37. Ibid.

38. Soren Kierkegaard: "For a crowd is untruth," in *Existentialism from Dostoevsky to Sartre,* ed. & intro. Walter Kaufman (New York: New American Library, 1975), p. 94.

39. *Way to Wisdom,* p. 126. In 1924 Steiner made the same point: "For at the very frontier where the knowledge derived from sense-perception ceases, there is opened through the human soul itself the further outlook into the spiritual world." *Anthroposophical Leading Thoughts,* trans. George and Mary Adams (London: Rudolf Steiner Press, 1973), p. 13.

40. *Way to Wisdom,* 127–128.

41. Cf. Simone Weil's emphasis on *amor fati,* love of fate.

42. *Karl Jaspers: Basic Philosophical Writings,* ed., trans., intro. Edith Ehrlich, Leonard H. Ehrlich, and George B. Pepper (Athens, Ohio: Ohio University Press, 1986), Part Seven: "Encounters with Limit Situations, Journal Entries 1939–42," p. 542. Jaspers and his wife Gertrude moved to Basel, Switzerland, in 1947. He died in 1969, Gertrude died in 1974.

43. Rudolf Steiner, *Intuitive Thinking as a Spiritual Path* (Great Barrington, Mass.: Steinerbooks, 1995); original translation, *Philosophy of Freedom* (London: Rudolf Steiner Press, 1970).

44. Rudolf Steiner, *How to Know Higher Worlds,* Afterword, Arthur Zajonc (Great Barrington, Mass.: Steinerbooks, 1994).

45. See especially Teilhard's masterpiece, *The Human Phenomenon,* trans. Sarah Appleton-Weber (Portland, Ore.: Sussex Academic Press, 1999); and Ursula King,

The Spirit of Fire: The Life and Vision of Teilhard de Chardin (Maryknoll, N.Y.: Orbis Books, 1996).

46. Bertrand Russell, *The Problems of Philosophy* (New York: Oxford University Press, 1959), p. 161.

47. Plato, *The Republic*, VI, 517.

10

The World's Great Wisdom

An Integral Overview

ROGER WALSH

For thousands of years in hundreds of countries, millions of people have sought to understand the fundamental questions of life. Many of these seekers died unknown and their discoveries died with them. Yet others taught or wrote and thereby contributed their hard-won wisdom to an ever-growing stream of insights and practices that matured into the world's religions, literatures, psychologies, and philosophies. For the first time in history, all these traditions are available to us and, as this book demonstrates, we are now heirs to the world's wisdom. This is a priceless gift.

Yet it is also a challenging gift. Not all claims for sagacity are sagacious, and all traditions contain brilliance and nonsense. Religions, in particular, are a confusing mix of profound transrational insight, brilliant rational analysis, and mythic prerational superstition. As Huston Smith, one of the world's preeminent religious scholars put it, "I regard the world's religions as the winnowed wisdom of the human race—with a lot of dross, of course" (Smith, 1991, p. 225).

Separating the wisdom from the dross is not always easy. It requires a rare combination of deep scholarship, personal immersion, and contemplative practice in the tradition. Fortunately, all the contributors to this volume possess this combination, and have winnowed and distilled their traditions' wisdom for us.

The next challenge is to compare and, where possible, to integrate the wisdom claims from these diverse traditions. This chapter attempts to begin this process by using integral theory—probably the most encompassing conceptual framework currently available—to offer an overarching framework that can compare traditions and approaches and begin to situate and integrate the world's wisdom claims into a larger picture.

The Goals of This Chapter

So the first goal of this chapter is to view wisdom from an integral perspective. The second is to clarify assumptions about the nature of wisdom, since many studies describe and define wisdom rather fuzzily, leaving crucial assumptions unarticulated. A third aim is to clarify the relationship between wisdom and development. Many traditions and researchers assume that it is associated with higher levels of development, but the nature of this association remains vague.

The fourth goal is to identify and differentiate the varieties of wisdom(s). We are heirs to a 2,500-year-old Western philosophical division of wisdom into two kinds: *sophia* and *phronesis* (theoretical and practical wisdom). Contemporary researchers seem to have implicitly accepted this category system, even though it has major problems. For example, the exact nature of *sophia* and *phronesis,* as well as the distinctions between them are unclear. The terms have not been precisely defined; have been used ambiguously, and employed in different ways by different philosophers (Curnow, 1999; 2010).

Moreover, contemplative traditions point to an additional and radically different kind of wisdom: a transconceptual seeing into the nature of self and reality. As Richard Trowbridge points out, this kind of wisdom has been almost entirely overlooked by contemporary researchers, even though it represents the culmination of many contemplative traditions. Clearly, it is time to reexamine the varieties of wisdom. The final goal of this chapter is an encompassing one: to point toward the possibility of a global view of wisdom.

Historical Approaches to Wisdom

So what is wisdom? This is an ancient question, and the earliest recorded answers are found in India's Vedas and the proverbial advice of Egyptian, Hebrew, and Mesopotamian literature (Crenshaw, 2010). Much of this consists of advice about acts and their consequences or karma: do this and good things will happen; do that and you'll be sorry.

In later revealed traditions, a recurrent theme is that wisdom is unveiled as a divine gift, and can be cultivated by pondering and aligning one's life with it. For example, in traditional Islam, "Wisdom derives from placing the revelation from God at the center of one's life, reflecting on it, and making it the basis of one's action" (Tharchin, 2000, p. 439). Likewise, in Christianity, "Christians are thus considered to be 'wise' to the extent that their words and actions reflect and conform to the teaching and practice of Jesus" (Dysinger).

However, revelation-centered wisdoms are only one form of religious sagacity. All authentic religions—including revealed traditions such as Christianity and Islam—contain contemplative or mystical branches. These are crucially important because they practice contemplative disciplines—for example, meditation, contemplation, and yoga—that foster an array of psychological and spiritual skills such as concentration, insight, emotional maturity, and wisdom. When these skills mature, they result in maturation to transpersonal states and stages that can culminate in a direct insight into reality. This insight yields a radically different (transrational, transconceptual, or transcendental) kind of wisdom known, for example, as *jnana* (Hinduism), *prajna* (Buddhism), *ma rifah* (Islam), or *gnosis* (Christianity).

With the emergence of philosophy came the first systematic analyses and divisions into different kinds of wisdom. The most influential have been the Greek distinction between *sophia* (knowledge of first causes) and *phronesis* (practical wisdom) (Curnow, 2011) as well as the analogous Buddhist distinction between *prajna* (transcendental insight) and *upaya* (skillfulness in serving and enlightening others).

The recent emergence of scientific, and especially psychological, research has birthed new perspectives and definitions of wisdom. Not surprisingly, these tend to focus on mental processes and capacities, on what can be measured, and therefore on *phronesis* rather than *sophia*.

Unfortunately, there is little overlap between contemporary definitions or between them and earlier views (Thomas, 2006). This is hardly surprising considering the wide variety of eras, cultures, approaches and perspectives, and given that sagacity "is perhaps the most complex characteristic that can be attributed to individuals or to cultures" (Birren & Svensson, 2005, p. 28).

This embarrassing richness of ideas about the nature of wisdom raises important questions. First, "Are all these contemplatives, sages, scholars, and scientists talking about the same thing?" Certainly a contemplative's meditative introspection, a philosopher's conceptual analysis, and a scientist's objective measurements are very different methods, will yield different data, and may imply different "wisdoms."

But are they simply focusing on different *aspects* of wisdom, or are there actually multiple kinds of wisdoms? In ontological terms, "Is wisdom one or many?" In other words, "Are we dealing with a unitary phenomenon or with multiple phenomena?"

If sagacity is multiple—i.e., if there are multiple kinds of wisdom—then the next questions become: "What is the relationship between these kinds of wisdoms?" "Are they overlapping or discrete?" And if discrete, "Are they incommensurate or can they be integrated in some way?"

Let's try to ground these questions in specific examples. Yoga, for instance, claims to culminate in transconceptual wisdom (*jnana*) that is radically and incommensurately distinct from wisdom based on conceptual understanding. This is a claim for two discrete and incommensurate kinds of wisdom.

There also seem to be varying depths of understanding or conceptual wisdom. For example, a contemplative's conceptual wisdom will (hopefully) be greater after thirty years of practice than after five. Yet these different degrees of insight and understanding can probably be ordered in a developmental hierarchy. Principles for ranking them include the sequence in which they emerge, the richness, range, and depth of the understandings they encompass, as well as the degree of integration of these understandings. Conceptually based wisdoms, then, would be overlapping varieties that can be integrated developmentally, an integration that integral theory can facilitate.

Integral Theory

Integral theory was birthed in the 1990s by an independent scholar named Ken Wilber. Since then it has expanded into an international, interdisciplinary movement known as integral studies (Esbjorn-Hargens, 2010). Its aim is to provide an encompassing conceptual framework that draws on and integrates diverse schools, disciplines, and perspectives: ancient and modern, East and West, scientific, philosophical, and religious.

What follow are, first, a synoptic outline of the integral framework, and then an exploration of its implications for understanding wisdom. For fuller accounts of integral theory see Ken Wilber's modestly titled *A Theory of Everything* (2001) (especially chapter 3), *Integral Spirituality* (2000), and his magnum opus *Sex, Ecology, Spirituality* (1995). Readable introductions include *A Brief History of Everything* (1996) and an excellent article by Sean Esbjörn-Hargens (2009; 2010).

Integral theory emphasizes five major dimensions: (1) domains of reality (the four quadrants), (2) levels of development, and (3) lines of development, (4) states of consciousness, and (5) types of personality.

The Four Quadrants

Wilber begins with dimensions or domains of reality. He points out that there are two great realms: subjective and objective, otherwise known as interior and exterior, or I and It.

Moreover, individuals are never entirely alone. Rather, they are always related to others and part of collectives. Each individual is therefore a *holon*: both a whole unto itself, and a part of something larger. The interior subjective aspect of collectives constitutes intersubjective culture. This is the realm of We, of shared experiences, beliefs, and values. The exterior objective aspect of collectives constitutes the interobjective domain of social and ecological systems or societies. Together these four domains of reality constitute "the four quadrants."

	INTERIOR	**EXTERIOR**
	I	*IT*
INDIVIDUAL	INTENTIONAL	BEHAVIORAL
	SUBJECTIVE	OBJECTIVE
	WE	*ITS*
COLLECTIVE	CULTURAL	SOCIAL
	INTERSUBJECTIVE	INTEROBJECTIVE

Figure 1. The Four Quadrants

Each person, each one of us, has all four domains. Each of us has an interior subjective realm of thought and feeling, as well as an outer objective realm of brain and behavior. Each of us also participates in, and is partly constituted by, our intersubjective culture and ethos comprised of, for example, collective beliefs and values. At the same time we also participate in, and are partly constituted by, collective material instantiations such as, institutions, economics, and books.

The four quadrants are interdependent and irreducible. They are interdependent because they form and inform the others, such that each of us shapes and is shaped by phenomena in all four quadrants. They are irreducible because you cannot adequately explain phenomena in one quadrant in terms of others. For example, you cannot adequately explain subjective experiences, beliefs, and values merely in terms of social structures (e.g., as Marxist economic theory tried to), or in terms of culture (as some postmodernists attempted) or neuroscience (as neural reductionism attempts).

Each quadrant also reflects a perspective, a way of looking, and what aspect we see reflects our perspective. Integral theory argues that understanding any phenomenon adequately requires investigating all of its four quadrants, and using methods appropriate to each quadrant.

For example, suppose you want to research the insights and wisdom cultivated by contemplative practices. Then yes, you can measure brain EEG activity and that will inform you about neural correlates. However it will tell you nothing about:

- The actual experience (for that you need meditation and phenomenology)

- Or the developmental level required to experience it (for that you need developmental structuralism)

- Or how we and our culture interpret these insights (for that you need hermeneutics)

- Or how societies instantiate and institutionalize these insights, and then how these institutions determine the likelihood of other people having such insights (that requires social systems analyses)

Integral theory therefore emphasizes the need for a plurality of perspectives and epistemologies—which it calls Integral Methodological Pluralism—that systematically applies methodologies appropriate to each of the four quadrants (Wilber, 2005). (For a fuller discussion see Wilber, 2006).

Where Is Wisdom? The Four Quadrants and the "Location" of Wisdom

The four quadrants offer one answer to a recurring research question: "Where is wisdom found?" Is it a characteristic of individuals only, or can cultures, societies, and institutions also embody wisdom? Integral theory suggests that aspects of wisdom are found in all four quadrants.

In individuals, sagacity appears as, for example, subjective insights and understandings, as well as objective behavior and neural activity. In collectives, wisdom is embedded subjectively in the cultural ethos: the innumerable shared beliefs, values, ethics, and ideas of a culture. These cultural elements embody the insights and understandings of countless individuals past and present. In turn, these collective cultural expressions form and inform (the wisdom of) individuals, so that, as the prolific Berlin research group led by Paul Baltes concluded, "Cultural memory is the mother of wisdom" (Baltes & Staudinger, 2000, p. 123).

Sapience is also expressed in collectives as objective social constructions that materially embody and institutionalize individual and collective wisdom. Examples include legal, educational, and political systems, contemplative institutions, as well as art and books. Paul Baltes saw wisdom as rare in individuals, "In general, wisdom is foremost a cultural product deposited in books of wisdom rather than in individuals" (Baltes, Gluck, & Kunzmann, 2002, p. 331).

Of course, collectives embody not only wisdom, but also much foolishness. The amounts of wisdom and foolishness, as well as their ratio, reflect the past evolution and present maturity of cultures, and are probably of monumental importance in deciding their fate. The ratio of wisdom to foolishness—which we might call the *sagacity:stupidity ratio*—may well be one of the most important cultural factors determining individual and collective well-being, as well as how much cultures support or suppress the search for wisdom: that is, whether cultures are *sophiatrophic* or *sophiatoxic*. Most important of all, the sagacity:stupidity ratio will likely determine the fate of societies, our species, and our planet.

In summary, integral theory suggests that we should look for expressions of wisdom in all four quadrants. And that means that we need to use multiple methods. Further implications will become apparent after we examine other dimensions of the integral model, beginning with levels of development.

Levels of Development

All things change, and organic things change in remarkable and systematic ways. As individuals they develop; as collectives they evolve. Consequently, development and evolution constitute a central dimension of integral theory.

Psychologists often describe development as maturing through three broad levels: preconventional, conventional, and postconventional. Wilber and contemplative disciplines suggest that many developmental lines can mature further into transconventional levels.

Wilber has been especially interested in, first, comparing and integrating different developmental theories, and second, mapping the higher reaches of development by integrating psychological research with contemplative reports. The result is the beginning of what he calls a "full spectrum model." This model aims to map development from preconventional childhood stages through conventional adult and then into postconventional adult levels. Beyond this Wilber explores post-post-conventional stages (which I will call transconventional or transpersonal). These higher stages are usually only found in advanced contemplatives, and as yet are rarely recognized or researched by Western psychologists.

Examples of such transconventional/transpersonal stages include Indian Vedanta's *vijnana mayakosha* (higher mind), and *ananda mayakosha* (bliss mind). Other examples include Cook-Greuter's (Cook-Greuter, 2010) *construct aware* and *unitive* ego stages, as well as the remarkable Indian philosopher-sage Aurobindo's (Aurobindo, 1982) *higher mind, illumined mind, intuitive mind, and overmind.*

Both ancient contemplatives and contemporary researchers imply that wisdom is related to development. For example, the original Buddhist term for meditation was *bhavana* (literally, mental development), while in Taoism the term is *lien-hsin* (refining the mind) (Wong, 1997). Likewise, some researchers link the emergence of wisdom to the higher levels of cognitive development (Kramer, 2003).

Postconventional, and transpersonal stages are important for many reasons. First, they point to our developmental potentials. Second, contemplative traditions imply that transpersonal stages and states are intimately linked to wisdom as both cause and effect. Wise insights, understandings, and behavior are said to foster transpersonal development, which in turn fosters further insights. For example, the first practice of Buddhism's Eight-Fold Path is "Right Understanding," because without some understanding of the nature of life and our existential dilemma, people see no reason to undertake contemplative practices. However, once begun, these practices then foster further understanding and wisdom through successively deeper stages.

The crucial point is that contemplative disciplines have discovered insights, lifestyles, and practices that can catalyze development in general, and wisdom in particular, to postconventional and even transconventional levels (Walsh, 1993; in press; Walsh & Shapiro, 2006; Wilber, 1996; 2000; 2001; 2005). This, of course, is a discovery of enormous significance, especially since Western culture and education struggle to bring people up to conventional levels and, at best, to early postconventional levels.

Developmental Lines

But of course people and minds are not unitary entities. There are multiple mental functions or mental modules, and over time these develop and are then known as developmental lines. Examples include cognitive, moral, ego, and perhaps wisdom lines.

Developmental lines are only loosely linked and can therefore develop unevenly in sundry patterns. For example, a dangerous sociopath might be an intellectual giant and a moral dwarf; a saint could be exceptionally morally mature yet cognitively average.

This raises an obvious question: Is there a characteristic developmental pattern associated with wisdom, and if so, what is it? As yet we have few clues. For example, wisdom scores seem to be associated with higher levels of intelligence and reflective thinking (Ardelt, 2009; Baltes & Staudinger, 2000). However, it is unclear to what extent these high scores actually reflect higher developmental stages rather than simply strengths or intensities.

What Is the Relationship Between Development and Wisdom?

The exact relationship of wisdom to development may be complex. In fact, researchers have suggested several distinct kinds of relationships.

Wisdom Linked to a Specific Stage (or Age)

"Age should speak; advanced years should teach wisdom" (Job 32:7 Bible, New International Version). The best-known example of linking wisdom to a specific stage (or age) is Erik Erickson's famous suggestion that wisdom can most readily emerge in life's final stage. However, there are problems with this idea, as well as with the general approach of tying wisdom to one stage.

Importantly, it suggests that sagacity can't be much expected in prior stages. Yet tying the birth of wisdom specifically to life's end runs counter to the painful fact that this is exactly when crucial energetic and social resources are waning. Moreover, counter to popular opinion, researchers find little improvement on wisdom scores with age (Baltes & Staudinger, 2000; Sternberg, 1998).

Erickson ruefully confessed in late life that his younger pronouncements on the growth possibilities of old age now felt overly optimistic. In his eighties he lamented that "the demand to develop Integrity and Wisdom in old age seems to be somewhat unfair, especially when made by middle-aged theorists—as, indeed, we then were" (Hoare, 2000, p. 79). Eventually he came to see the final goal or achievement of life, not as wisdom, but as faith (Brugman, 2010).

Indian perspectives offer instructive comparisons. By contrast with Erickson, the Buddha lamented the limited progress possible to people taking up contemplative practices late in life: *ars longa, vita brevis*. In Hinduism, wisdom is esteemed as a lifelong pursuit, though the pursuit takes different forms—e.g., student, householder, and renunciate—at different ages (Feuerstein, in press).

Why Doesn't Wisdom Increase with Age?

Why should wisdom, which intuitively seems so closely linked to life experience, not increase significantly as one ages and acquires ever more life experience? This question has puzzled researchers for years (Sternberg, 2005). Yet the finding makes sense if we consider (at least parts of) wisdom as a form of expertise, and if we consider exactly how expertise is acquired. What kind of expertise might wisdom be? Well, according to Baltes and Staudinger, wisdom is "expertise in the conduct and meaning of life" (2000, p. 124).

In recent years, researchers have developed a rich understanding of how expertise is acquired across domains ranging from athletics to academics. One of the central findings is that mere experience or practice does not necessarily lead to improvement. You can play golf or chess, teach, write, or (sadly) practice a profession such as psychotherapy for decades without necessarily improving. Just because you walk for decades doesn't mean you improve at it.

What is required is not just practice but what is called "deliberate practice." With deliberate practice, you consciously seek to improve, focus on and practice tasks you don't do well, carefully assess your performance, obtain feedback and mentoring, and sustain these efforts over time (Ericsson et al., 2006; Ericsson, Prietula, & Cokely, 2007).

What might this imply for the cultivation of wisdom? I suspect what it means is that wisdom requires a strong, lifelong commitment to reflecting on and learning from all life experiences. Certainly this idea accords with recommendations from sages. Confucius described his own path as beginning when "At fifteen I set my heart on learning" (Lau, 1979, p. 63), while the

Buddha stated that "He who would, may reach the utmost height—but he must be eager to learn" (Smith, 1991, p. 391). Likewise in Judaism, "The wise man learns from every phrase he hears, from every event he observes, and from every experience he shares" (Hoffman, 1985, p. 94). This is a very, very different attitude from much contemporary conventional living, which involves hours of mind-numbing television and tranquilization by trivia: a conventionality that existentialists denigrate as, for example, "automation conformity" (Erich Fromm) or "everydayness" (Heidegger) (Walsh, 2001). Small wonder, then, that for so many, age increases wisdom so little.

Wisdom as a Specific (Higher) Stage of a Specific Line
(Postformal Operational Cognition)

Another possible relationship between wisdom and development is that wisdom is linked to the development of a specific line, especially cognition. Piaget identified formal operations as the highest stage of cognitive development. However, higher postformal operational stages have been suggested by both contemplative practitioners, such as Aurobindo, and by contemporary researchers, such as Bruner, Flavell, Sinnott, and Wilber. Several researchers have gone farther to suggest that wisdom is associated with postformal operational cognition (Kramer, 2003).

PROBLEMS WITH POSTFORMAL OPERATIONAL COGNITION

However, there are three problems with tying wisdom to a specific cognitive stage, even an advanced one such as postformal operational:

- First, it ignores the role of other developmental lines. Due to developmental imbalance, one could exhibit mature cognitive development but immature ego and moral development (Wilber, 2006). Yet mature levels of all three may be essential for wisdom.

- It suggests that wisdom won't emerge prior to the appearance of a specific cognitive stage, in this case postformal operational thought. This places a floor on wisdom, and means that it cannot appear in less mature stages and forms.

- It overlooks the possibility of still higher stages such as Aurobindo's "illumined mind" or Wilber's (2006) "violet cognition." Thus, it also sets a ceiling on wisdom.

If these arguments are correct, then they suggest that postformal operational cognition might be a major facilitator of wisdom, yet not be required for less mature forms nor sufficient for more mature forms.

INTERACTION HYPOTHESES

A recurrent idea in contemporary research is that sagacity arises from an interaction among psychological capacities, and that the strength or developmental level of the capacities is crucial. Three kinds of interaction are frequently mentioned—combination, balance, and integration—though none have been specified precisely.

Wisdom as a Combination of Capacities

These theories suggest that wisdom emerges from a combination of capacities. For example, Monika Ardelt (2009) defines wisdom as a "combination of cognitive, reflective, and affective personality characteristics"(pp. 11–12). However "combination" is a vague term, and tells us little about the nature of the relationship or interaction between capacities. The choice of a vague term is certainly understandable at this early stage of research, but will hopefully yield to more precise terms as research matures. However, other researchers have suggested particular kinds of relationships between capacities, specifically *balance* and *integration*.

Wisdom From Balance

Balance theories imply that sagacity emerges when two or more capacities are at optimal proportionate levels. For example, Birren & Fisher (1990) suggest that "Throughout life, wisdom develops as a balance of cognition, volition (conation), and affect" (p. 321). Three questions immediately emerge:

- A balance of what? For example, what kinds of capacities need to be in proportion? Are they invariably other virtues? Or can they also be neutral capacities such as concentration that can be used for good or bad?

- What aspects of the capacities are crucial? Is it their strength, their developmental level, or both?

- What does balance really mean? Presumably it implies that some sort of proportion between two or more capacities is crucial for the emergence of wisdom. But what kind of proportion? Obviously many balance theories are as yet imprecise.

However, their current imprecision does not mean that balance theories are necessarily wrong. In fact, there are venerable philosophical and contemplative examples. For example, "the interdependence of virtues" is an ancient philosophical idea going back to the Stoics who held that "every virtue requires other virtues to complete it" (Murphy, 1992, p. 558), while Christian contemplatives claim that "the virtues are linked one to another" (St. Nikodimos & St. Makarios, 1993, p. 160).

However, wisdom balance theories are proposing more than an interdependence of virtues; they are proposing an interdependent emergence of an additional virtue, in this case wisdom. Are there any specific examples of this kind of emergence? Yes there are, and Buddhist psychology (Abhidharma) offers two.

The first example is the "seven factors of enlightenment": seven qualities or capacities that are crucial to fostering mental maturation, wisdom, and enlightenment. These are comprised of three calming factors (calm, concentration, and equanimity) and three energizing factors (effort, energy, and rapture), and a superordinate factor of mindfulness.

The calming and energizing factors need to be of comparable strength to balance each other and to avoid the disabling extremes of sleepiness and agitation respectively. Moreover, when all seven are strong and balanced then there is the possibility of a breakthrough into transconceptual awareness known as "cessation" and its resultant transconceptual wisdom (Kornfield, 1993; Vaughan, 1979).

The second example from Buddhist psychology is "the five spiritual faculties." These consist of mindfulness, and two pairs of mental qualities that must be in balance: energy and concentration, faith and wisdom. Energy unbalanced by concentration leads to agitation, while concentration without sufficient energy produces lethargy. Likewise, faith devoid of wisdom collapses into blind belief, while wisdom without faith is said to result in egocentric cunning (Nyanatiloka, 1980). As the *Visuddhimagga,* a 1,500-year-old classic Buddhist text (Buddhaghosa & Nanamoli, 1999), puts it "For one strong in faith and weak in understanding has confidence uncritically and groundlessly. One strong in understanding and weak in faith errs on the side of cunning and is as hard to cure as one sick of a disease caused by medicine. With the balancing of the two a man has confidence only when there are grounds for it" (ch. IV, §47, ¶1).

When all five qualities are sufficiently strengthened and balanced they are said to become "unshakeable" and are then known as the "five spiritual powers." Like the seven factors of enlightenment, they facilitate spiritual maturation and the cessation experiences that are central to classical Buddhist enlightenment. So as these examples from Buddhist psychology demonstrate, balance theories can be venerable and valuable, but to be really fruitful they need to be more carefully specified than contemporary research has done.

Integration Hypotheses

A further kind of interaction between developmental capacities is frequently suggested as essential for sagacity: integration. For example, wisdom is said to result from the integration of emotion and cognition (Shearer, 1989) and from an "unusually integrated personality structure" (Orroll & Perlmutter, 1990, p. 160).

But what does "integration" mean here? Once again, the hypotheses are none too specific. Presumably, integration implies some sort of harmonious, facilitative interaction between capacities. But so too does balance. So does the idea of integration add anything to the idea of balance? If so, none of the integration hypotheses seems to suggest what this addition might be.

However, one possibility is that a mental function might foster (or cease to inhibit) other functions and/or beneficial interactions between them. For example, let's consider the possible role of defense mechanisms in integration and wisdom. Defenses can repress emotions, distort cognition, and redirect motivation in unhealthy ways. They can also dissociate mental functions so that they are no longer readily available.

As an example, consider the case of a talented woman with high postformal intelligence, idealistic motives, and a strong tendency to love. But let's also assume she has a poor self-image, severe insecurity, and "normal neurotic defense mechanisms" (Vaillant, 1977). Consequently, she *displaces* her love away from people (who are too threatening) onto animals, *represses* her idealism (which is incongruent with her poor self-image), and uses her powerful intellect to *rationalize* her suboptimal behavior. Consequently, her positive emotions, motives, and intellect function suboptimally, and keep her locked into unhealthy, unsatisfying, and unwise ways of being and living.

Now let's assume that she goes into psychotherapy. There she gradually improves her self-image, releases insecurity, and adopts more mature defense mechanisms such as humor, altruism, and sublimation. Now her idealistic motives can be acknowledged, her love expressed, and her intellect used in the service of these healthy, mature motives and emotions. As her motives, emotions, and intellect are increasingly aligned toward a common goal—for example, loving and serving others—we can say they are becoming increasingly integrated. Over time, she may well learn how to achieve her goals more effectively and thereby grow in practical wisdom.

This case example suggests two possible ways in which capacities might become integrated and thereby foster practical wisdom. The first is through healthy psychodynamics, and the second is through an alignment of capacities toward a common goal. As an aside, the absence of psychodynamics from discussions of wisdom research seems a major oversight, both because of their power and pervasiveness, and because both ordinary defenses and higher level metadefenses can inhibit exceptional functioning (Maslow, 1970), quite likely including wisdom.

But What Kind of Wisdom?

There has been an implicit assumption in combination, balance, and integration hypotheses that all varieties of wisdom require the same kind of balance or integration. However, different varieties of wisdom may well differ in their requirements. For example, practical wisdom may require far higher levels of interpersonal sensitivity than does subjective wisdom. When discussing facilitative capacities, we need to specify the kind of wisdom.

Wisdom as an Emergent of Higher Levels of Multiple Lines

Here the idea is that wisdom may emerge when two or more mental capacities become sufficiently mature and/or healthy. For example, this is an implication of the Berlin group who describe "wisdom as excellence in mind and virtue" (Baltes, 2004; Baltes & Staudinger, 2000).

A similar emergence principle is also found in contemplative disciplines. For example, they suggest that when multiple capacities and virtues are cultivated sufficiently, then a variety of insights into the mind and life can emerge and yield intuitive, conceptual, and transconceptual wisdom. Contemplative traditions differ in their emphasis on specific capacities and virtues. However, there is widespread agreement on the importance of seven interdependent capacities: mature ethics, emotions, motives, concentration, generosity, wisdom, and sensitivity of awareness (Walsh, 1993; 2001). Cultivating any subset of these tends to cultivate others. This is another example of the recurrent idea of the interdependence of virtues.

My own suggestion is that wisdom is a function of the maturation of multiple developmental lines. Which lines? Well, central ones probably include cognitive, worldview, ego, moral, motivational, emotional, interpersonal, and perceptual lines. In other words, the amount and level of a person's sagacity will be a function of the extent that these lines (and doubtless others) mature. Moreover, the relative maturity of different lines will probably vary from one kind of wisdom to another with, for example, interpersonal maturity being more important for practical than for conceptual wisdom.

Wisdom as a Distinct Developmental Line

Just as we consider cognition, affect, and motivation as largely separate capacities and developmental lines, so too we might consider wisdom. Confucianism may offer an example of this view. The Confucian idea, originally suggested by the sage Mencius (372–289 BCE), is that wisdom develops from a "seed" which is the capacity to discern right from wrong (Kalton, in press).

Against this suggestion of a single developmental line is the fact that wisdom is doubtless dependent on many other capacities such as cognition and motivation. But of course these other capacities are also complex and interdependent. The psyche functions as an organic whole, and to tease out one capacity is in part an artifact of our focus and methods.

What are the implications of considering wisdom as a distinct developmental line? One is that we would expect to find, not a sudden emergence of wisdom at a specific developmental stage, but rather a continuum or spectrum, though perhaps, like cognition, with quite different processes and expressions at different stages. Perhaps we might expect a range of expressions from, say, survival skills and street cunning at the lower end, to midlevel interpersonal skills and existential insights, through to high level transpersonal understanding and transconceptual insights at the upper end.

Summary of Levels and Lines

When we apply a developmental perspective to different hypotheses about the nature and genesis of wisdom, we can recognize seven major families of hypotheses. These are, first, *specific stage hypotheses,* which see wisdom (1) as (an emergent of) a specific developmental stage, for example, Erikson, or (2) as a specific higher stage of a specific developmental line, for example, postformal operational cognition.

Then we have three *interaction hypotheses,* which see wisdom as the result of interactions between two or more developmental capacities: (3)

wisdom as a combination of capacities; (4) wisdom as an emergent of balance between two or more capacities; and (5) wisdom as an emergent of integration between two or more capacities. Finally, we have (6) wisdom as a function of higher levels of multiple lines and (7) Wisdom as a distinct developmental line.

So which hypothesis is correct? Well, that may be the wrong question. First, because what we see and measure as wisdom will depend on our perspective. Second, because wisdom is doubtless the product of multiple developmental processes and so several of these hypotheses may offer parts of the answer. Finally, there are likely several distinct kinds of wisdom, and different processes may contribute differentially to each. However, what is clear is that we will need to sharpen our thinking about the developmental nature of wisdom.

States of Mind

Whereas stages of development persist, "states of mind"—otherwise known as "states of consciousness"—fluctuate. In fact, all of us cycle through multiple states daily, such as those of dreaming and dreamless sleep, as well as waking states that vary in, for example, alertness and clarity.

States of mind (SOM) can be ranked relative to the ordinary waking state according to their functional capacities (Tart, 2001). When we do so, three major classes emerge:

- *Lower states* of reduced function such as delirium and intoxication;

- *Functionally specific states* in which some capacities are enhanced and others reduced, e.g., meditative states of great concentration but reduced perceptual sensitivity;

- *Higher states,* which retain usual abilities while including heightened or additional capacities, e.g., meditative mindfulness with its heightened introspective and perceptual sensitivity.

Contemplative disciplines make several radical claims about SOM. First, they suggest that all of us potentially have available to us families of functionally specific and higher states, and that contemplative practices can foster these. Examples from yoga include functionally specific states of intense concentration, such as *nirvikalpa samadhi,* and higher states such as *sahaj samadhi.*

Moreover, they claim that many of these contemplative SOM—also called altered states of consciousness—can offer multiple psychological, somatic, and spiritual benefits. These states may heal, catalyze development, cultivate specific capacities such as positive emotions, as well as produce insights, understanding, and wisdom (Goleman, 1996). In other words, contemplative disciplines suggest that certain kinds of insight, understanding, and wisdom are more likely to occur in specific states of mind, and some may occur *only* in specific states. For example, "It is axiomatic in the yogic tradition that 'knowledge is different in different states of consciousnesses" (Shearer, 1989, p. 26). Likewise, In Taoist contemplation, by reaching a state of stillness and stability through practices such as "entering stillness" or "fasting the heart-mind" people can attain "The Great Pure Realm" and recognize that they are actually an integral part of the Tao (Wong, 1997). However, contemplative traditions aim not just to glimpse altered states and higher perspectives, but to stabilize them. The goal is to transform transient states into enduring traits, higher states into higher stages, peak experiences into plateau experiences, and epiphanies into personality (Goleman, 1996; Tart, 2001). The religious scholar Huston Smith put it poetically when he suggested that the goal is "to transform flashes of illumination into abiding light." The result is that brief glimpses extend into continuous vision, novel perspectives become permanent metaperspectives, and new insights develop into enduring understandings.

In short, certain functionally specific and higher states may be doorways through which wisdom—in the form of valuable insights, understandings, perspectives, and resultant ways of life—can emerge and find expression. Equally important, contemplative disciplines have developed specific practices and inner technologies to cultivate these states and their insights.

But Can We Recognize Wisdom?

So wisdom can be cultivated. However, there is a crucial question: Will it be recognized? Answer: not necessarily! For the insights and wisdom of higher developmental states and stages may not be fully comprehensible to those of us at earlier stages. For example, some forms of sagacity may require advanced cognitive capacities such as postformal operational cognition or Aurobindo's intuitive mind. Therefore, aspects of this sagacity may be incomprehensible to people at earlier cognitive stages. This is the phenomenon of *stage-specificity*.

Likewise, the insights and wisdom of higher states may not be fully comprehensible to those of us without direct experience of these states due to *state*-specificity (Tart, 2001). Without such direct experience, sage insights and ideas remain what Immanuel Kant called "empty concepts," and the deeper meaning of these concepts—or what philosophers call their "higher grades of significance"—will escape us (Schumacher, 1977).

But what is most problematic is this: we won't recognize that their real meaning and significance are escaping us. Perhaps the best way of illustrating this is with a story.

Imagine an animal finding a novel object. This object is dark and light, has an unfamiliar smell, and tastes terrible. Needless to say, the animal spits it out in disgust.

Now imagine that a woman from an illiterate tribe discovers the object. It is very curious indeed—it opens and closes, is soft and flexible, and has squiggly marks on it. Being a bright woman, she soon makes a wonderful discovery: This object is superb for starting fires. Then a Western child finds the object and immediately recognizes it as a book. However, because he cannot read, he hasn't a clue what it says. Next, the same object is picked up by a contemporary adult. She begins reading it, but quickly throws it away, because she cannot understand it, and it makes bizarre claims about the nature of reality. Then a physicist picks up the book. He opens it and is awed to realize that it describes a profound new understanding of quantum physics. Finally, the book is found by a woman who is both a physicist and contemplative. She also appreciates the brilliant quantum physics and delights in the new understandings it offers, while simultaneously recognizing the limited ability of all words and concepts to grasp the fundamental nature of reality.

This simple story offers several crucial insights. First, each animal, child, and person was correct in their perception. It was nonnutritious, it was useful for starting fires, it was a book—everyone's perception and understanding were correct. However, their perception and understanding were also partial, and contained no information that the object held deeper meanings (higher grades of significance) waiting to be understood.

The crucial point is that we can completely overlook higher grades of significance, yet be completely unaware that we are missing them. In his widely influential critique of scientific materialism, *A Guide for the Perplexed*, the British economist E. F. Schumacher described the dilemma as follows:

> When the level of the knower is not adequate to the level [or grade of significance] of the object of knowledge, the result is not factual error but something much more serious; an inadequate and impoverished view of reality. (Schumacher, 1977, p. 42)

The challenging implication is this. Without direct experience, we may be like the child or ordinary adult looking at the book. We may read sage concepts, we may hear wise ideas, and we may even appreciate some of their beauty. However, without direct experience of the requisite higher states and stages, the full significance of these ideas escapes us. And trickiest of all, we will not realize that it is escaping us.

In contemplative terms, higher wisdom remains "self-secret" (Tibetan Buddhism) or *sod* (hidden, Judaism) until one "opens the eye of contemplation" (Christianity) and develops the necessary "*adaequati*" (Schumacher, 1977; Walsh, 1993; Walsh & Vaughan, 1993). In fact, history is filled with accounts of people now recognized as sages—most famously Socrates and Jesus—whose transconventional views and lifestyles were mistaken for heresy or insanity and resulted in persecution and even execution (Feuerstein, 2006).

So not only will wisdom itself mature with later developmental stages and states of mind, but so also the sophistication of one's understanding of wisdom. With higher developmental stages we might expect to find views of wisdom that are more complex, deep, differentiated, nuanced, encompassing, integrated, and contextualized. Hopefully, we will one day see, not only maps of the way wisdom matures across developmental stages, but also maps of the ways in which understanding of the nature of wisdom matures.

Types

The final major dimension of integral theory is "types." These are relatively stable orientations such as Jung's introversion and extroversion, and the "big five" personality factors.

An obvious question is whether wisdom may be correlated with, or even intimately linked to, certain personality types. For example, could wise people simply be open-minded introverts? In fact, some types—such as high intelligence and open mindedness—do display modest correlations with wisdom-related performance (Baltes & Staudinger, 2000). Yet sagacity is clearly not simply a (function of) type, and so we need not consider it in detail as we examine the varieties of wisdom.

The Varieties of Wisdom

For thousands of years, philosophers have distinguished two kinds of individual wisdom: subjective and objective, theoretical and practical, traditionally called *sophia* and *phronesis,* and similarly in Buddhism, *prajna* and *upaya.* However, there is an obvious question: Are these two categories sufficient? Or do we need to add further and more refined distinctions? Let's turn to practical wisdom first and begin by defining it.

Practical Wisdom

Practical wisdom is skill in responding to the central existential issues of life skillfully and benevolently.

Life presents us with a wide array of existential issues that range from personal survival and suffering to relationships, society, and politics. An obvious question is, therefore, "Is practical wisdom domain specific?" In other words, can we be relatively wise in one area of life, and less so, even foolish, in others?

It certainly seems so. For example, political wisdom is not always accompanied by parental wisdom, as Gandhi—who is widely revered as a saint on the basis of his political activities—painfully demonstrated. He announced that "'All of India is my family'. . . . But he never quite learned to be a father to his sons." Rather, he expected them to be "junior saints," even to the point of denying them a formal education "on the grounds that character was more precious than learning" (Fischer, 1954, pp. 127,128). The results were less than optimal.

So what accounts for domain differences in practical wisdom? Personality and proclivity, to be sure. But a further factor is probably the different amounts of time and attention given to them, with resultant differences in domain-relevant knowledge and skills. Gandhi gave enormous amounts of time to his political work and significantly less to his family. Yet the cognitive processes involved are probably similar across domains. Therefore, it seems reasonable to think of practical wisdom as a single type with multiple expressions.

Subjective Wisdom: The Several Faces of Sophia

Subjective wisdom is a different matter. The exact nature of *sophia* and how it differs from *phronesis* were ambiguous throughout Greek history, and when I wrote to Trevor Curnow seeking clarification, he responded that "tidiness is not out there to be found in the case of *sophia*" (personal communication, 2010). Aristotle described *sophia* as knowledge of first principles or causes. However, it is not at all clear exactly what kind of knowledge it entails or how it is acquired (Curnow, 1999; 2011).

One way of acquiring it may be intuition, and there is certainly widespread public belief in intuition's importance. In fact, when I've spoken on wisdom, a common audience response is, "These intellectual ideas are all very well, but I've met some amazing people, such as grandmothers and tribal people, who wouldn't understand any of this. They can't tell you how they do it, yet everyone turns to them with their problems and they are respected as wise elders."

This, of course, is tacit knowledge, knowledge that can't be easily verbalized or communicated, and Sternberg (1998, p. 351) considers "Tacit knowledge as the core of wisdom," or at least of practical wisdom. This is consistent with two central ideas of intuition, both of which are supported by considerable research. Namely, that we can know much more than we can conceptualize, and that we can know much more than we know (Meyers, 2004; Vaughan, 1979).

Yet some wisdom can be communicated; otherwise, there would be no wise books or teachers. So subjective wisdom may be comprised of both tacit and explicit knowledge, of both intuitive and conceptual processes. And this suggests that we need to distinguish two kinds of subjective wisdom: intuitive apprehension and conceptual understanding.

Intuitive apprehension may well be sufficient for acquiring much subjective wisdom and expressing it as practical wisdom. Yet conceptual analysis and understanding can enrich intuitions in multiple ways, such as by examining, extending, and articulating them, drawing out implications, and linking them into networks of insights and ideas. In fact, at postformal operational levels, intuition and analysis may merge so that one "sees" the interconnections of networks of ideas, which is why Wilber (2001) describes this level of cognition as "vision logic." For Aurobindo (1982), this capacity for vision logic emerges at the transpersonal developmental stage which he called the "higher mind," which "can freely express itself in single ideas, but its most characteristic movement is a mass ideation, a system or totality of truth-seeing at a single view; the relations of idea with idea . . ." (p. 940).

So far, we have differentiated *sophia* or subjective wisdom into two kinds of knowledge and two corresponding cognitive processes for acquiring it. Yet there may be further distinctions to be teased out of *sophia*. For contemplative disciplines insist on the possibility and importance of a radically different subjective wisdom.

The contemplative claim is that specific states of mind permit a direct transconceptual insight into the fundamental nature of reality and self. This insight is said to be neither a conceptually mediated understanding, nor even a cognitively mediated intuition. Rather, it is said to be transconceptual and transrational, a direct apprehension of consciousness by consciousness, Mind by Mind, Spirit by Spirit. Examples of one family of such states—states of pure awareness or pure consciousness—include "cessation" (Theravadin Buddhism), *Ayin* (Judaism), "mindless awareness" (Christianity's Meister Eckhart), "no mind" (Zen), *nirvikalpa samadhi* (yoga), or what Robert Forman (1997) calls a "pure consciousness event." The result is a transconceptual apprehension and wisdom known as, for example, *jnana* (Hinduism), *prajna* (Buddhism), *maʿrifah* (Islam) or *gnosis* (Christianity).

The reason that transconceptual apprehension is essential is that, as the *Tao Te Ching* put it "Existence is beyond the power of words to define" (Bynner, 1944, p. 25). In the words of the great Indian philosopher Radhakrishnan, "The real transcends, surrounds and overflows our miserable categories" (1940/1959, p. 43). In short, the very nature of reality is said to be inherently transconceptual, and so a transconceptual apprehension is essential for deep insight and wisdom.

So widespread is this claim of a contemplative apprehension "higher than discursive reasoning" that Aldous Huxley named it "The Second Doctrine of the Perennial Philosophy" and claimed that "it is to be found in all the great religions of the world" (1972, p. 15). Transconceptual apprehension has also been an important part of Western philosophy and its understanding of wisdom, though a part almost entirely lost to contemporary academics (McDermott, in press; Trowbridge, 2011).

So radically distinct is this epistemological mode and the wisdom it yields that it is said that "The wise are completely free from all concepts about the true nature of reality" (Gyamtso, 2003, p. 42). However, like intuition, this transconceptual wisdom or gnosis can subsequently be partly elaborated into concepts, and even inspire whole psychologies and philosophies such as Buddhist Abhidharma psychology and Vedantic philosophy.

Not surprisingly, these radical epistemological claims have sparked fierce academic debates about their validity. The best known debate is between constructivists such as Steven Katz (1983) and contemplatively sympathetic philosophers such as Robert Forman (1997). Katz argues that all experience is necessarily constructed and limited by historically and culturally situated cognition, and so any and all claims for transconceptual knowing are necessarily false. Yet, the philosopher Donald Rothberg (1989) points out that Katz's argument is itself historically and culturally limited, while Wilber (2001) points out that it is self-defeating.

However, the important points for wisdom studies are the following: Across cultures and centuries, contemplatives have claimed that it is possible to cultivate transconceptual insights and that an extremely important and powerful kind of wisdom ensues. This wisdom is radically different from ordinary intuition and conceptual understanding in both its nature and results. For it is not only illuminating, but also potentially liberating, being capable of significantly healing, deconditioning, and freeing the mind from its conventional "consensus trance" (Tart, 2001). Such wisdom is said to help catalyze an "awakening" of the mind to radically more mature, healthy, and veridical states variously described as, for example, enlightenment, liberation, introversion (St Augustine in Christianity), *Ruach Hakodesh* (Judaism), *fana* (Islam), *satori* (Zen), or the Jade Pure Realm (Taoism) (Goleman, 1996; Wong, 1997).

Equally important, contemplatives claim to have developed mental disciplines—sapiential and soteriological technologies—to realize this wisdom. In fact, some of these disciplines recognize and foster all three kinds of subjective wisdom through a specific sequence of practices. For example, in yoga, one first listens to (*sravana*) and reflects on (*manana*) teachings to develop conceptual understanding. Then one meditates on them (*nididhyasana*) to gain a deeper intuitive apprehension, and finally one enters a state of intense concentration (*samadhi*) in which transconceptual insight (*jnana*) emerges (Free John, 1988; Feuerstein, in press). An analogous process occurs with the Christian contemplative practice of *lectio divina*. Here reading (*lectio*) leads to conceptual reflection (*meditatio*), and culminates in interior silence and insight (*contemplatio*) that becomes "too deep for words" (Hall, 1988). An important implication, as with virtues in general, is that different kinds of wisdom may be mutually facilitating.

The Varieties of Sagehood

If there are different kinds of wisdom, then this implies that there may be different kinds of sages. A sage might be remarkably wise in one arena, less so in others. What kinds of sages might we expect? One way of pointing to an answer is to suggest exemplars.

For an exemplar of practical wisdom, Mother Teresa would certainly rank high on many people's list, because of both her remarkable altruism and practical skill in creating a worldwide charity. Yet while achieving all this, she suffered a decades-long existential despair, a prolonged dark night of the soul (Kolodiejchuk, 2007).

An exemplar of transconceptual wisdom might be Ramana Mahashi (1988), who was widely revered for his deep realization and transconceptual wisdom, and regarded as one of India's greatest twentieth-century sages. Yet he showed little interest in conceptual analysis, and chose a monastic life where practical wisdom, other than occasional teaching, was little needed.

Aurobindo, on the other hand, is considered one of India's greatest philosopher-sages: a person who combined transconceptual and conceptual wisdom to extraordinary degrees. For intuitive wisdom, a perennial archetype is the wise grandmother: an elder who may have little education, analytic skills, or contemplative experience, yet whom everyone turns to for comfort and advice with life concerns.

A master sage would embody high degrees of all four wisdoms. Are there any such people? Hopefully so, and one possibility might be the Dalai Lama. He has done decades of intense contemplative practice and intellectual training, is widely regarded as having deep *prajna* and impressive intuitive sensitivity, and possesses remarkable existential and philosophical insight (I once saw him debate the chair of philosophy at Harvard University and hold his own). He also displays remarkable interpersonal skills, and many people, including Western scientists, report that their lives were permanently changed by brief interactions with him. The psychologist Dacher Keltner gave a moving account of the effects of one such brief encounter:

> Goose bumps spread across my back like wind on water, starting at the base of the spine and rolling up to my scalp. A flush of humility moved up my face from my cheeks to my forehead and dissipated near the crown of my head. Tears welled up, along with a smile. . . . For several weeks I lived in a new realm. My suitcase was missing at the carousel following the plane flight home—not a problem, I didn't need those clothes anyway. Squabbles between my two daughters . . . [produced] no bristling reaction on my part, just an inclination to step into the fray and to lay out a softer discourse and sense of common ground. (Keltner, 2009, p. 175)

This is an example of what contemplatives call "transmission:" the induction of a sage's state of consciousness by contact or encounter. And this is one reason why contemplative traditions the world over regard spending time in the company of the wise as one of the best means for cultivating wisdom (Walsh, 1999).

Conclusions about the Varieties of Wisdom

The traditional Western philosophical lumping of all wisdom into only two categories—*sophia* and *phronesis,* subjective and practical—is insufficiently precise. We can retain the category of *phronesis* or practical wisdom for now. However, we need to distinguish at least three epistemologically, cognitively, and phenomenologically distinct modes of subjective wisdom: intuitive apprehension, conceptual understanding, and transconceptual insight.

Are there further distinctions to be made? Probably so. The above is only an initial exploration, and future studies will doubtless add further refinements, such as distinguishing different kinds of intuition.

Moreover, there are doubtless multiple levels of wisdom(s). Conceptual, intuitive, and practical wisdom probably mature as people develop through both stages and states. Most importantly, contemplative traditions have developed methods for both cultivating and assessing higher levels of sagacity. Methods for cultivating wisdom include, for example, systematic reflection, investigation, meditation, and ethical training, while assessment is usually done intuitively, but sometimes with standardized tests such as Zen koans (Walsh, 2001). These methods are among the most important of all the jewels in humankind's treasury of wisdom.

Acknowledgments

Parts of this chapter are based on earlier articles: Walsh, R. (2009). The state of the integral enterprise, Part I. *Journal of Integral Theory and Practice, 4*(3), 1–12; Walsh, R. (2011). The varieties of wisdom. *Research in Human Development, 8*(2), 109–127; Walsh, R. (2012) Wisdom: An integral view. *Journal of Integral Theory and Practice, 7*(1), 1–21.

References

Ardelt, M. (2009). How similar are wise men and women? A comparison across two age cohorts. *Research in Human Development, 6,* 9–26.

Aurobindo. (1982). *The life divine.* Ponicherry, India: Sri Aurobindo Ashram.

Baltes, P. B. (2004). *Wisdom as orchestration of mind and virtue.* http://library.mpib-berlin.mpg.de/ft/pb/PB_Wisdom_2004.pdf.

———, Gluck, J., & Kunzmann, U. (2002). Wisdom: Its structure and function in regulating successful life span development. In C. R. Snyder & S. J. Lopez (Eds.), *Handbook of positive psychology* (pp. 327–347). Oxford: Oxford University Press.

Baltes, P. B., & Staudinger, U. M. (2000). Wisdom: A metaheuristic (pragmatic) to orchestrate mind and virtue towards excellence. *American Psychologist, 55,* 122–136.

Birren, J., & Fisher, L. (1990). The elements of wisdom: Overview and integration. In R. Sternberg (Ed.), *Wisdom: Its nature, origins, and development* (pp. 317–332) New York: Cambridge University Press.

Birren, J., & Svensson, C. (2005). Wisdom in history. In R. Sternberg & J. Jordan (Eds.), *A Handbook of wisdom* (pp. 3–31). Cambridge: Cambridge University Press.

Brugman, G. M. (2010). Wisdom and aging. In J. Birren & K. W. Schaie (Eds.), *Handbook of psychology of aging* (pp. 445–469). Amsterdam: Elsevier.

Buddhaghosa & Nanamoli (Trans.). (1999). *The path of purification.* BPS-Pariyatti Editions, Onalaska, Wa. (Buddhist Publication Society), 1999. Retrieved from: http://en.wikipedia.org/wiki/Indriya.

Bynner, W. (Trans.). (1944). *The way of life according to Lao Tzu.* New York: Perigee/ Putnam.

Cook, F. (1977). *Hua-yen Buddhism: The jewel net of Indra.* University Park, Pa.: Pennsylvania State University Press.

Cook-Greuter, S. (2010). Second-tier gains and challenges in ego development. In S.Esbjörn-Hargens (Ed.), *Integral theory in action* (pp. 303–321). Albany: State University of New York Press.

Crenshaw, J. (2010). *Old Testament wisdom,* 3rd ed. Louisville: Westminster John Knox.

Curnow, T. (1999). *Wisdom, intuition and ethics.* Abingdon, UK: Ashgate.

————. (2010). Personal communication.

————. (2011). Sophia and phronesis: Past, present and future. *Research in Human Development, 8*(2), 95–108.

Dysinger, L. (in press). Wisdom in the Christian tradition. In R. Walsh (Ed.), *The world's great wisdom.* Albany: State University of New York Press.

Ericsson, K. A., Charness, N., Faltovich, P., & Hoffman, R. (Eds.) (2006). *The Cambridge handbook of expertise and expert performance.* Cambridge: Cambridge University Press.

————, Prietula, N., & Cokely, E. (2007). The making of an expert. *Harvard Business Review, 85*(7/8), 115–121.

Esbjörn-Hargens, S. (2009). An overview of integral theory: An all-inclusive framework for the 21st Century. *Integral Institute, Resource Paper No. 1,* March 2009, http://integrallife.com/node/ 37539.

————. (Ed.). (2010). *Integral theory in action.* Albany: State University of New York Press.

Feuerstein, G. (2006). *Holy madness: Spirituality, crazy-wise teachers, and enlightenment,* Rev. ed. Prescott, Ariz.: Hohm Press.

————. (in press). Wisdom: The Hindu experience and perspective. In R. Walsh (Ed.), *The world's great wisdom.* Albany: State University of New York Press.

Fischer, L. (1954). *Gandhi.* New York: New American Library.

Forman, R. (Ed.). (1997). *The problem of pure consciousness: Mysticism and philosophy.* New York: Oxford University Press.

Free John (1988). *The basket of tolerance.* Clearlake, CA: Dawn Horse Press.

Garfield,J. (1995). *The fundamental wisdom of the middle way: Nāgārjuna's* Mūlamadhyama-kakārikā. New York: Oxford University Press.

Goleman, D. (1996). *The meditative mind: The varieties of meditative experiences.* New York: Tarcher.

Gyamtso, K. T. (2003). *The sun of wisdom: Teachings on the Noble Nagarjuna's fundamental wisdom of the middle way.* Boston: Shambala.

Hall, T. (1988). *Too deep for words: Rediscovering* lectio divina. New York: Paulist Press.

Hoare, C. (2000). Ethical self, spiritual self: Wisdom and integrity in the writings of Erik H. Erikson. In M. Miller & S. Cook-Greuter (Eds), *Creativity, spirituality, and transcendence: Paths to integrity and wisdom in the mature self* (pp. 75–98). Stamford, Ct.: Ablex.

Hoffman, E. (1985). *The heavenly ladder: A Jewish guide to inner growth.* San Francisco: Harper & Row.

Huxley, A. (1972) Introduction. In Prabhavananda & Isherwood (Trans.), *The song of God: Bhagavad Gita* (pp. 11–22). Hollywood: Vedanta Society.

Kalton, M. (in press). The Confucian pursuit of wisdom. In R. Walsh (Ed.), *The world's great wisdom*. Albany: State University of New York Press.

Katz, S. (Ed.). (1983). *Mysticism and religious traditions*. Oxford: Oxford University Press.

Keltner, D. (2009). *Born to be good: The science of a meaningful life*. New York: W. W. Norton.

Kolodiejchuk, B. (2007). *Mother Teresa: Come be my light*. New York: Doubleday.

Kornfield, J. (1993). The seven factors of enlightenment. In R. Walsh & F. Vaughan (Eds.), *Paths beyond ego* (pp. 67–69). New York: Tarcher/Putnam.

Kramer, D. (2003). The ontogeny of wisdom in its variations. In J. Demick & C. Andreoletti (Eds.), *Handbook of adult development* (pp. 131–168). New York: Plenum.

Lapsley, D. (2006). Moral stage theory. In M. Killen & J. Smetana (Eds.), *Handbook of moral development* (pp. 37–66). Mahwah, N.J.: Lawrence Erlbaum Assoc.

Lau, D. (Trans.). (1979). *The analects of Confucius*. New York: Penguin Books.

Maslow, A. (1970). *Religions, values and peak experiences*. New York: Viking.

———. (1971). *The farther reaches of human nature*. New York: Viking.

McDermott, R. (in press). Wisdom in Western philosophy. In Walsh, R. (Ed.), *The world's great wisdom*. Albany: State University of New York Press.

Meyers, D. (2004). *Intuition*. New Haven: Yale University Press.

Murphy, M. (1992). *The future of the body: Explorations into the further evolution of human nature*. New York: Tarcher/Putnam.

Nyanatiloka. (1980). *Buddhist dictionary*. Kandy, Sri Lanka: Buddhist Publication Society.

St. Nikodimos & St. Makarios (G. Plamer, P. Sherrard & K. Ware, trans.). (1993). *Prayer of the heart: Writings from the Philokalia*. Boston: Shambhala.

Orroll, L., & Perlmutter, M. (1990). The study of wise persons. In R.Sternberg (Ed.), *Wisdom: Its nature, origins and development* (pp. 160–180). New York: Cambridge University Press.

Radhakrishnan, S. (1940/1929). *Indian philosophy. Vol. 1*. Bombay: Blackie & Sons.

Ramana Maharshi (1988). *The spiritual teachings of Ramana Maharshi*. Boston: Shambhala.

Rothberg, D. (1989). Understanding mysticism: Transpersonal theory and the limits of contemporary epistemological frameworks. *ReVision, 12*(2), 5–22.

Schumacher, E. (1977). *A guide for the perplexed*. New York: Harper & Row.

Shearer, P., (Trans.) (1989). *Effortless being: The yoga sutras of Patanjali*. London: Unwin.

Shedlock, D., & Cornelius, S. (2003). Psychological approaches to wisdom and its development. In J. Demick & C. Andreoletti (Eds.), *Handbook of adult development*. New York: Springer.

Smith, H. (1991). *The world's religions*. San Francisco: Harper Collins.

———. (2005). Do drugs have religious import: A forty year follow-up. In R. Walsh (Ed.), *Higher Wisdom: Eminent elders explore the continuing impact of psychedelics*.

———. (2009). *Tales of wonder: Adventures chasing the divine, an autobiography*. New York: HarperOne.

————, & Novak, P. (2003). *Buddhism: A concise introduction.* San Francisco: Harper San Francisco.

Sternberg, R. (1998). A balance theory of wisdom. *Review of General Psychology, 2,* 347–365.

————. (2005). Older but not wiser? The relationship between age and wisdom. *Aging International 30*(1), 5–26.

Tart, C. (2001). *States of consciousness.* 2nd ed. New York: iUniverse.

Tharchin. (2000). *A commentary on the Dudjom Tersar Ngondro.* Watsonville, Cal.: Vajrayana Foundation.

Thomas, D. (2006). Receiving and acquiring wisdom in Islam. *Journal of Chinese Philosophy, 33*(3), 439–452.

Trowbridge, R. (2011). Waiting for *sophia*: Thirty years of conceptualizing wisdom in empirical psychology. *Research in Human Development, 8*(2), 149–164, DOI: 10.1080/15427609.2011.568872.

Vaillant, G. (1977). *Adaptation to life.* Boston: Little Brown.

Vaughan, F. (1979). *Awakening intuition.* New York: Doubleday.

Wallace, A., & Shapiro, S. (2006). Mental balance and wellbeing: Building bridges between Buddhism and psychology. *American Psychologist, 61,* 690–701.

Walsh, R. (1993). Hidden wisdom. In R. Walsh & F. Vaughan (Eds.), *Paths beyond ego* (pp. 223–226). New York: Tarcher/Putnam.

————. (1999). *Essential spirituality: The seven central practices.* New York: Wiley & Sons.

————. (2001). Authenticity, conventionality, and angst. In K. Schneider, J. Bugental, & J. Pierson (Eds.), *The handbook of humanistic psychology* (pp. 609–620). Thousand Oaks, Cal.: Sage.

————. (2010). Contemplative therapies. In R. Corsini and D. Wedding (Eds.), *Current psychotherapies.* 9th ed. (pp. 454–500). Belmont, Cal.: Thomson Brooks/Cole.

————. (Ed.). (in press). *The world's great wisdom: What sages say about living wisely and well.* Albany: State University of New York Press.

Walsh, R., & Shapiro, S. (2006). The meeting of meditative disciplines and Western psychology: A mutually enriching dialogue. *American Psychologist, 61*(3), 227–239.

Walsh, R., & Vaughan, F. (Eds.). (1993). *Paths beyond ego: The transpersonal vision.* New York: Tarcher/Putnam.

Wilber, K. (1995). *Sex, ecology, spirituality: The spirit of evolution.* Boston: Shambhala.

————. (1996). *A brief history of everything.* Boston: Shambhala.

————. (2000). *Integral psychology.* Boston: Shambhala.

————. (2001). *A theory of everything: An integral vision for business, politics, science and spirituality.* Boston: Shambhala.

————. (2005). *A sociable God: Toward a new understanding of religion.* Boston: Shambhala.

————. (2006). *Integral spirituality.* Boston: Shambhala.

Wong, E. (1997). *The Shambhala guide to Taoism.* Boston: Shambhala.

Yalom, I. (1980). *Existential psychotherapy.* New York: Basic Books.

11

Reviving Wisdom

What Will It Take?

ROGER WALSH

Wisdom has fallen on hard times. Once revered as one of the greatest of all virtues, it is now eclipsed by the success of science and technology as well as the torrent of new information and data. The costs of this eclipse are all around us. We see them in the suffering of individual lives, in social strife, and in global crises that threaten both our planet and our species.

In fact, the need is greater than ever. So great is our technological power that the state of the world now reflects the state of our minds, and what we call our global crises are actually global symptoms: symptoms of our psychological and spiritual immaturities, our individual and collective pathologies. In short, our global crises reflect our lack of wisdom, and humankind is now in a race between sagacity and catastrophe. What can we do?

What Can We Do To Revive Wisdom?

Clearly, the first task is to recognize and emphasize wisdom's importance. The challenge is to draw attention to the timeless amid the flood of transient information, the profound amid an ocean of superficiality, and the meaningful while confronting an onslaught of media sensationalism. Contemporary culture has mastered the art of what Kierkegaard called "tranquillization by the trivial," and valuing wisdom runs counter to powerful cultural trends, social institutions, and economic forces. Fortunately, there are major resources available to us.

Cross-Cultural Studies

As this book makes clear, the philosophies, psychologies, and religions of many cultures are rich wisdom resources. The time has come to mine them. Focusing purely on Western resources and disciplines is clearly no longer sufficient.

Contemplative Practices

A recurrent theme across cultures is that contemplative disciplines offer valuable ways to cultivate several kinds of wisdom. Until the 1970s, disciplines such as meditation and yoga were dismissed in the West as esoteric oriental practices. Their rapid proliferation in the West—both by the introduction of Eastern practices and the rediscovery of Western ones—has been one of the more subtle yet potentially most valuable cultural shifts of recent decades. Tens of millions of Westerners now practice them along with hundreds of millions of people worldwide. More than five thousand research studies demonstrate their remarkably wide-ranging benefits, which span somatic, psychological, spiritual, developmental, and relational effects (Sedlemeier et al., 2012; Walsh, in press).

A crucial claim of these disciplines is that they can foster psychological maturation and the growth of multiple virtues, including wisdom. Considerable research evidence now demonstrates their ability to foster psychological maturation as well as virtues such as calm, equanimity, empathy, and compassion. Will we soon find evidence that they also foster wisdom? Quite possibly.

Education

In the developing world, the major educational challenge is simply keeping children in school and establishing basic literacy. Elsewhere, the very nature of education—its vision, goals, and methods—are hotly debated.

One recurring debate centers on the mission of education. Should education focus primarily on preparing students for employment and economic productivity? Or should it focus on preparing them for life by emphasizing, for example, personal enrichment, relational skills, high ideals, and high culture? This is often framed as a debate over the relative value of the humanities versus science and technology. However, we can also see it as a tension between providing technical skills and fostering psychological maturation, between making a living and making a life, between acquiring knowledge and cultivating wisdom.

A related question concerns the types of knowing that we should value and cultivate. Today, the emphasis is almost entirely on training the intellect, and other modalities—such as imagination, intuition, contemplation, and emotional learning—are largely neglected. This neglect reflects "an unquestioned assumption at the deepest levels of Western thought and culture" (McDermott, 2005, p. 6). Yet these other modalities were traditionally valued as elements of an effective wisdom education.

Obviously, we need an integral education that values multiple modes of knowing and learning as well as multiple goals. However, equally obviously, political and economic pressures continuously emphasize economically valued skills, and other values are easily displaced. The challenge is to maintain an integral balance. But even if we succeed, a crucial question remains.

Can Wisdom Be Taught?

A major challenge is that we know very little about how to teach wisdom. Unfortunately, this is true even in areas where it is most clearly needed. For example, psychotherapists clearly require wisdom, and fortunately they tend to score high on measures of it (Baltes & Staudinger, 2000).

Yet though psychotherapists require wisdom, what they are taught are psychological theories and techniques. Why? Because, even in this profession, wisdom is undervalued, and also because we (and I certainly include myself here, since I teach psychotherapy) know very little about how to teach it (Golding, 1996).

So does anyone know how to teach wisdom? Well, contemplative traditions and some philosophies claim to know. As this book demonstrates, Asian traditions, ancient Western philosophies, and contemplative disciplines all emphasize teaching and transmitting multiple virtues, including wisdom. So what do they recommend? The following are recurrent recommendations:

1. Lifestyle: A moderate lifestyle that emphasizes voluntary simplicity so as to minimize distractions and trivial pursuits.

2. Relationships

   • A teacher who can teach and transmit wisdom

      The wise man tells you
      Where you have fallen
      And where you may yet fall—
      Invaluable secrets!

Follow him, follow the way . . .
Find friends who love the truth. (The Buddha, Byrom,
   1976, p. 31)

- A community of fellow wisdom seekers: "Let your house
  be a meeting place for the wise" advises an ancient Jewish
  text, "and drink in their words with thirst" (Hoffman, 1985,
  p. 77).

3. Intellectual activities

- Study of wisdom texts

  - Memorization of key ideas so as to internalize them and
    then apply them spontaneously (Hadot, 1995).

  - Reflection on texts, ideas, and existential issues: "There is
    layer upon layer [of meaning] in the words of the sages.
    In your reading of them, penetrate deeply. . . . Be sure to
    ponder what you read. Then you'll see the meaning leap
    right out from the text" (Chu Hsi, NeoConfucian scholar)
    (Gardner, 1990, pp. 129, 141).

  - Dialogue, for example, Socratic dialogue and Tibetan Bud-
    dhist debate

4. Investigation

- Self-examination so as to "know yourself": In the West, the
  best-known claim for the importance of self-examination
  was Socrates's "The unexamined life is not worth living"
  (*The Apology*, 38a), but the importance of self-examination
  is widely recognized across cultures. For example, the great
  Confucian sage Mencius argued that "By exhaustingly
  examining one's own mind, one may understand his nature"
  (Creel, 1953, p. 210).

- Investigating one's experience, for instance, with meditation. For example, in Buddhism, such investigation is highly
  valued as one of the "seven factors of enlightenment."

5. Personality transformation

- Purification so as to winnow away destructive motives and
  emotions—such as greed, fear, anger, and jealousy—that

inhibit wisdom. For example, Mohammad claimed that "Greed steals away wisdom from the heart of the learned" (Angha, 1995, p. 70).

- Cultivation of other virtues—such as ethics, love, and generosity—that facilitate the cultivation and expression of wisdom (Walsh, 1999). This is the idea of the "interdependence of virtues."

6. Contemplative practices such as Christian contemplation, Confucian quiet sitting, Sufi *dzikr*, and Taoist yoga.

In short, sapiential philosophies and contemplative traditions emphasize that the cultivation of deep wisdom requires a multifaceted life discipline and life transformation.

Translating Perennial Wisdom for a Postmodern World: A Call for "Gnostic Intermediaries"

Teaching wisdom poses a further problem. Many ideas and texts are couched in archaic terms or foreign languages. Therefore, making them available to our postmodern world will demand translating them into contemporary languages and concepts.

This sounds simple but is actually demanding. In fact, it may demand what Carl Jung (1966) called "gnostic intermediaries." What is a gnostic intermediary? Jung used the term to refer to Wilhelm, the translator of the *I Ching,* who Jung suggested was able to transmit, not only the ideas, but also the underlying wisdom of the *I Ching.* Jung does not seem to have developed the concept further, but we can amplify it as follows (Walsh, 2009).

First, let me offer a definition. A *gnostic intermediary* is a person who effectively translates and transmits wisdom from one culture or community to another. This translation/transmission can be across cultures (e.g., Indian yogic wisdom to Western culture) or across times (from archaic languages and concepts into contemporary forms, for example, communicating early Christian contemplative wisdom to contemporary Christian communities).

What does this require? Well, it seems to require three tasks and three corresponding capacities:

- First, one must imbibe the wisdom one seeks to transmit and become wise oneself. Since while one can *have* knowledge, one must *be* wise. This, of course, is a major task. In fact, when we are talking about profound contemplative wisdom it can take a lifetime.

- The second requirement for gnostic intermediaries is linguistic and conceptual competence. They must master the language and conceptual system of the culture from which they wish to draw as well as of the culture to which they wish to communicate. For professionals who wish to communicate to their peers, this means mastering one's professional conceptual framework, for example, philosophy, psychology, or science.

- The third requirement is translational. Gnostic intermediaries must be able to translate wisdom from the wisdom-bearing culture or tradition into the language and conceptual system of the recipient community. The goal is to make the wisdom understandable, legitimate, and, hopefully, compelling.

This is the challenge and opportunity of our time for those who would draw from and communicate the world's wisdom. It is a large task. However, it is also an essential one, for we are drowning in information but bereft of wisdom. We are clearly in a race between wisdom and world disaster, between sagacity and catastrophe. We are in great need of wisdom and of gnostic intermediaries to communicate it.

Acknowledgment

The last section of this chapter draws on part of an article: R. Walsh, "The Transmission of Wisdom: The Task of Gnostic Intermediaries."

References

Angha, N. (Ed.). (1995). *Deliverance: Words from the Prophet Mohammad.* San Rafael, Cal.: International Association of Sufism.

Baltes, P. B., & Staudinger, U. M. (2000). Wisdom: A metaheuristic (pragmatic) to orchestrate mind and virtue towards excellence. *American Psychologist, 55,* 122–136.

Byrom, P. (Trans.). (1976). *The Dhammapada: The sayings of the Buddha.* Boston: Shambhala.

Creel, H. (1953). *Chinese thought from Confucius to Mao Tse-Tung*. Chicago: University of Chicago Press.

Gardner, D. (Trans.). (1990). *Chu Hsi: Learning to be a sage*. Berkeley: University of California Press.

Golding, J. (1996). The question of wisdom in the contemporary academy. In K. Lehrer, B. Lum, B. Slichta, & N. Smith (Eds.). *Knowledge, teaching and wisdom*. Dordrecht: Kluwer Academic Publishers, pp. 267–277.

Hadot, P. (1995). (A. Davidson, Ed.) *Philosophy as a way of life*. (M. Chase, Trans). Oxford: Blackwell.

Hoffman, E. (1985). *The heavenly ladder: A Jewish guide to inner growth*. San Francisco: Harper & Row.

Jung, C. (1966). Spirit in man, art and literature. *Collected works of C.G. Jung, Vol. 15*. Princeton: Princeton University Press.

McDermott, R. (2005). An Emersonian approach to higher education. *Revision, 28*(2), 6–16.

Sedlmeier, P., Eberth, J., Schwarz, M., Zimmermann, D., Haarig, F., Jaeger, S., et al. (2012). The psychological effects of meditation: A meta-analysis. *Psychological Bulletin, 05*(2), 309–316.

Walsh, R. (1999). *Essential spirituality: The seven central practices*. New York: John Wiley.

Walsh, R. (2009). The transmission of wisdom: The task of gnostic intermediaries. *Journal of Transpersonal Research, 1*, 114–117.

Walsh, R. (in press). Contemplative psychotherapies. In D. Wedding & R. Corsini (Eds.). *Current psychotherapies, 9th ed.* Belmont, Cal.: Thomson, Brooks/Cole.

Contributors

Father Luke Dysinger, OSB, MD, DPhil, is a Benedictine monk, Catholic priest, and family practice physician. He received his BA and MD degrees from the University of Southern California and his doctorate in theology from Oxford University. He is a professor at St. John's Seminary in Camarillo, California, where he teaches graduate courses on spirituality, history, and ethics. He has written extensively on the Desert Fathers and on early Christian traditions of prayer and spiritual direction. His publications include numerous articles on contemplative prayer, the practices of psalmody and *lectio divina,* and a book on the fourth-century desert father Evagrius Ponticus, *Psalmody and Prayer in the Writings of Evagrius Ponticus.*

Georg Feuerstein, PhD, MLitt (1947–2012), was an Indologist and one of the world's foremost authorities on Yoga, who became interested in Yoga at the age of thirteen, and wrote his first book on it at nineteen. His lifelong passion was to make traditional yogic wisdom accessible to modern spiritual seekers and to foster dialogue between traditions. To further this goal he founded the Yoga Research and Education Center in California and in 2004 Georg and his wife Brenda, founded Traditional Yoga Studies in Canada where Brenda continues to serve as the director. He published more than fifty books, twenty edited volumes, and some two hundred articles, and his work received several awards and honors. Among his writings are *The Yoga Tradition, The Encyclopedia of Yoga and Tantra, The Bhagavad-Gita,* and *Tantra: The Path of Ecstasy.* Inspired by the ancient Hindu ideal of the forest-dweller, he entered into semiretirement in Canada in 2004 in order to vigorously pursue spiritual practice. For more information see www.traditionalyogastudies.com.

Ari Goldfield, JD, is a Buddhist teacher who had the unique experience of being continuously in the training and service of his own teacher, the Tibetan master Khenpo Tsültrim Gyamtso Rinpoche, for eleven years. From 1998–2006, Ari served as Khenpo Rinpoche's oral translator and secretary on seven round-the-world teaching tours, received extensive instruction from

Rinpoche, and meditated under Rinpoche's guidance in retreats. Ari is also a published translator and author of books and articles on Buddhist philosophy and meditation, including *The Sun of Wisdom: Teachings On Nagarjuna's Fundamental Wisdom of the Middle Way* and *Stars of Wisdom: Analytical Meditation, Songs of Yogic Joy, and Prayers of Aspiration* (Shambhala Publications), as well as numerous songs of realization. He holds a BA from Harvard College and a JD from Harvard Law School, both with honors. He and his wife, Rose Taylor, currently teach internationally from their home base in San Francisco under the auspices of Wisdom Sun, the practice and study community they established in 2011 (www.wisdomsun.org).

Michael C. Kalton, PhD, graduated from Harvard University with a joint degree in East Asian languages and civilization and comparative religion. He has done extensive research on the Korean Neo-Confucian tradition, and published *To Become a Sage: The Ten Diagrams on Sage Learning by Yi T'oegye* (Columbia University Press), which was awarded the International T'oegye Studies Award, and *The Four-Seven Debate: An Annotated Translation of the Most Famous Controversy in Korean Neo-Confucian Thought* (State University of New York Press). Since 1990 he has been a professor of Interdisciplinary Studies at the University of Washington, Tacoma, and his work has expanded into contemporary environmental concerns and into systems theory, especially Complex Adaptive Systems, systems that learn and evolve. He sees a deep and creative synergy between premodern Neo-Confucian thought and self-cultivation and these areas of contemporary thought and concern. Publications exploring these themes include: "Extending the Neo-Confucian Tradition: Questions and Reconceptualization for the Twenty-first Century," *Journal of Chinese Philosophy* (1998); "Sagely Learning," in *Confucian Spirituality*, Vol. 11 of *World Spirituality: An Encyclopedic History of the Religious Quest*, Crossroad Publishing (2004); and "Confucian Trajectories on Environmental Understanding" in *Confucianism in Context*, State University of New York Press (2010).

Livia Kohn, PhD, graduated from Bonn University, Germany, in 1980 and joined Boston University as professor of Religion and East Asian Studies. She has also worked as visiting professor and adjunct faculty at several universities including Eötvös Lorand University in Budapest and the Stanford Center for Japanese Studies in Kyoto. Her specialty is the study of the Daoist religion and Chinese long life practices. She has served on multiple committees and editorial boards, and organized a series of major international conferences on Daoism. She retired from active teaching in 2006 and now lives in Florida, from where she leads workshops, trips, and conferences and serves as the executive editor of the *Journal of Daoist Studies*. Her many books include *Taoist Meditation and Longevity Techniques, Daoist Mystical Philosophy, Laughing at the Dao, Daoism Handbook, Daoism and Chinese Culture, Introducing Daoism,* and most recently, *Daoist Dietetics* and *Sitting in Oblivion*. For further information see www.liviakohn.com and www.threepinespress.com.

Robert McDermott, PhD, is president emeritus of the California Institute of Integral Studies and chair of its program in Philosophy, Cosmology, and Consciousness. Previously, he was professor and chair of the department of philosophy and of the program in religion at Baruch College of the City University of New York. He has served as president and chair of the board of many institutions, including secretary of the American Academy of Religion, and founding chair of the board, Sophia Project for Mothers and Children at Risk of Homelessness, in West Oakland. His publications include *Radhakrishnan, The Essential Aurobindo, The Essential Steiner, The Bhagavad Gita and the West,* and *The New Essential Steiner,* as well as many essays on philosophy, religion, and American thought. He is currently writing *Unique Not Alone— Steiner and Others*. He has received Fulbright and National Endowment for the Humanities grants.

Reza Shah-Kazemi, PhD, of the Institute of Ismaili Studies in London is an internationally renowned scholar of Islam and comparative religion. His many books include *The Sacred Foundations of Justice in Islam* and *My Mercy Encompasses All: The Koran's Teaching on Compassion, Peace and Love*. His interfaith works include *Paths to Transcendence: According to Shankara, Ibn Arabi, and Meister Eckhart* and *Common Ground between Islam and Buddhism* which was co-authored with the Dalai Lama. He is currently editor-in-chief of the forthcoming *Encyclopedia Islamica*.

Rabbi Rami Shapiro is an award-winning writer and educator whose poems and essays have been anthologized in more than a dozen volumes, and whose prayers are used in prayer books around the world. He received rabbinical ordination from the Hebrew Union College–Jewish Institute of Religion and holds both PhD and DDiv degrees. A congregational rabbi for twenty years, Rabbi Rami is currently adjunct professor of Religious Studies at Middle Tennessee State University where he also co-directs the creative writing program. He is director of Wisdom House, a center for interfaith study, dialogue, and contemplative practice at the Scarritt-Bennett Center in Nashville. In addition to writing books, Rami writes a regular column for

Spirituality and Health magazine called "Roadside Assistance for the Spiritual Traveler," and blogs at rabbirami.blogspot.com. His most recent books are *Recovery: The Sacred Art* (Skylight Paths), and *The Angelic Way* (BlueBridge). He can be reached via his Web site, rabbirami.com.

Roger Walsh, MD, PhD, DHL, graduated from Queensland University with degrees in psychology, physiology, neuroscience, and medicine and then came to Stanford University as a Fulbright scholar. He is currently professor of psychiatry, philosophy, and anthropology, and a professor in the religious studies program at the University of California at Irvine. His interests include topics such as contemplative practices, psychological well-being, religion and spirituality, transpersonal and integral studies, and the psychological roots of our global crises. His research and writings have received more than twenty national and international awards and honors while his teaching has received one national and six university awards. His publications include *Essential Spirituality: The Seven Central Practices* and *The World of Shamanism,* and together with his wife, the psychologist Frances Vaughan, *Paths Beyond Ego: The Transpersonal Vision.* For more information see www.drrogerwalsh.com.

Index

Made in the USA
Middletown, DE
10 February 2015